The Structural Prevention of Mass Atrocities

This book offers a different approach to the structural prevention of mass atrocities. It investigates the conditions that enable vulnerable countries to prevent the perpetration of such violence.

Structural prevention is commonly framed as the identifying and ameliorating of the 'root causes' of violent conflict, a process that typically involves international actors determining what these root causes are, and what the best courses of action are to deal with them. This overlooks why mass atrocities do not occur in countries that contain the presence of root causes. In fact, very little research has been conducted on what the causes of peace and stability are, particularly in countries located in regions marred by civil war and mass atrocities. To understand better how such vulnerable countries prevent the commission of mass atrocities, this book proposes an analytical framework which enables not only an understanding of risk that arises from the presence of root causes, but also of the factors that build resilience in countries, and consequently mitigate and manage such risk. Using this framework, three countries – Botswana, Zambia and Tanzania, are analysed to account for their long-term stability despite their location in neighbourhoods characterized by decades of civil war, ethnic repression and mass atrocities.

This work is a significant contribution to the field of genocide studies and crimes against humanity and will be of interest to students and scholars alike.

Stephen McLoughlin is a Post-doctoral Research Fellow at the Griffith Asia Institute and Centre for Governance and Public Policy, Griffith University.

Routledge Studies in Genocide and Crimes against Humanity
Edited by Adam Jones, University of British Columbia in Kelowna, Canada.

The *Routledge Series in Genocide and Crimes against Humanity* publishes cutting-edge research and reflections on these urgently contemporary topics. While focusing on political-historical approaches to genocide and other mass crimes, the series is open to diverse contributions from the social sciences, humanities, law, and beyond. Proposals for both sole-authored and edited volumes are welcome.

The Structural Prevention of Mass Atrocities
Understanding risks and resilience
Stephen McLoughlin

The Structural Prevention of Mass Atrocities

Understanding risk and resilience

Stephen McLoughlin

Routledge
Taylor & Francis Group

LONDON AND NEW YORK

First published 2014
by Routledge
2 Park Square, Milton Park, Abingdon, Oxon OX14 4RN

and by Routledge
711 Third Avenue, New York, NY 10017

Routledge is an imprint of the Taylor & Francis Group, an informa business

© 2014 Stephen McLoughlin

The right of Stephen McLoughlin to be identified as author of this work has been asserted by him in accordance with the Copyright, Designs and Patent Act 1988.

Trademark notice: Product or corporate names may be trademarks or registered trademarks, and are used only for identification and explanation without intent to infringe.

British Library Cataloguing in Publication Data
A catalogue record for this book is available from the British Library

Library of Congress Cataloging in Publication Data
McLoughlin, Stephen.
    The structural prevention of mass atrocities : understanding risk and resilience / Stephen McLoughlin.
        pages cm. – (Routledge studies in genocide and crimes against humanity)
    Summary: "This book offers a different approach to the structural prevention of mass atrocities. It investigates the conditions that enable vulnerable countries to prevent the perpetration of such violence"– Provided by publisher.
    Includes bibliographical references and index.
    1. Atrocities–Prevention. 2. Crimes against humanity–Prevention. I. Title.
    HV6322.M45 2014
    363.32'17–dc23
                2014002025

ISBN: 978-0-415-70613-1 (hbk)
ISBN: 978-1-315-88684-8 (ebk)

Typeset in Times New Roman
by Taylor & Francis Books

Contents

List of tables

Acknowledgements

There are many people whose guidance and support were given throughout the writing of this book. I owe great a debt to three friends and colleagues who read every chapter, and provided detailed and very insightful feedback. In particular, Alex Bellamy's guidance and advice has been crucial at every stage of this project. It was his expertise and enthusiasm which drew me back to Brisbane to embark on this research, and his suggestion in 2007 that I look into conflict prevention as a possible PhD topic was the genesis of this book. Deborah Mayersen has been enormously supportive over the last few years, and our informal chats about our overlapping research interests has yielded some great collaborative work, with more to come, I am sure. I am grateful to Sara Davies for her insightful observations – her suggestions and feedback made a substantial difference to the final draft.

I am grateful to my family – without their love and support I would never have even contemplated starting this project. I am grateful to my good friends who read different chapters and offered valuable suggestions. Catherine Smith read the whole book and provided very thoughtful and detailed feedback. Jess Gifkins and Jacqueline Medvecka read different case study chapters – their comments and suggestions were greatly appreciated. I also want to thank Pedram Rashidi, Tina Donaghy, Riaz Hooshmand, Samand Hooshman, who along with Jacqueline gave much support through their friendship and company, especially during our weekly coffee sessions. Thanks go to Chris Irons and David Rose, whose regular company and support I really valued. Thanks also to my friends and colleagues at the Asia Pacific Centre for the Responsibility to Protect – Alex Pound, Annie Pohlman, Sarah Teitt, Hong Hai Nguyen, Charlie Hunt, Kim Nackers, Raymond Lau, Marie Hobman, Tim Dunne and Noel Morada.

I would also like to thank the Griffith Asia Institute and its director, Andrew O'Neil. The GAI has been my base through the final stages of this project, and I am grateful for the solid support both the GAI, and the Centre for Governance and Public Policy (both at Griffith University) have given me as an early career researcher.

I am also grateful to Adam Jones, whose meticulous feedback in the final stages of this project helped to greatly enhance the final product. His support for the manuscript was instrumental in transforming it into a published book. It is a great honour to have it released as part of his Genocide and Crimes Against Humanity book series.

Finally, I want to thank Shirin. Her love and support and her enthusiasm for this project – through both ups and downs – sustained me these last few years, and her meticulous editing of successive drafts has much improved it. All errors of course, are my own.

Introduction

In the 1990s, Zaire's[1] dramatic downward spiral into state failure, war and atrocities seemed to typify everything that was wrong with Africa. Early in the decade, growing calls for democracy through widespread student protests were brutally suppressed by Mobutu Sese Seko's corrupt regime. After a very brief period of power sharing, Mobutu provoked conflict with the opposition leader's ethnic group, sowed division and fear, and provoked the displacement of over 100,000 people (Meredith 2006: 391–92). This occurred in a broader context of decaying infrastructure, poorly functioning government institutions and an absence of basic services. In the wake of the Rwandan genocide, this corrupt and deeply unstable state became the incubator of a protracted transnational war that claimed the lives of more than 3 million people (Meredith 2006: 544).

Yet in neighbouring Zambia, a very different story unfolded. There, growing unrest and widespread protests proclaimed the same demands for greater democracy, in a similar context of prolonged economic decline and mounting poverty. However, unlike Mobutu, Zambia's longstanding autocratic ruler, Kenneth Kaunda, relented in the face of public pressure. The multi-party elections he sponsored in 1991 produced his emphatic defeat (Phiri 2006: 166–76). Kaunda accepted the results, and cooperated in a peaceful transfer of power to the new leader, Frederick Chiluba (DiJohn 2010: 31–32).

What prevented Zambia from following a path similar to Zaire? This story of resilience amidst the challenges associated with war and atrocities is the subject of this book. Often overlooked, countries like Zambia hold valuable insights into why some countries avoid mass atrocities[2] despite having much in common with countries that have succumbed to such violence.

The protection of populations from genocide and mass atrocities is most effective when these crimes are prevented from occurring in the first place. The recent tragedy of Darfur has shown how difficult it is to stop mass killing once it has started. Prevention, therefore, is the best form of protection. In addition, prevention is much cheaper than reaction. The Carnegie Commission's 1997 report, *Preventing Deadly Conflict*, concluded that despite the costs that preventive action inevitably demands, they 'are minuscule when compared with the costs of deadly conflict and of the rebuilding and psychological healing in its aftermath' (Hamburg and Vance 1997: xlvi).[3] The United Nations' (UN) preventive deployment in Macedonia in 1992 and the combination of preventive diplomacy and peace keeping in Burundi in 1994 are evidence of the positive impact that prevention can have (Ackermann 2000, 2003: 345; Bjorkdahl 2006; Bjorkdahl 1998: 46; Evans 2007; Evans 1996: 63; Menkhaus 2004: 422; Wallensteen 2002: 224). Both countries were spared the enormous economic, political and social costs of rebuilding with which their neighbours continue to struggle.[4] Although much controversy still exists regarding the interventionist character of some direct prevention strategies (see, for example, Welsh 2010),[5] long-term prevention enables far greater space for global consensus. The delayed and constrained UN Security Council resolution on Darfur in 2007 (S/RES/1769), and the recent failure to table a Security Council resolution on Syria (see UN News 2011), demonstrate how difficult it is to agree on an effective response to mass violence once it is underway. By contrast, the daily cooperation among governments, international, regional and sub-regional organizations, private actors and civil society on projects related to good governance, economic development and social stability demonstrates that consensus about strategies of atrocity prevention is far from impossible. Furthermore, greater investment in effective prevention is likely to decrease the number of cases of mass atrocities that require a response (Bellamy 2010: 167), making such violence more difficult for the international community to ignore if and when it does occur.

Although the UN, regional organizations, many national governments and civil society organizations have developed increasingly sophisticated strategies to target escalating tension through preventive diplomacy, peace operations and sanctions, such measures will have limited long-term benefits unless the underlying causes of violence are also addressed. This sentiment was voiced in a 2009 report on conflict prevention by Secretary-General Ban Ki-moon: 'if we do not deal with the root causes of conflict – and offer sustainable solutions – we will be left with humanitarian emergencies and peacekeeping operations without end' (Ban 2008: 14). Often the success of preventive action is measured by highly publicized responses to escalating tensions, such as in Kenya in 2008.[6] Africa's Elders were lauded for their role in stopping the Kenyan violence, yet very little work was done to address the root causes (Hansen 2009: 8). Long-term or structural prevention is premised on identifying and addressing root causes of deadly violence. This entails developing strategies and programmes targeted at 'the deep-rooted socio-economic, cultural, environmental, institutional and other structural causes that often underlie the immediate political symptoms of conflicts' (Annan 2001: 2). This approach is also echoed in the prevention of genocide and mass atrocities (see, for example, Ban 2009a: 19).

However, long-term prevention is limited by a tendency to focus on what goes wrong, and overlooks good practices that occur in a number of countries that contain risk. Focusing only on the identification of root causes, while neglecting local sources of stability and risk mitigation, precludes an understanding of how states themselves effectively manage the tensions asso-ciated with atrocity risk. This imbalance has been acknowledged by many scholars and policy makers, who have pointed out that little is known about the causes of peace, the societal processes that build resilience against vio-lence, and the societies that manage to de-escalate tensions when they occur, such as Zambia (Lund 1996: 52; Wolter 2007: 50).

As a consequence, this approach to long-term prevention is problematic for two main reasons. First, while most scholars investigating mass atrocities identify local and national interactions and patterns of behaviour as central to the structural causes of such violence, prevention is overwhelmingly framed as a process decided and implemented from the outside by international actors. Second, premising long-term prevention on the identifying and addressing of root causes assumes a linear inevitability between cause and outcome. Yet such an assumption contradicts what is known about the crime of genocide and other major episodes of mass violence – that the commission of such crimes is rare. As Bartoli, Ogata and Stanton note, 'Most states do not commit genocide most of the time. State interest normally does not coincide with genocidal intent, and the predisposition of governments is generally non-genocidal' (Bartoli *et al.* 2009: 21). An assumption of causal inevitability over-looks the fact that many countries that demonstrate risk of future atrocities never experience such violence.

Premising prevention solely on identifying risk fails to explain why some at-risk countries experience mass atrocities, yet others do not. Similarly, there are countries located in neighbourhoods characterized by protracted civil wars and the commission of mass atrocities that have not themselves been marked by such mass violence. The cases examined in this book – Botswana, Zambia and Tanzania – provide three such examples. Indeed, research that emphasizes identifying root causes as a starting point for prevention tends to neglect the processes and dynamics that provide insights into how risk is mitigated by local and national sources. Secretary-General Ban Ki-moon acknowledged this omission, stating that 'more research and analysis is needed on why one society plunges into mass violence while its neighbours remain relatively stable' (Ban 2009a: 10–11).

Premising long-term prevention on understanding the relationship between risk and mitigation is important for three reasons. First, it allows for a re-evaluation of the relationship between root causes and the occurrence of mass atrocities. Structural factors that contribute to risk do not have a direct causal connection to mass violence. Thus while their presence indicates risk, they do not suggest an inevitable linear path towards mass violence. Second, it gen-erates a repository of good practices based on what goes right within coun-tries that exhibit factors associated with heightened atrocity risk. Such a repository can provide insights into how to respond to comparable manifes-tations of risk in other places. Third, these insights are important for inter-national practitioners and policy makers, as they direct them towards local sources of resilience, and are therefore likely to be more effective in violence prevention. The more resilient a society is, the less likely it is to experience atrocities. Thus, the most effective thing the international community can do is to identify local sources of resilience and support them. This leads to a facilitative approach to prevention, rather than a prescriptive one.

My aim in this book is to examine how, in specific contexts, the risk of mass atrocities is mitigated by these local and national sources of resilience. Although much has been written about the root causes of genocide and mass atrocities, very little study has been devoted to why such violence does *not* occur when root causes, preconditions and risk factors[7] *are* present. Consequently, there is very little understanding of why atrocities do not occur in high-risk environments. However, there is much to be learnt from such cases, especially when they contain numerous significant risk factors.[8]

This book develops an analytical framework that explores the relationship between risk and mitigation, in order to achieve greater clarity about what some states already do to develop resilience against the risk of mass atrocities, with the goal of gaining greater insight into the structural prevention of such violence. The process of mitigating the risk posed by the presence of preconditions is deeply contextual. However, this book will demonstrate that general positive factors are instrumental in encouraging stability and building resilience. These include a government that promotes an inclusive national identity, fosters social cohesion, provides essential services equitably, steers away from political competition marked by divisive ethnic or religious difference, and provides equal economic opportunities. Understanding the way these conditions take shape over time is important because it grounds prevention in local processes, advanced by those who have the greatest investment in developing peace and avoiding violence. Understanding the complex relationship between risk and resilience enables international actors to encourage practical methods that work in preventing mass atrocities.

Theories of prevention tend to be arranged in a two-tiered hierarchy. Direct (or 'operational') prevention entails measures to prevent the escalation of tensions into violence, while structural prevention refers to actions that seek to address the root causes of potential violent conflict (Hamburg and Vance 1997: xix). The idea of preventing war has existed for centuries (Ackermann 2003: 340), and although it was clearly mandated in the UN Charter (Bellamy *et al.* 2004: 250; United Nations 1945), it was not until the end of the Cold War that the notion started to take shape and find institutional support.

An attempt was made to establish an early warning system in the UN Secretariat in the 1980s (see, for example, Boothby 2004: 252; Dedring 1998: 48; Peck 1998: 72; Sutterlin 2003: 18). It was Secretary-General Boutros Boutros-Ghali's release of *An Agenda for Peace* that first mentioned the importance of addressing root causes (Boutros-Ghali 1992: 2; Menkhaus 2004: 421). The need to address the 'immediate as well as the root causes of conflict' was underscored in *Supplement to An Agenda for Peace* (Boutros-Ghali 1995: 19), an approach pioneered by the Organization for Security and Co-operation in Europe (OSCE) (Miall 1999: 116). Prevention was firmly categorized as a two-tiered concept in the Carnegie Commission's report, *Preventing Deadly Conflict* (Hamburg and Vance 1997). This approach to conflict prevention was adopted by Kofi Annan in his report, *Prevention of Armed Conflict* (2001), and was acknowledged by the Security Council in resolution 1366, which prioritized both the need to address the root causes of conflict and direct prevention measures (United Nations Security Council 2001a). Subsequent reports by Annan, as well as his successor, Ban Ki-moon, emphasized this notion of structural prevention (Annan 2003, 2006; Ban 2008).

This two-tiered model has largely characterized strategies for atrocity prevention as well. Just as it took a number of decades for the UN system to begin to institutionalize and formalize its efforts in conflict prevention, so too has it taken many decades to do the same for genocide and other mass atrocities. Despite the Genocide Convention endorsing the prevention of genocide alongside its punishment, it was not until 2004 that the Office of the Special Adviser on the Prevention of Genocide (OSAPG) was established to deal specifically with the prevention of genocide and mass atrocities.

The OSAPG's commitment to prevention includes both operational and structural strategies. Regarding operational prevention, it provides advocacy based on its own early warning analysis. It premises structural prevention on an understanding of root causes (OSAPG 2011a), which according to the Special Adviser are based on 'inequalities between identity groups' (OSAPG 2011b). The OSAPG states that such activity includes promoting equitable economic development and political representation, as well as fostering tolerance amidst social diversity – clearly linking the risk of genocide to a broad range of tensions and inequalities inherent in many societies. Prevention, for the Special Adviser, involves both long-term strategies and proximate strategies.

The two-tiered approach to prevention is also emphasized in the principle of the Responsibility to Protect (R2P). The International Commission on Intervention and State Sovereignty (ICISS) report defined the 'responsibility to prevent' as addressing 'both the root causes and direct causes of internal conflict and other man-made crises putting populations at risk' (ICISS 2001: xi). Although R2P was streamlined in 2005 to refer specifically to the four crimes of genocide, ethnic cleansing, crimes against humanity and war crimes, it clearly prioritized prevention, stating, 'this responsibility entails the prevention of such crimes, including their incitement' (United Nations General Assembly 2005). Developing this, Secretary-General Ban Ki-moon's report *Implementing the Responsibility to Protect*, emphasized the need to address the root causes of mass atrocities, particularly where inequalities prevailed (Ban 2009a: 19).

The structural prevention of mass atrocities is less controversial than direct preventive strategies, but there are three key problems with the way the concept is framed. First, premising prevention on the identification and removal of root causes assumes a linear inevitability of cause and outcome. This contradicts what most scholars of genocide and mass atrocities have concluded – that is, long-term structural factors known as root causes have a tenuous causal link with mass violence. While they create the conditions that are conducive to atrocities, these conditions are not sufficient in and of themselves to cause directly such episodes of violence (see, for example, Fein 1979; Harff 2003; Kuper 1981; Somelin 2007). In fact, the perpetration of mass atrocities is rare – the exception rather than the norm. According to Genocide Watch's survey of countries that experienced significant risk of genocidal violence between 1945 and 2008,[9] for every country that reached stage seven (genocidal as well as non-genocidal massacres), there were two that did not (Genocide Prevention Advisory Network 2009). Chirot and McCauley (2006: 95) point out that genocide, a crime that occurs predominantly during violent conflict, is 'far less common than warfare itself'. Therefore, it is clear that risk often exists without inevitably resulting in mass atrocities. Clearly a gap exists between this assumption, embedded in the concept of structural prevention, and the findings of research conducted on the causes of mass atrocities.

This leads to a second problem. If the concept of structural prevention is concerned solely with root causes, it becomes blind to variations among states at risk. It is clear that some states displaying risk factors experience mass atrocities while others do not, but assuming the linear inevitability of mass violence precludes an understanding of the processes that build resilience and mitigate such risk. The idea that prevention could be based on local strategies which address such problems is almost non-existent in the literature – investigating what goes right is almost completely overlooked in genocide studies and by prevention scholars. The Human Security Report Project (2011: 61) draws attention to the fact that there has been insufficient attention paid to the causes of peace.[10] Clearly the literature pays little attention to the successful cases. As I have pointed out, there are many cases in which the risk of mass atrocities is apparent, but atrocities have not resulted. In failing to understand why atrocities have *not* occurred, we miss an opportunity to gain insights from local and national processes that have effectively prevented such violence.

The third problem is that the concept of structural prevention has prioritized the role of international actors, with regard both to identifying root causes and determining which strategies will be implemented to ameliorate them (see, for example, Hamburg 2008; Lund 2004; Moolakkattu 2005; Wallensteen 2002). This external focus encourages a prescriptive approach to long-term prevention, rather than supporting local processes that build resilience and stability. In this way, policies related to the prevention of mass atrocities run the risk of perpetuating a cycle of external diagnosis and external troubleshooting without regard for context-specific factors that strengthen a country's immunity to mass atrocities.

The structural prevention of both violent conflict and mass atrocities needs to consider a broader framework, one that goes beyond root causes to incorporate an understanding of how actions and processes that encourage stability and build resilience in communities and countries mitigate the risk of mass violence. This resonates strongly with the approach advocated by the UN

Special Adviser on the Prevention of Genocide, who emphasizes that the prevention of genocide and other mass atrocities depends on the effective management of diversity within states. By facilitating such management, the Special Adviser argues, genocide prevention achieves its greatest success. Likewise, with regard to preventing the four mass atrocity crimes, Bellamy argues that such protection is 'universal and enduring – it applies to all states, all the time' (Bellamy 2010: 158). Given this, Bellamy claims that the key question is 'how it is best exercised' (Bellamy 2010: 158). Understanding how diversity is managed, particularly in states where social cleavages or 'fissures' are salient, clarifies not only how states carry out their responsibility to protect their populations, but how they do so in the presence of risk. When risk is inherent in a state, whether through internal conditions of social, political and economic inequality, or location in a region characterized by the commission of mass atrocities, understanding the measures that governments and other actors take to mitigate such risk can provide key insights into long-term prevention.[11] In this way, a consideration not only of 'risk factors', but of the factors that mitigate against risk, permits the accumulation of a repository of states' 'best practices' in fulfilling their responsibility to protect.

Broadening the framework to incorporate mitigating factors puts greater focus on the responsibility of the state. To ask the question, 'What are states already doing?' sheds analytical light on the first pillar of R2P, and shifts the emphasis from a third-party approach to structural prevention. One question that is overlooked in the discussions on prevention is how states effectively prevent violence through their own range of policies and actions, particularly in the face of risk. Paragraph 138 of the World Summit Outcome Document states that it is states' responsibility to protect their populations from the four crimes (United Nations General Assembly 2005). In a similar manner, Annan's reports on the prevention of violent conflict also stress the primary responsibility of the state to engage in conflict prevention (Annan 2001: 2; Annan 2003: 2; Annan 2006: 1). Given this, it is surprising that there is little systematic analysis on how state institutions and communities mitigate the risk of mass violence. Ban Ki-moon, in his report *Implementing the Responsibility to Protect*, points out that more research is needed on why some states commit mass atrocities while others do not. Another way of expressing this would be to say that researchers should aim to understand how some states effectively carry out their responsibility to protect their populations, or how the first pillar of R2P can be applied successfully. In order to do this, the concept of prevention needs to be broadened, so as not simply to focus on identifying and addressing 'root causes' of potential violence, but to identify and understand conditions that foster resilience, particularly in the face of risk. In this sense, research on this aspect of prevention needs to understand both risk and mitigation.

I propose an alternative approach to the structural prevention of mass atrocities, which allows for an understanding of the way that 'what goes right' impacts on risk factors, or so-called root causes. This is a model that provides a framework for understanding how risk of mass atrocities is mitigated by conditions that foster greater resilience or, in the words of the Special Adviser, help to 'manage diversity' (OSAPG 2011b).

However, to move beyond the language of root causes, I follow the lead of scholars Barbara Harff and Ted Gurr, who have done extensive research into early warning indicators for genocide and politicide,[12] and more broadly for violence between minority groups. Both Harff (2003) and Gurr (1993) have cautiously steered away from making direct causal links to future episodes of mass violence. Rather, they highlight risk by identifying 'preconditions' – general conditions that have often preceded genocide and politicide. These preconditions do not necessarily directly cause mass violence, but, as Harff argues, such episodes rarely occur in their absence. In this way, such pre-conditions give us some idea of risk. Other genocide scholars have also high-lighted the need to understand the general circumstances in which most atrocities are perpetrated (Fein 1979; Hilberg 1985; Kuper 1981; Midlarsky 2005). Most contend that while genocide is the product of calculated plans by elites, it is necessary to move beyond this direct causal path to understand also the circumstances that facilitate the emergence of such elites in the first place. These conditions, which are not themselves necessarily the result of particular government or elite policies, create the structural foundations for genocide and mass atrocities. Although such conditions do not always result in genocide and mass atrocities (in fact they generally do not), over the last century genocide and mass atrocities have rarely occurred in their absence.

My aim in this book is to propose an approach to the structural prevention of mass atrocities that acknowledges that such long-term risk factors do not necessarily result in a violent outcome. Instead, it seeks to shift the emphasis of prevention from external diagnosis and action to one that seeks to under-stand what vulnerable countries currently do to manage such risk. In order to enhance such an understanding, I advance a framework that broadens the widely accepted notion of structural prevention to incorporate an under-standing not only of root causes or risk factors of mass violence, but also the factors that enhance stability and resilience.

After setting out my framework, the book then considers three cases: Botswana, Zambia and Tanzania. These are important cases because they are located in regions that have, over many decades, been characterized by con-flict, political repression and mass atrocities. Being located in a violent region is itself a risk factor for political instability and mass violence, according to the Political Instability Task Force (PITF) (Goldstone *et al.* 2005; Goldstone and Ulfelder 2004). Despite this, none of these countries have, since indepen-dence, experienced mass atrocities on their soil,[13] suggesting that the associated risk has been effectively managed over time. Nonetheless, these countries all contain some of the risk factors commonly associated with genocide and mass atrocities, making them particularly interesting for our purposes. In Bots-wana, these include social division, ethnic discrimination, human rights vio-lations and economic inequality. In Zambia, social division, limited democracy, limited rule of law and economic inequality have increased the risk of atrocities. In mainland Tanzania,[14] social division, limited democracy, limited rule of law and inequality of economic opportunity exist. Finally, Zanzibar's risk factors include prior atrocities, social division, discrimination, human rights violations, limited democracy, limited rule of law and economic inequality.

This book seeks to go beyond the existing notion that those countries that have not experienced genocide or mass atrocities lack the same measure of risk as those countries with such a history. The contribution it makes is two-fold: first, it highlights a need to go beyond root causes, in particular, examining the relationship between risk and mitigation demonstrating that effective prevention is not simply about creating a non-event, but also exhibits a range of other benefits that contribute to the social, political and economic health of a country. The book also questions the notion that structural prevention is a process that is planned and carried out principally by international actors. Instead, it is a complex and deeply contextual process best understood by local actors – one in which international actors ought to play a facilitative rather than a prescriptive role.

Notes

1 The Republic of Zaire was renamed the Democratic Republic of Congo in 1997.
2 Mass atrocities in this book refer to genocide, politicide (political mass murder as defined by Barbara Harff), ethnic cleansing, and other systematic attacks against civilian populations that constitute crimes against humanity or war crimes, as defined by the Rome Statute (United Nations 1998).
3 This is based on the assumption that every form of preventive action carried out would otherwise have resulted in violent conflict or atrocities. However, there is no direct causal link between the 'root causes' of violent conflict and mass atrocities. Thus, it is highly likely that a substantial portion of the preventive action invested by the international community was directed to circumstances which would not have otherwise turned violent. Seen in this light, the cumulative cost of prevention increases substantially. See, for example, Valentino 2011.
4 Although Burundi has experienced significant violence since 1994, there is widespread consensus that the preventive deployment coupled with mediation efforts there was effective in Burundi taking a different path from Rwanda. See, for example, Wolff 2006.
5 For example, early warning, preventive diplomacy, sanctions and peacekeeping missions.
6 This is a problem because prevention is usually still accompanied by loss of life, and late prevention is not always successful.
7 Throughout this book, I use the terms 'root causes' and 'risk factors'. Root causes refer to the structural underlying factors that are regarded to be at the root of conflict and mass violence. Ethnic divisions and prejudice, poor governance and economic inequalities are examples of such. While 'risk factors' refer to the same phenomena, the difference is that the term 'root causes' suggests that there is a strong link between these factors and the violent outcome, whereas 'risk factors' is less deterministic. The term 'risk factors' is used to emphasize the fact that prior to past atrocities, certain structural conditions tended to be present, although their

precise causal relationship with mass atrocities is not certain. As I will explain in Chapter 3, I prefer to use the term 'risk factors' to demonstrate risk because there is no certainty that the existence of such factors will inevitably lead to mass atrocities.

8 I identify and explain these risk factors as part of my analytical framework in Chapter 3.

9 Stage four or above, according to Stanton's (1996) 'eight stages of genocide'.

10 For one notable exception, see Adolf 2009. However, it is not directly relevant to this study, as it largely deals with historical epochs reaching back to antiquity. Where it does focus on the twentieth century, the emphasis is mostly on international peace, or peace between nation-states.

11 In response to the World Summit Outcome Document, Secretary-General Ban Ki-moon identified three pillars as constituting the core of R2P: states' responsibility to protect; the responsibility of the international community to assist in the prevention of genocide, war crimes, ethnic cleansing and crimes against humanity (where needed); and the international community's responsibility to take action when a state is 'manifestly failing' to protect its citizens from these crimes. See Ban 2009a: 2.

12 Politicide refers to 'political mass murder' (see Harff 2003: 57). The term compensates for the exclusion – in the Genocide Convention – of the eradication of groups defined by political affiliation.

13 One exception is Tanzania's semi-autonomous region of Zanzibar, where a bloody revolution was staged in early 1964, shortly after the islands gained independence. Zanzibar and Tanganyika did not form the United Republic of Tanzania until later that year. Thus, technically it could be argued that there have been no atrocities in Tanzania as it is known today. Nevertheless, the country is still a valid subject for case study analysis, as it has enjoyed relative stability since 1964 despite sharing a border with many countries that have experienced great upheaval and mass violence.

14 As I will explain in Chapter 6, I have conducted separate analyses of mainland Tanzania and Zanzibar due to their distinct histories and circumstances.

1   A review of prevention

In his 2008 book, *Preventing Genocide*, David Hamburg drew on a two-pronged definition of prevention, originally articulated in the Carnegie Commission's 1997 report, *Preventing Deadly Conflict*. Operational prevention – 'measures applicable in the face of immediate crisis' – and structural prevention – 'strategies to address the root causes of deadly conflict' (Hamburg and Vance 1997: 69) – were identified as the two key approaches. This distinction has underpinned prevention in the UN system, both in the development of institutional capacity and in numerous reports written subsequently by Secretaries-General Kofi Annan and Ban Ki-moon. As Hamburg was also co-architect of the Carnegie Commission's report, it is interesting to consider his use of public health analogies to illustrate both proximate and long-term preventive strategies. Operational preventive measures, such as 'early, skilful, and respectful preventive diplomacy', were likened to 'expert care of a sprained ankle' (Hamburg 2008: 5). Structural prevention, which entailed 'helping a troubled nation to build a democratic, equitable, socio-economic infrastructure', was comparable to 'promoting a healthy lifestyle and environment ... for a society that is accustomed to health-damaging habits such as cigarette smoking' (Hamburg 2008: 5).

Such analogies are useful for illustrating, in general terms, the benefits of multi-dimensional preventive strategies that do more than address the most visible signs of dangerous risk escalation. However, they also reveal blind spots. Two in particular stand out: the first is an assumption that the existence of root causes assumes an inevitable violent outcome. The second is a tendency to make a distinction between external prevention actors and internal prevention recipients, much like the relationship between a doctor and a patient. What these blind spots overlook are the myriad domestic sources of resilience that contain insights into the way that risk of violent conflict or mass atrocities is managed over time. This is particularly relevant for structural prevention, as the effectiveness of long-term strategies becomes more difficult to prove the further upstream from potential violent outcomes they are implemented. Understanding what already works in countries that manage challenges associated with the long-term risk of mass atrocities is surely an important dimension of structural prevention.

To discuss these challenges, this chapter commences with an overview of prevention in the UN system and beyond, since 1945, with a particular emphasis on developments in the post-Cold War era. I then discuss the policy implications of structural prevention, with specific reference to the concerns that in aiming to address the root causes of potential violence, the utility of prevention as a policy and analytical tool may become diminished in its attempts to 'make it be all things to all people' (Luck 2002: 256). The third section then addresses two major limitations inherent in the concept of structural prevention. The general argument is that these limitations, which are inherent in the way that structural prevention has been conceptualized, overlook what communities and states already do to build resilience and mitigate the risk of genocide and other mass atrocities.

The evolution of prevention since 1945

Conflict prevention and the UN

There is nothing novel about the idea of preventing war. Ackermann points out that a number of preventive measures were agreed on and implemented as a result of the Congress of Vienna in 1815, seeking to bring about the peaceful settlement of disputes between various principalities and states (Ackermann 2003: 340). Although the terms 'prevention' or 'preventive diplomacy' were not used,[1] the North Atlantic Treaty Organization (NATO), the Marshall Plan, as well as the European Union (EU) can all be seen as efforts to provide the institutional and infrastructural groundwork for the fostering of cooperation and the peaceful settlement of hostilities (de Maio 2006: 132).

Prevention is also central to the UN. The UN Charter clearly mandated the prevention of violent conflict, and established it as its central principle (Bellamy *et al.* 2004: 250). The opening lines, 'To save succeeding generations from the scourge of war ... to reaffirm faith in fundamental human rights ... justice and respect ... for international law ... to promote social progress ...' (United Nations 1945), brought together the basic ingredients of a broad notion of prevention which included both immediate concerns ('the scourge of war') and more structural concerns (human rights, international law, social progress). Further articles give shape to this approach. For example, Article 1 reinforces the UN's primary principle by articulating its purpose as taking 'effective collective measures for the prevention and removal of threats ... to the peace' (United Nations 1945). In Article 2, paragraph 5, member states are requested not to assist other states that are subject to UN preventive/ enforcement action. Responsibility is given to the UN Security Council, in Article 24, paragraph 1, to maintain peace and security, and this is followed up in Article 34, which highlights the importance of investigating any dispute or situation that might lead to a threat to international security, implying that action can legally be taken well prior to a conflict breaking out (United

Nations 1945). This preventive action is reinforced in Article 40, which gives the Security Council the authority to 'call upon the parties concerned' to adopt 'provisional measures' in an effort to offset an escalation to violent conflict. In fact, membership of the UN itself was declared to be open only to 'peace-loving states which accept the obligations contained in the present Charter, and in the judgement of the organization, are able and willing to carry out these obligations' (United Nations 1945).[2]

Despite conflict prevention being the 'first promise in the Charter' (Hampson *et al.* 2002: 1), it has been one of the most difficult areas not only to devise and implement policy, but also to articulate and map out how such a goal could be understood and reached. This is also reflected in the way that conflict prevention has arisen and evolved as a concept, particularly since the end of the Cold War. Secretary-General Javier Pérez de Cuéllar raised one major limitation in 1982 regarding Article 99, which stated that 'The Secretary-General may bring to the attention of the Security Council any matter which in his opinion may threaten the maintenance of international peace and security' (United Nations 1945: 15/99). De Cuéllar brought to light the inadequacy of UN early warning capacity in his annual report of the same year (Dedring 1998: 48). In the report he stated he was unable to give the Security Council reliable and timely updates on developments that might lead to international disputes if not dealt with appropriately and swiftly. This concern was triggered by the war in the Falkland Islands between the UK and Argentina, which was said to have caught the UN Secretariat by surprise, to the extent that it did not have a map of the islands at the time the invasion commenced (Peck 1998: 72). Eventually, in 1987, the Office of Research and Collection of Information (ORCI) was set up to provide timely early warning, as well as engage in policy planning, disseminate information, thus aiming to improve the UN's capacity for responding to situations that were deemed at risk of escalating into violent conflict (Boothby 2004: 252). However, as part of a number of reforms initiated by Boutros Boutros-Ghali (and due to the political controversy of the Office having the capacity to collect information that could be used against some member states), ORCI was shut down in 1992, with some of its functions of information collection being transferred to the UN Secretariat-based Department of Political Affairs (DPA) (Sutterlin 2003: 18).

With the Cold War over, and optimism spreading about the potential for the UN Security Council to make more effective use of its Chapter VII powers, Boutros-Ghali was called upon to provide a report that would address the way this renewed international consensus could be galvanized to meet current issues of security (Luck 2006: 52). The subsequent report, *An Agenda for Peace*, went beyond the original request of the Council to provide proposals that would 'improve the capacity of the United Nations for preventive diplomacy, for peacemaking and for peacekeeping' (Boutros-Ghali, quoted in Meisler 1995: 287). This, and the *Supplement to An Agenda for Peace* three years later, stressed the need for greater coordination and resources to engage in preventive diplomacy, as well as for post-conflict peace-building efforts to address the underlying causes of conflict (Boutros-Ghali 1995; Menkhaus 2004: 421).

Conflict prevention beyond the Cold War

Although the UN Charter clearly mandated the prevention of violent conflict, the focus until the end of the Cold War had been on inter-state conflict. Following this, and in response to a greater concern for the number of internal conflicts that were taking place, the Secretariat, in response to a request from the Security Council, began to develop a framework for dealing with intra-state conflict. Boutros-Ghali's *An Agenda for Peace* outlined this framework.

An Agenda for Peace represented what Carment and Schnabel (2003: 12) call an 'attitudinal shift' in conflict prevention. This was evident in the first visibly successful preventive operation in Macedonia, which commenced in the same year (1992). In addition, it posited that long-term peace efforts must extend beyond the security paradigm to address systemic inequalities such as poverty and human rights violations. In effect, it stimulated the coordination of agencies to 'integrate conflict prevention strategies' with the UN system, especially those dealing with development projects (Duggan 2004: 246–47). Although the *Supplement to An Agenda for Peace* placed greater emphasis on addressing the underlying causes of intra-state conflict, one conceptual limitation in addressing these causes was the tendency to associate peace building with post-conflict reconstruction, rather than preventive efforts prior to crises. By contrast, Evans contends that peace building is what stable prosperous nations do as a matter of course, and this is an essential ingredient in the long-term establishment of peaceful societies (Evans 1993: 40). Nevertheless, both *An Agenda for Peace* and the *Supplement to An Agenda for Peace* placed new emphasis on the need for the UN to address not only inter-state but also intra-state conflict, highlighting the UN's responsibility to mitigate disputes as early as possible through preventive diplomacy, as well as addressing underlying causes.

Many of the themes in these two reports were developed further in *Preventing Deadly Conflict*, published by the Carnegie Commission (Hamburg and Vance 1997). The steps toward an institutional approach to conflict prevention were crystallized and extended, and this was to become a conceptual cornerstone of the UN's approach to conflict prevention. In its report, the Commission presented three broad aims. The first was to mitigate the long-term risk of violent conflict through assisting states to foster 'security, well-being and justice for their citizens' (Hamburg and Vance 1997: 69), the protection of human rights and the promotion of fair and equitable economic circumstances. The second aim was to prevent disputes that had already started from escalating further; third was to prevent past conflicts from reigniting. This led to the repackaging of preventive activity into two main categories: structural prevention and operational prevention. Structural prevention refers to action that seeks to address the underlying causes of violent conflict (Hamburg and Vance 1997: xix). Also referred to in the report as peace building,[3] such action is associated with creating equitable, social, economic, political and humanitarian circumstances within which a society can operate, without subjecting its citizens to mounting grievances, which increase the likelihood of conflict. Operational prevention refers to action that is taken to prevent an already tense situation from escalating into violent conflict. Known also as direct prevention, it involves such activities as fact finding, preventive diplomacy and preventive peace keeping.[4]

The Carnegie Commission's report clarified and broadened the concept of prevention. The commission expanded it to include not only diplomacy, sanctions and preventive deployment, but also peace building, which had previously been associated largely with post-conflict reconstruction. This two-tiered approach to prevention set a precedent in that it framed prevention as addressing early warning signs of impending conflict and the perceived underlying causes – or risk factors – of conflict. If these 'root causes' were addressed through more equitable development and governance, then the possibility of conflict erupting would be greatly lessened. Such a concept of prevention, Lund (2002: 160) suggests, reaches out 'to a wide range of policy sectors and organizations'. This was certainly the authors' intention: upon establishing the new parameters of the term, the commission posited that 'its approach to prevention was broad' (Hamburg and Vance 1997: xix). The authors claimed there needed to be an 'international commitment' to this broad concept of prevention, as this was the only way to ensure a progressive approach to combating the vast range of factors that contributed, both over the short term and the long term, to the outbreak of violent and deadly conflict (Hamburg and Vance 1997: xvii). This articulation of prevention reflected in part what had already been initiated by the OSCE, which had been engaged in structural prevention (emphasizing the need to address the root causes of conflict) as early as 1992 (Miall *et al.* 1999: 116).

UN Secretary-General Kofi Annan adopted this two-tiered approach to conflict prevention. In his report *Prevention of Armed Conflict* (2001), Annan called for the establishment of a 'culture of prevention' throughout the UN system. This amounted to the adoption of what he coined a 'prevention lens', or prevention mainstreaming, for any project by any agency engaged in activities that were in some way related to operational or structural prevention. The report set a precedent by combining what had been separate concerns of security and development. For UN agencies to adopt a prevention lens would mean, for example, that agencies such as the United Nations Development Programme (UNDP), which had traditionally distanced themselves from the political affairs of nation-states, were now being called on to consider the implications that projects would have on the overall security of countries concerned (Annan 2001: 1).

Annan's report contains 29 recommendations, targeting the UN's main bodies as well as addressing the need for coordination between its departments, agencies and programmes, encouraging and often urging reform that would amount to greater coordination and capacity to engage in conflict prevention, both at the operational and structural levels. In legitimizing his call to adopt a 'culture of prevention', Annan evoked both Chapter II and Article 55 of the Charter, which respectively mandated the peaceful settlement of disputes and linked development with peace, stating that 'when sustainable development addresses the root causes of conflict, it plays an important role in preventing conflict and promoting peace' (Annan 2001: 18).

Two focal points for prevention within the UN system were identified: the DPA and the Interdepartmental Framework for Coordination (Framework Team). Annan urged member states to give the DPA greater capacity to identify early warning cases, and as overseer of all preventive activities in the system. Greater support was also urged for the UNDP in an effort to bring about more sustainable and equitable development, and to prevent more effectively the lack of human security contributing to conflict triggers, thus easing the 'security' mandate of the DPA (Annan 2001: 7). The Framework Team was established in 1994, and consists of 'fourteen different departments, agencies, programmes and offices', which meet monthly to 'exchange information from their respected areas of competence and to assess the potential for armed conflict, complex emergencies or other circumstances that might provide a prima facie case for United Nations involvement' (Annan 2001: 22). Coordinated efforts within the UN system presided over by the DPA and the Framework Team were essential to move towards a 'culture of prevention', as central to such a culture is the developing of 'long-term and integrated strategies, combining a wide range of political, economic, social and other measures aimed at reducing or eradicating the underlying causes of conflict' (Annan 2001: 18).

The culture of prevention that Annan envisaged involved a shift of emphasis in the large number of bodies, departments and agencies affected, and also required much greater coordination among these groups. With the overall aim of eradicating the root causes of conflict, the UN system required a consensus on causes and risk factors which could then in turn inform a wide range of projects (Annan 2001: 10). Without such broad coordination and consensus-building efforts, UN preventive efforts would remain ad hoc, and limited in their ability to succeed.

It was the ongoing lack of institutional coordination that highlighted Annan's *Progress Report on the Prevention of Armed Conflict* (Annan 2006). Admitting that 'an unacceptable gap remains between rhetoric and reality' (Annan 2006: 4), Annan declared that the primary obstacle was the inability of the UN to provide leadership and coordination with regards to the many and complex initiatives that were already underway. This coordination 'has fallen short of providing a coherent, over-arching strategy, both in the field, and at Headquarters' (Annan 2006: 26), with the DPA remaining 'significantly under-resourced' and consequently 'not always in a position to respond'; it 'needs to be better equipped to do so' (Annan 2006: 26). While Annan refers to a 'newly strengthened Framework Team', its ability to serve as a focal point for structural prevention continues to be hindered as 'the United Nations system lacks a comprehensive repository for the knowledge gained in its diverse conflict prevention activities – its institutional memory in this field is fragmented and incomplete' (Annan 2006: 27).

The 2006 report on the prevention of conflict indicated that there had been greater discussion of the concept of prevention, but little in the way of results. The report was also noted for its expansion of the concept to include 'systemic prevention', referring to actions and initiatives that aim to lessen the risk of conflict, such as reducing the illicit trade of weapons, confronting environmental degradation and regulating industries that are known to fuel conflict (Annan 2006: 1). There remain two major obstacles to effective prevention by the UN – early warning capacity and coordination of the variety of structural prevention projects that currently operate on an ad hoc basis. Another oversight is the lack of consideration of how states themselves carry out prevention, despite a repeated emphasis on their primary responsibility in this area (Annan 2006: 1, 5, 15). While Annan strongly promoted a 'culture of prevention' on the one hand, and stressed the primary responsibility of states on the other, there was no suggestion as to how these two ideas overlapped. Indeed, there was no discussion of ways that states already carried out this responsibility, nor an examination of how cases of local and national resilience to conflict might impact the way that the UN's preventive activities might be shaped, in order to facilitate positive domestic processes.

Prevention of genocide and mass atrocities

The prevention of genocide, along with its punishment, was legally sanctioned in 1948, with the signing of the Genocide Convention, yet it took many decades for the UN system to begin to institutionalize efforts to prevent this crime. It was not until 2004 that a specific office was set up for this purpose.[5] Nevertheless, there is evidence that the UN had been involved in campaigning against possible genocidal outbreaks and other mass atrocities prior to this, albeit in an ad hoc fashion. As the concept of prevention began to take shape following the end of the Cold War, the same framework was adopted for the prevention of mass atrocities, as seen in key reports on the principle of the Responsibility to Protect (R2P).

For over four decades after the convention entered into law in 1951, no formal efforts to prevent genocide were established, nor was the parlance of the convention utilized in cases where acts of genocide were imminent or already underway. While it defined the crime of genocide and achieved consensus on the need to prevent and punish, it did not specify strategies relevant to these ends (United Nations 1948a). Until the establishment of the Office of the Special Adviser on the Prevention of Genocide (OSAPG) in 2004, there were no departments or programmes within the UN system that directly addressed the issue of genocide prevention. However, this did not mean that there was no activity related to genocide prevention prior to the OSAPG. Rather, the means for engaging in such action, and the language adopted for this purpose, usually avoided any association with the term 'genocide'. An example cited by Kuper is the campaign against Iran's treatment of Bahá'ís in the early 1980s. After the 1979 revolution in Iran, Bahá'ís were specifically targeted, with many arrested, tortured and killed, in an orchestrated effort by the revolutionaries to coerce them into abandoning their religion (Bigelow 1992: 120). In response, Bahá'í communities throughout the world initiated a broad international campaign. The UN Sub-Commission on Prevention of Discrimination and Protection of Minorities eventually adopted the issue in 1980. This led to direct communication between the UN secretary-general and the government of Iran. Both the General Assembly and the Economic and Social Council publicly raised the issue. Together, these actions have been regarded as pivotal in limiting the persecution of the Bahá'ís in Iran, and as Kuper points out, in averting a potential genocide. However, despite the attention it received in the UN, and an abundance of evidence to indicate that there had been attempts to destroy a religious group,[6] these events were never referred to as potential genocide. Instead, as Kuper points out, strategies of genocide prevention were articulated 'under the more acceptable categories of violations of human rights, racial discrimination and religious persecution' (Kuper 1985: 163–64). The desire to avoid using the language of genocide was widespread throughout the Cold War, as major powers 'went to enormous lengths to avoid having to invoke the Convention' (Levene 2004: 155). The outcome of this avoidance was tragically observed a few years after the Cold War, in Rwanda, with 'Western inability or unwillingness to pronounce genocide after April 6, 1994, or do anything to activate the UN to halt it' (Levene 2004: 156).

The two-tiered approach to prevention in relation to mass atrocities became more apparent with the development of the principle of R2P. In its 2001 report by that title, the ICISS followed the Carnegie Commission's lead by emphasizing both long-term and proximate approaches to prevention: 'Encouraging more serious and sustained efforts to address the root cause of the problems that put populations at risk, as well as more effective use of direct prevention measures, is a key objective of the Commission's efforts' (ICISS 2001: 20). When member states endorsed the principle of R2P at the 2005 World Summit, they acknowledged the role that both direct and structural prevention played in ensuring the protection of populations from the crimes of genocide, war crimes, ethnic cleansing and crimes against humanity. In emphasizing the role of individual states in carrying out their responsibility, the document stressed, 'this responsibility entails the prevention of such crimes, including their incitement' (United Nations General Assembly 2005). Subsequent to the international endorsement of the Responsibility to Protect principle, structural prevention of the four included crimes – genocide, ethnic cleansing, war crimes and crimes against humanity – has continued to be articulated in a similar way. UN Secretary-General Ban Ki-moon's 2009 report, *Implementing the Responsibility to Protect*, for example, emphasized the need to address the 'underlying fissures in the social and political fabric particularly in states and regions where ethnic tensions run high and deep inequalities among groups persist' (Ban 2009a: 19).

Prior to the World Summit, Kofi Annan's High Level Panel on Threats, Challenges and Change (HLP) posited that the prevention of genocide and mass atrocities, along with a range of other threats, such as conflict, terrorism and infectious diseases, needed to be confronted primarily through national development. It argued that compounding poverty and ethnic or territorial inequalities provokes grievances that substantially raise the likelihood of civil violence (HLP 2004: 23–24). The HLP therefore, focused principally on advocating structural preventive strategies, aimed at dealing with the root causes of atrocities.

Ten years after the Rwandan genocide, Secretary-General Annan established the OSAPG. The Office's approach to prevention can be divided into both operational and structural strategies. In terms of operational prevention, it engages in advocacy in response to its own early warning analysis, while its structural preventive strategies are somewhat broader. The Office stressed, 'To prevent genocide and genocidal conflicts, it is critically important to understand their root causes' (OSAPG 2011a), which 'revolve around inequalities between identity groups' (OSAPG 2011b). The Office then stated that such activity includes the promoting of equitable economic development and political representation, as well as the fostering of tolerance amidst social diversity – linking the risk of genocide to a broad range of tensions and inequalities inherent in many societies. For the Special Adviser, prevention clearly involves both long-term strategies and proximate strategies.

Regional organizations and prevention

A number of regional and sub-regional organizations have also been proactive in prioritizing and institutionalizing preventive policies (Ackermann 2003: 340; Bellamy 2009: 137). The EU, itself an example of an organization with the purpose to mitigate or prevent conflict, has also organized a number of 'assessment missions' to Indonesia, Nepal, Fiji and Papua New Guinea, in order to develop the capacity for conflict prevention and crisis management in local communities (Ackermann 2003: 344; Bellamy 2008: 137). It also established the Göteborg Programme in 2005, which engages in a variety of international projects committed to the prevention of conflict, as well as improving coordination with other regional organizations (Hamburg 2008: 243). For its part, the OSCE contains a number of institutions that are active in a wide range of preventive activities, from structural prevention through its Office for Democratic Institutions and Human Rights (ODIHR) to preventive (and quiet) diplomacy through the Office of the High Commissioner on National Minorities (Ekeus 2003, 2006; Hamburg 2008: 247–49). Indeed, the OSCE pioneered the institutionalization of long-term prevention, at a time in the early 1990s when such notions had only begun to be proposed in the UN (Ackermann 2003: 344). The African Union (AU) provides a range of institutional mechanisms for conflict prevention, largely housed in the Peace and Security Department, which contains a Conflict Management Division. It also runs the Continental Early Warning System, 'in order to facilitate the anticipation and prevention of conflicts in Africa' (African Union 2011). Other organizations, such as the Organization of American States (OAS), the Economic Community of West African States (ECOWAS), the Asian Regional Forum (ARF) within the Association of Southeast Asian Nations (ASEAN), and NATO, have incorporated programmes that engage in both direct and structural prevention of violent conflict.

Summary

Since the end of the Cold War, the concept of prevention has gained in attention and clarity, both at the UN and in regional organizations. Increased interest is evident in resolving and preventing intrastate conflicts, many of which were characterized by atrocities against civilians. The UN has formalized prevention, both for conflict as well as mass atrocities in a range of departments and agencies, with the OSAPG in the Secretariat, as well as the role of the DPA in providing an 'anchor' for the UN's efforts at peace making and conflict prevention. Regional organizations such as the EU, OSCE and AU have pioneered a range of approaches that have challenged policy makers to move beyond traditional methods of prevention, resting largely on preventive diplomacy and preventive deployments. However, despite more than two decades of renewed interest in prevention, many challenges remain. The end of the Cold War coincided with the commission of mass atrocities in the Caucasus and the Balkans, including the genocidal massacre in Srebrenica. The genocide in Rwanda, in particular, tragically highlighted the international community's ambivalence toward preventing mass violence. Calls by Kofi Annan in 2001 for the UN system to develop a 'culture of prevention' have not yet materialized. In a 2006 progress report, Annan himself acknowledged that a gap remained between rhetoric and action; in 2009, Ban Ki-moon stated: 'The United Nations and its Member States remain unprepared to meet their most fundamental prevention and protection responsibilities' (Ban 2009a: 6). Despite prevention being one of the principal priorities of the UN, limitations clearly remain. These limitations reflected problems intrinsic to the concept of prevention, highlighted below.

Operational prevention or structural prevention?

The prevention of violent conflict, and mass atrocities in particular, has become more institutionalized, but still faces constraints in its capacity to develop fully a system-wide 'culture of prevention'. Political problems are indicative of the challenges inherent in the coordination and commitment needed to translate the idea of prevention into a set of practical and effective policies, or a framework for an array of developmental, environmental, legal and social programmes already in place. Inherent in these challenges is the question of whether or not the two-pronged definition of prevention is too broad to warrant effective implementation.

Indeed, some scholars have pointed out that the concept tries to incorporate too much, running the risk of becoming irrelevant (de Wilde 2006; Luck 2002; Moolakkattu 2005; Swanstrom 2005). Edward Luck (2002: 256) referred to this as the 'dilemma of comprehensiveness', meaning that prevention, in trying to be too many things to too many people, has spread itself too thinly to be effective. Luck contended that to overcome the risk of irrelevance, there needed to be a solid and practical set of initiatives which would move the idea of prevention from rhetoric to action. Otherwise, there was a danger that conflict prevention would follow the well-worn path toward 'rhetorical glory and programmatic irrelevance' (Luck 2002: 257). For Luck, this meant focusing initially on operational prevention. This, he posited, would enable the UN to harness the policy tools that it already had in place for conflict and dispute resolution, and thus would be a logical way of approaching conflict prevention from a policy perspective (Luck 2002: 259). Such an approach would give priority to operational prevention as 'an immediate policy option', one that would enable the 'broad' concept of prevention to live beyond the realms of rhetoric (Luck 2002: 268).

Luck's claim – that we need a greater initial emphasis on operational prevention – is logical, but may not be practical. Key member states have always shown a great reluctance to permit any substantial injection of resources into a UN early warning system – the necessary cornerstone of operational prevention, as evidenced by the short-lived efforts within the ORCI in the late 1980s and early 1990s, as well as the financial constraints imposed on the DPA. Attempts to operationalize early warning in ORCI were met with resistance from many member states, and this was manifested in its limited resources and incapacity to fulfil its role of collecting and analysing information. Peck argued that many of these member states had two concerns: one was the suspicion that preventive diplomacy and early warning were part of a hegemonic and interventionist agenda by Northern states, and second, a belief that Northern states had little interest in the South's social and economic needs (Peck 1998: 69). This suspicion can be attributed to the perceived links between operational prevention and 'Western intervention', as reflected in the lack of funding for the DPA.

The DPA's constraints are not limited to early warning and analysis. Until recently, the department's budget was so small that it was unable to finance adequate field missions for fact finding and diplomacy. Of the two funds set up for conflict prevention since 1999, little more than US$50 million has been donated by member states after ten years. This limited access to funds led the UN Secretariat to claim that there have been 'deliberate' attempts to keep the

DPA from fulfilling the goals of coordinated prevention (Bellamy 2009: 115–16). The Human Security Report observed that the DPA is overstretched to the point that it is unable to engage in preventive diplomacy, and is hamstrung in dealing with crises (Human Security Report Project 2011: 65). Although the General Assembly agreed to expand the budget of the DPA in 2009, its capacity for early warning, fact finding and preventive diplomacy remains limited (Zenko and Friedman 2011: 23). At the same time, the department has been broadening its mandate, engaging in more 'long-term' preventive projects 'better associated with structural prevention – projects to strengthen human rights and the rule of law, carry out security sector and socio-economic reform, or promote dialogue in polarized societies' (UNDPA 2008). The more distance between prevention and military options, the less resistance seems to be encountered from member states.

Preventive strategies that neglect to address the structural risk factors associated with genocide and mass atrocities may have limited value. There is broad consensus on the notion that most genocides are deliberate and planned acts carried out for the most part by political elites (see, for example, Fein 1979; Kuper 1981; Midlarsky 2005; Semelin 2007). Bearing this in mind, it is arguable that such strategies of preventive diplomacy, sanctions or peace making to prevent such occurrences of mass atrocities once such violence is imminent are unlikely to yield positive results if a government (or other elites) has already decided to carry out such action. Past interventions in Kosovo in 1999 and Libya in 2011 demonstrate that often only the costly option of military intervention is likely to have an effect, and this, as Levene (2004: 158) claimed, works only in rogue or 'failed' states. This kind of 'technical fix', Levene rightly argued, could equally be applied to any operational preventive strategy that attempted to solve the problem 'without dealing with its root cause' (Levene 2004: 158). Preventing genocide and mass atrocities by addressing their root causes means addressing the conditions that allow for actors with violent exclusionary policies to gain power (see, for example, Kuper 1981: 51). In short, there is much political resistance by member states to the use of operational prevention measures within the UN system, and much of the scholarship on the prevention of genocide and mass atrocities makes strong claims for the need to address the underlying causes that give rise to more visible escalating factors.[7]

Conceptual limitations of structural prevention

While structural prevention is indeed a necessary dimension in the mitigation of risk against mass atrocities, the concept – as articulated originally in the Carnegie Commission's report – is not without its problems. By framing structural prevention as the identification and addressing of root causes, researchers and policy makers are faced with two major limitations. First, the public health model approach to long-term prevention has encouraged a tendency towards external diagnosis and prognosis, prioritizing the role of international actors in determining the root causes of potential conflict, as well as the correct strategies to deal with them. Second, this notion of prevention assumes that the existence of root causes will necessarily result in a violent outcome if not dealt with, suggesting a linear connection between cause and outcome. These limitations exclude a consideration of the local and national capacities for building resilience to the risk posed by such root causes, and as a consequence overlook the role that domestic actors play in the prevention of mass atrocities.

Emphasis on international actors

Research and policy making on conflict/atrocity prevention is almost entirely focused on the role of international actors, consequently neglecting what states and communities already do themselves to manage diversity and mitigate risk. Principal proponents of prevention include the UN, regional organizations, international nongovernmental organizations (NGOs) and wealthy nations acting as donors. It is rare in the literature on structural prevention to consider the role of local and national actors. I do not mean to suggest that international actors do not make valuable and often crucial contributions in terms of structural prevention. Rather, my point is that the role of such actors is discussed without considering what local and national actors might already be doing to mitigate the risk of mass violence. Consequently, the role international actors play in prevention is not discussed in terms of how they may facilitate processes that already work.

In the literature on structural prevention, key preventive actors are almost always external to the places deemed at risk. Indeed, some definitions of prevention explicitly exclude local and national actors in places of concern (see, for example, Stewart 2005: 13; Wallensteen 2002: 214). Other sources, in discussing prevention actors, typically identify the UN, regional organizations, international NGOs and Western liberal-democratic states as the key players. Local communities and national governments in places where preventive strategies are directed are mentioned – if at all – mostly in passing (see, for example, Carment and Schnabel 2003: 18–20; Hampson and Malone 2002: 8–10; Lund 2002: 159–63; Kapila and Wermester 2002: 299; Sriram and Wermester 2003: 393; Hamburg 2008: 5–6). This is reflected in the key (mostly edited) publications on prevention that have appeared over the last decade – in chapters devoted to the role of preventive actors, international and regional organizations are featured prominently, as are (albeit to a lesser extent) national external actors and international NGOs (Carment and Schnabel 2003; Hampson *et al.* 2002; Sriram and Wermester 2003; Schnabel and Carment 2004; Hamburg 2008). There are a few exceptions to this. For example, Dress and Rosenblum-Kumar (2002: 230) stress that a *broad* spectrum of preventive actors – from local to international – can improve the capacity for such action. Chirot and McCauley (2006: 155) go further by examining a range of state policies aimed at managing tension between identity groups in countries, such as India, Switzerland and Canada, where ethnic and religious diversity exists.

Overlooking domestic examples of success in the effective management of risk and diversity accentuates the culture of external diagnosis and trouble-shooting, and gives preventive action a paternalistic character, particularly when it is rare for such research to consider what is already happening to prevent conflict and mass atrocities.[8] Moreover, strategies aimed at preserving or restoring peace generally require commitments that last years or decades – well beyond the immediate interests of external parties who often lack the necessary perseverance for sustained long-term effectiveness (see, for example, Lederach and Appleby 2010: 24).

Even when the parlance of prevention shifts to incorporate greater state responsibility domestically/internally, there remains much ambiguity about how this is actually carried out. State responsibility is repeatedly stressed in numerous UN reports on prevention. Kofi Annan's first report on prevention stated: 'the primary responsibility for conflict prevention rests with national governments, with civil society playing an important role' (Annan 2001: 2). Subsequent reports by both Annan and Ban Ki-moon echoed this (Annan 2006: 1; Ban 2008: 2; Ban 2009a: 8). However, there is almost no guidance on how to recognize fulfilment of that obligation. Much is known about the absence of responsibility, but little about its presence. More recently, a con-sensus has emerged regarding the prevention of mass atrocities, as seen in the overwhelming number of member states that vocally endorsed the principle of the Responsibility to Protect in the General Assembly in 2009 (Ban 2009b: 1). Significantly, the three-pillar strategy of the principle, as articulated in the 2005 World Summit Outcome document, clearly identified state responsibility as of primary importance in atrocity prevention. This was an endorsement of a principle for the prevention of mass atrocities that does not assume third party diagnosis and prognosis as the starting point.[9] Given this, it is surpris-ing that so little research investigates how states effectively carry out this responsibility, and little attention is paid to what limited research exists.

Assuming the inevitability of violent outcomes

Premising prevention on the identification and removal of root causes assumes a linear relationship between cause and outcome – that such violence will inevitably occur if the root causes are not dealt with. It suggests that the existence of conditions that constitute root causes necessitates their removal, and that doing so will result in the prevention of mass atrocities. For example, in his 2008 report on prevention in Africa, Ban Ki-moon emphasized, 'if we do not deal with the root causes – and offer sustainable solutions – we will be left with humanitarian emergencies and peacekeeping operations without end' (Ban 2008). Often the linear relationship between cause and violent outcome is suggested through the positioning of root causes as the first of a number of stages, or phases, eventually culminating in violence. The stages of conflict typically progress from 'pre-violence', or 'potential violence' – representing the existence of root causes – then usually pass through periods of 'gestation' and 'escalation' (see, for example, Draman 2003: 234; Rothchild 2003: 44–56; Stanton 1996). While there are caveats,[10] the assumption of a linear relationship between cause and outcome nonetheless remains. Framing structural prevention within a 'conflict continuum' (Dress and Rosenblum-Kumar 2002: 241) or a 'temporal continuum' (Talentino 2003: 71) invites a certain policy logic – that not only is it better to tackle these problems earlier rather than later, but that not tackling such problems at an early stage will inevitably result in the need to deal with more complex challenges later on. Dress and Rosenblum-Kumar (2002: 241) advocate the need to 'develop interventions aimed at poverty alleviation, social empowerment, and reducing horizontal inequality'. Draman regards such early stage prevention by international actors (particularly the UN) as 'morally imperative', and crucial to ensuring the genie does not escape the bottle (Draman 2003: 241; see also Eliasson 1996: 318). Once such root causes are known to exist, there is a need to act, lest these causes are allowed to progress from the stage of pre-violence to one of gestation.

However, just as some contend that preventive approaches in public health tend to lead to over-diagnosis, there is a similar risk that theorists of conflict and mass atrocities prevention may conclude wrongly that violent outcomes are inevitable if action is not taken. Indeed, there is a general consensus that long-term risk factors have at best a tenuous causal link with mass violence. While they create the conditions that are conducive to atrocities, these preconditions are not sufficient in and of themselves directly to cause such episodes of violence (see, for example, Fein 1979; Harff 2003; Kuper 1981; Midlarsky 2005; Semelin 2007). In fact, the perpetration of mass atrocities is rare – the exception rather than the norm. According to Genocide Watch's survey of countries that experienced significant risk of genocidal violence between 1945 and 2008,[11] for every country that reached stage seven (genocidal, as well as non-genocidal massacres), there were two that did not (Genocide Prevention Advisory Network 2009). Chirot and McCauley (2006: 95) point out that genocide, a crime that occurs predominantly during violent conflict, is 'far less common than warfare itself'. Risk often exists without inevitably resulting in the perpetration of mass atrocities. Clearly there is a gap between the assumptions embedded in the concept of structural prevention, and the findings of the research on the causes of mass atrocities.

To suggest – as the concept of structural prevention does – that it is necessary to ameliorate root causes once they have been identified, runs counter to what is known about the long-term causes of mass atrocities. If, as the scholarship on comparative genocide studies suggests, the existence of root causes does not indicate an inevitable violent outcome, what other outcomes are common? In countries that contain these root causes, the local dynamics and processes that steer them away from violent outcomes are clearly worthy of investigation, and are potentially a valuable insight into national sources of resilience that deter violent outcomes. However, under-standing the capacity of the sovereign to prevent genocide and mass atrocities, and examining the policies of those who have done so, have not been hitherto a priority within the literature on structural prevention.

In fact, such positive dynamics are also largely overlooked in comparative genocide studies. Despite a consensus that high risk-prevalence is not suffi-cient for the perpetration of mass violence, very little research has been con-ducted into the reasons why many societies that evince these root causes and risk factors have *not* experienced violent outcomes. Such scholarship itself has a tendency to focus on 'what goes wrong'. Methodologically, the approach amongst most comparative genocide scholars is to select a number of cases of past genocides and to examine their contributing factors – those factors that are common across cases – then form the theoretical bases found in com-parative genocide studies (see, for example, Straus 2012: 343; McLoughlin and Mayersen 2013).[12] While such research has yielded valuable knowledge on the antecedents of past genocide, very little has been learned about which factors deter the outcome of violence where risk exists. Such knowledge is clearly valuable for the long-term prevention of genocide and other mass atrocities.[13]

The way forward

These limitations suggest that structural prevention needs to be framed more broadly, by incorporating an understanding of how long-term risk is miti-gated by local and national sources of resilience. The policy focus for pre-vention, Susan Woodward argued, 'should not be on causes as conventionally understood but on how mechanisms that keep limits on the use of violence as a means to political ends are destabilized or restored' (Woodward 2007: 158). Prevention needs to include not just fixing what is wrong, but ensuring that what is 'right' and positive remains strong. As Detlev Wolter attested, 'Such research is almost entirely focussed on what is wrong with societies and fails to provide a framework for identifying and assessing the forces that work, in every society, against conflict' (Wolter 2007: 50). This, in fact, is the essence of peace building, as articulated both by Gareth Evans and the Carnegie Com-mission's Report, *Preventing Deadly Conflict*. Evans stated that peace build-ing comprises actions that stable countries do as a matter of course (Evans 1993: 50), and the Carnegie Commission's Report declared that structural prevention is in essence peace building (Hamburg and Vance 1997: xxxviii). In this way, structural prevention can be seen not simply as preventing something, but as creating the basis for stable and equitable societies and states. In order to understand what mechanisms are needed to 'keep limits on the use of violence', it is necessary, Woodward argued, to understand not only the causes of conflict, but the causes of violence, and hence the way that it may be translated for political ends, even if its origin served a different pur-pose. In this sense, she highlighted the importance of Stathis Kalyvas's work as an important contribution to our growing understanding of root causes of intra-state conflict (Woodward 2007: 156). Kalyvas's contribution to the debate on root causes was to highlight what he claimed was a distinction between the political causes of civil war, and the causes of violence in a civil war. This distinction is necessary, he argued, because there is a disjunction between what happens at the top and what happens on the ground. Civil wars, he claimed, are 'ambiguous'. There is a range of goals and actors, which means that the fighting carried out at a local level might be at odds with the interests promoted by the centre (Kalyvas 2003: 476). 'It is the convergence of local motives and supralocal imperatives that endows civil wars with their particular and often puzzling character', he argued (Kalyvas 2003: 487). This again has relevance particularly for structural prevention. This understanding of the complexity and multilayered character of civil wars stresses the need to explore ways to 'prevent translation into violence and provide ways of managing social tension' (Kalyvas 2003: 485). In other words, the goal of long-term prevention is better served not only by identifying and addressing root causes and risk factors, but by focusing on ways that tensions can be managed when they arise. The peace building that Evans pointed to as being the normal functioning of stable states may provide answers as to how disputes that naturally arise within groups are resolved without recourse to violence.

Conclusion

Preventing war – long recognized as the incubator of mass atrocity – has been the main goal of the UN since its inception. However, until the 1990s, attempts at atrocity prevention have been sporadic and ad hoc. Renewed interest since the end of the Cold War saw progress in clarifying the concept. Pioneering reports consolidated traditional approaches of preventive diplomacy and preventive deployments, but also encouraged a broader approach to address the long-term root causes of conflict and mass atrocities. This broader approach is not without its critics, with some claiming that it runs the risk of stretching the concept of prevention beyond practical use. However, long-term measures are generally less politically controversial, and reflect the desire of many developing states to receive greater developmental support.

Despite this, there is still a tendency in approaches to the structural prevention of mass atrocities to focus solely on the role of international actors in identifying root causes and determining solutions. This overlooks the repeated emphasis in UN reports on the primary responsibility that states have in prevention. However, very little research has been conducted into the preventive work that individual governments and communities do, particularly in countries that are located in regions characterized by civil war and atrocities.

This chapter has sought to demonstrate two things. For the prevention of mass atrocities, it is important to invest in long-term strategies prior to the emergence of a political elite with an exclusionary ideology (often with destructive policies). Although direct prevention is necessary for cases of escalating tension and violence, without addressing the structural factors that made such violence conducive in the first place, its effectiveness is limited. Second, although the tackling of root causes through structural preventive action needs greater priority, the current framing of structural prevention is highly restrictive, as it overlooks what states and their citizens are doing to mitigate the risk posed by 'root causes' and risk factors. As the Human Security Report of 2009/2010 observes, 'The causes of peace ... appear to interest scholars much less than the causes of war' (Human Security Report Project 2011: 61). This is a profound oversight, especially considering that research into the root causes of ethnic conflict and genocide points to sources being local. They are generally rooted in identity, patterns of social relations, and the behaviour of national institutions.[14]

The next chapter provides greater detail about the research into root causes. Given the local nature of many root causes, one must question the assumption that structural prevention requires external solutions, administered by external actors, to complex local problems. A broader approach to prevention is needed: one that considers not only the complex causal dynamics, but also the processes that work to build resilience in communities and states, and guard against outbreaks of mass atrocity.

Notes

1 Dag Hammarskjöld coined the term 'preventive diplomacy' in 1960.
2 A more detailed discussion of the UN Charter and its 'provisions' for prevention can be found in Dedring 1998: 46–48.
3 This is a notion of peace building that goes beyond an association solely with post-conflict reconstruction, as articulated in *An Agenda for Peace*. See, for example Evans 1993: 40.
4 For an example of the successful use of preventive diplomacy in response to mass atrocities, see Cohen 2008.
5 The Office of the Special Adviser on the Prevention of Genocide, based at the UN Secretariat.
6 Which, according to Article II of the Genocide Convention, comprises a 'genocidal act'.
7 This is not to say that the UN is unengaged in long-term prevention. Much of the work the UNDP does, for example tackling poverty, strengthening democracy and empowering women, strongly resembles structural prevention, although it is rarely framed as such.
8 Indeed, Oliver Richmond argues that reports such as the Carnegie Commission's *Preventing Deadly Violence* aim to preserve a 'specific' and 'prior understanding of what constitutes peace' (Richmond 2005: 12).
9 Although international assistance is the second pillar, and an international response to the failure of such responsibility through the UN's chapter VI and VII powers comprises the third pillar.
10 For example, the articulation of phases is not meant to be a restrictive guide (see, for example, Sriram and Wermester 2003: 20–29), and each episode of conflict or mass violence has its own unique contextually specific set of drivers.
11 Stage four or above, according to Stanton's (1996) 'eight stages of genocide'.

12 Such scholars include Fein (1979); Kiernan (2007); Mann (2005); Melson (1992); Midlarsky (2005); Semelin (2007); and Valentino (2004). While negative cases (non-genocidal cases) are sometimes referred to (as in Midlarsky's book, *The Killing Trap*), they are never included as one of the principal analytical subjects. One exception here is Mayersen and McLoughlin (2011), who provide a comparative analysis of one positive (Rwanda) and one negative (Botswana) case, in order to understand not only 'what goes wrong' but also 'what goes right' when the risk of genocide and mass atrocities are present. Also worth noting is Adam Jones's *Genocide: A Comprehensive Introduction* (2nd edition, 2010). In the final chapter, 'Strategies of Intervention and Prevention', he identifies a number of 'success stories' – countries and regions that have avoided genocide despite the presence of 'ethnoreligious divisions and, often, histories of intercommunal conflict' (Jones 2010: 582).

13 Chapter 2 provides a more detailed discussion of the research into causes of genocide and mass atrocities, according to scholars of comparative genocide studies, civil war and ethnic conflict.

14 It is also important to point out that the complex historical dynamics in all states preclude claims that such root causes arise in isolation of international influences. No state is immune to international influence, yet all states are faced with the challenges of using national institutions and organizations to manage the political, economic and social complexities that materialize over time.

2 Re-examining the root causes of mass atrocities

Scholarly research into the root causes of genocide and other mass atrocities reveals a remarkable range of factors at play. From the '*imaginaire* of the individual' (Semelin 2007: 10) to the destructive policies of exclusionary governments (Fein 1979; Kuper 1981), the causal path to mass atrocities is neither straight nor simple. Despite this, an overview of the broad research into such long-term causes illuminates two common elements. One is that the link between root causes and violent outcomes is at best a tenuous one. In particular, scholars of comparative genocide studies have stressed that the structural precursors to such violence are necessary but insufficient factors (Fein 1979; Chirot 1981; Kuper and McCauley 2006). Second, although there are some broad elements that act as common antecedents to episodes of mass atrocities, their precise nature is complex and contextually specific. It is logical to assume that the processes of risk mitigation are equally complex and contextually specific. Yet it is surprising that most scholars studying genocide and other mass atrocities provide recommendations for prevention that are largely formulaic, and rely on third-party intervention or punishment.

This chapter presents an overview of the scholarship on the causes of genocide and other mass atrocities. Theories of ethnic conflict and civil war, where atrocities are often committed, and theories of genocide and other forms of mass violence are outlined. The chapter then appraises these sources' suggestions and recommendations for prevention. I argue that throughout the claims of this broad scholarship, there is at best a tenuous causal link between root causes and violent outcome. However, the root causes of such violence are largely local in character, and deeply contextual. Despite this, most suggestions for prevention do not consider contextually specific responses to the risk that root causes pose. Instead, these suggestions overwhelmingly favour third-party interventions or punishment as a deterrent. Ironically, these recommendations give oxygen to the notion that long-term prevention is about the identification and amelioration of root causes, and that prevention is a process best steered by external actors. Nevertheless, a small pool of researchers offers alternative approaches emphasizing positive domestic processes that constructively manage diversity. Such approaches mitigate the risk associated with potential mass atrocities. Using these alternative approaches as a starting point, I make the case for the need to go beyond the root cause paradigm that underscores structural prevention. A more comprehensive approach to understanding prevention is required – one that incorporates a broader conceptual framework, and is informed by an understanding of the dynamic relationship between risk and resilience.

Mass atrocities: root causes and risk factors

Most mass atrocities are committed during war, and since the Second World War, most wars have been intra-state in character. According to Bellamy, since 1945, 67 per cent of episodes of mass atrocities were committed during armed conflict, and since 1980 this rose to 85 per cent (Bellamy 2011: 2). Therefore, to provide a comprehensive survey of research into the causes of these atrocities, theories of genocide and atrocities will be presented alongside theories of the types of armed conflict in which such atrocities commonly occur, such as ethnic conflicts and civil wars.

Ethnic conflict

Since the end of the Cold War, academic interest in intra-state conflicts characterized by ethnic tension has grown markedly. Researchers initially divided into those who claimed primordial ties were at the centre, and those who argued that political elites manipulated such notions for their own gain. Over the last decade, some theorists have incorporated both approaches into frameworks that aim to account for the complex factors contributing to such identity conflicts.

The theory of primordialism, as developed by Geertz (1973), Stack (1986) and Connor (1998), can be broken into two interconnected parts. Primordialists argue that in order to understand why ethnic conflict arises, it is first necessary to understand what binds the ethnic group. Primordialism means the identity of the group is based on traditions and ties deeply rooted in the past. This identity may have its origins in certain biological traits as well as in language, kinship and territory (Suny 2004: 28). Primordialists argue that ethnicity comes from 'a sense of peoplehood' (Stack 1986: 1), through bonds of kin, shared language and a number of common social practices, the bonds of which often transcend personal or collective interest in the present (Geertz 1973: 259). In this way, primordialists have attempted to conceptualize the intangibility of ethnicity rather than dismiss it outright (see, for example, Connor 1978: 390–91). Although such bonds are subject to change over time, they also contain an almost irrational resilience, which, according to Connor (1998: 5), 'is subconscious and emotional rather than conscious and rational'.

According to primordialists, conflict between ethnic groups occurs out of a hatred or fear of those who are different (Suny 2004: 28). This arises from a perceived threat to group existence or apparent incompatibility between different groups who live in close proximity to each other (Horowitz 1985:

175–81). The powerful unifying force of identity, as Stack argues, 'is often accompanied by a recognition of the differences that divide mankind' (Stack 1986: 3), or what Horowitz (1985: 144) refers to as a 'tendency to cleave and compare'. While this tension and apparent incompatibility between groups is clearly local in character, the primordialist approach does not effectively account for many groups cohabiting in cities, towns and regions peaceably for decades. Other theories that highlight the orchestration of ethnic difference for political ends by local and national elites show that ethnic difference on its own rarely accounts for violent conflict.

In contrast to primordialists, proponents of instrumentalism claim that in such conflicts, ethnicity is 'instrumental', but is not the sole or the principal cause. Instead, ethnicity is used, usually by political elites, to achieve a certain end: namely, to consolidate their own power amidst changing political and economic circumstances. The manipulation of the people by leaders or elites occurred, as Gagnon claims, in Yugoslavia in the early 1990s during the breakdown of the old communist power structure following the death of Tito. He claims that 'ethnic conflict along ethnic cleavages is provoked by elites in order to create a domestic political context where ethnicity is the only relevant identity' (Gagnon 1994: 132). Similar shifts of power also took place in the former Soviet Union, and triggered, as many have claimed, similar elite strategies of manipulation and provocation to cement their ongoing power during the transition that started during perestroika and continued after the collapse of the Soviet Union (Derlugian 1998; Lipschultz 1998; Roeder 1998).

Instrumentalists like Lipschultz (1998: 44) argue that ethnic conflict is 'about the struggle for state power'. The causes of these conflicts are found not only in the internal make-up of the countries, but in the 'global processes and forces impinging on these domestic configurations' (Lipschultz 1998: 44). In other words, if there is a struggle for power within a country or a region, then it is necessary to focus on the instability that triggered this struggle, and examine contingent forces both within and beyond the borders of the region. This instability is usually the result of changing economic forces, which in most cases are part of the transition toward a more liberal and globally connected market (Lipschultz 1998: 54). Lipschultz notes a tendency for 'political entrepreneurs' to take advantage of instability to consolidate or build on their own power; this often involves the manipulation of one ethnic group against another (Lipschultz 1998: 68). Referring to post-Soviet conflicts, Roeder suggests that conflicts that appear to be ethnic in nature in fact involve a variety of dynamics that aggravate ethnic tensions; ethnicity is not the 'root cause' of the conflicts. Instead, it is the behaviour of leaders that poses the most pressing problem (Roeder 1998: 78). Roeder claims that virtually all of these 'ethnic' conflicts 'focus on conflicts among political entrepreneurs within the administrative apparatus of the successor states' (Roeder 1998: 79). Mueller makes a similar point in his argument that the civil war in Bosnia was motivated not by ethnic hatred, but by a small number of criminals and militia groups commissioned by the Serbian government to create violent ethnic conflicts in generally peaceful and harmonious communities (Mueller 2000: 42).

However, a focus on the role of political elites is, as Kaufman argues, inadequate to understand fully the causes and nature of the violence that characterizes ethnic conflict. His proposed theory of symbolic politics is a hybrid of different explanations of ethnic war, including primordialism and instrumentalism (Kaufman 2001: 2). Kaufman draws upon both ethnic myths and ancient hatreds, but with the understanding that this ancient hatred is not so much ancient as recent – regenerated to suit current circumstances. These myths, therefore, are 'modern recastings' of something that may or may not have been true in the past (Kaufman 2001: 11). Ethnic mobilization arises when, first, there exists a 'conflict of interest', real or perceived; and second, 'mythically based' feelings that can be tapped and mobilized (Kaufman 2001: 12). This does not mean that war is automatically the outcome, as is evident during the breakdown of the Soviet Union, where nine out of the 15 new states experienced war. However, in all of those nine places, certain risk factors were evident, and can be seen as preconditions for ethnic war. They include the existence of ethnic myths and fears, and the capacity to act violently in response to these fears. A sense of chauvinism within the ethnic group is also often present. Hostile actions can be led either by the populace or by an elite group, but they almost always result from a sense of insecurity brought about by extremist politics, creating a problem that spirals into violence, and leaves no space for moderate views (Kaufman 2001: 12). In addition to myths, there usually exists a fear or real threat of extinction. When the state grants a licence to sublimate these fears in political unity and violent comradeship, the likelihood of ethnic conflict increases dramatically (Kaufman 2001: 30–32). Financial or military support from outside also raises the risk of violent conflict (Kaufman 2001: 33).

Like Kaufman, Toft's theory of 'indivisible territory' includes elements of both primordialism and instrumentalism. The notion of 'indivisible territory' is based on both intangible and instrumentalist perspectives, and explores how conflict arises when the two perspectives clash. According to Toft, violence is a very real possibility when, first, a minority ethnic group (within a larger state) makes a claim for the territory it inhabits; and second, when the state of which the ethnic group is a part regards this territory as 'indivisible' from the remainder (Toft 2003: 18). For these conditions to come about, an ethnic group's population must be concentrated in a specific region within the larger state (Toft 2003: 18).

For states, territory is power. In other words, 'territory (maintaining borders) is a matter of physical survival' (Toft 2003: 132). A challenge to this is usually met with opposition. If the state is composed of a number of different ethnic groups, each inhabiting and attached to specific regions, then Toft claims the issue of 'precedence' is pertinent (Toft 2003: 28). In other words, if one group's attempt to gain sovereignty opens the way for others, then the response is usually uncompromising refusal. Indivisibility increases the likelihood of violence, and although an ethnic group's connection to the land may not be based on notions of power and material gain, its confrontation with the state may still be rational. Toft posits that confronting the state may be rational if there is a good chance of the group achieving its aims or securing at least some benefits. In other instances, the choice to fight may have been provoked by the state; if conditions are particularly bad, there may be nothing to lose by fighting. The region in question may also have support from abroad, which may improve its chances of winning. Therefore, to understand the causes of ethnic conflict, it is important to understand what territory means to the actors in question.

These four approaches to ethnic conflict display some major differences. Proponents of primordialism, for example, place historically rooted identity at the heart of mobilization and violence, whereas instrumentalists regarded such identity as a tool with which political elites impose their goals. However, some scholars argue for understanding both the emotional power of identity and the role of elites in harnessing such emotion. Toft and Kaufman consider how these dynamics interacted. Despite differences in perspectives, all these theories point to local and domestic sources of violence – violence arising out of hatred and fear between groups, the manipulation of identity for political purposes, conflicting claims to territory, or the complex relationship between 'recast myths', ethnic mobilization and the capacity for elite or grassroots actors to respond to the hostility evoked by extreme politics.

Civil war

The evolution of theories of ethnic conflict throughout the 1990s took place within a broader evolution of understanding civil war since the Second World War. More recently, perspectives that use economics to explain conflict have grown in prominence (Zartman 2005: 258). The large-sample quantitative studies conducted by Collier and Hoeffler, Fearon and Laitin, and Sambanis offer valuable insights into the factors that correlate with civil war, although their conclusions varied. In addition to these studies, Kaldor and Kalyvas also make significant theoretical contributions.

Two large quantitative studies concluded that economic opportunity amidst widespread poverty is the key motivating factor in the onset of civil war. One study, developed by Collier and Hoeffler, measured the influence of a number of conditions on a dataset of 161 countries. The Collier/Hoeffler (CH) model contends that the failure of economic development contributes most significantly to internal conflict (Collier *et al.* 2003: 53). Grievance does not play a significant role in causing civil war onset, they argue; for civil war to break out, a number of conditions have to be in place, providing an opportunity for rebel groups to wage a sustained and effective fight. These include the availability of finance, a suitable terrain (to shelter insurgents) and a relatively low cost of fighting (usually the ability to draw from unemployed males in an economically depressed country) (Collier *et al.* 2005: 6). Like Collier and

Hoeffler, Fearon and Laitin argue that civil wars in the 1990s were not due to the end of the Cold War, nor to grievances held by identity groups. Rather, 'conditions that favor insurgency' were key (Fearon and Laitin 2003: 75). They included state weakness, poverty, a large population and instability (Fearon and Laitin 2003: 88).

In contrast to the CH model, Fearon and Laitin argue that 'primary commodity exports and rates of secondary school enrollment for males' have no bearing on the onset of civil wars (Fearon and Laitin 2003: 76). However, both studies claim that identity-related grievances have little correlation with the factors and conditions preceding civil war. In fact, such general correlates of war fail to account for why people choose to mobilize and fight rather than adopt another course of action. This is significant because many countries that possess such conditions have not experienced civil war. Burkina Faso, Zambia and Tanzania, to name a few, have all experienced prolonged conditions of poverty, and have been surrounded by countries of similar size and topography. Yet they have avoided civil war.

Identity-based grievances have also been recognized as important root causes of some civil wars. Sambanis, for example, argues that recognizing key differences between 'identity' and 'non-identity' civil wars could provide crucial insights into their root causes, and 'this can lead to the design of policy to better manage or prevent those wars' (Sambanis 2001: 259). Drawing on research into ethnicity and ethnic conflict, Sambanis developed a new model to account for the causes of 'identity wars'. Using a new data set from 161 countries over a 40-year period,[1] his model draws conclusions very different from those of Collier and Hoeffler. For these conflicts, a lack of democracy is an important predictor of civil war. There is also an important connection between the level of 'heterogeneity' in a country and the onset of war (Sambanis 2001: 260). Economic development is also important: Sambanis argues that the more developed a country, the greater the opportunity cost of waging war. Nevertheless, he argues that defusing ethnic conflict could be more effectively accomplished through greater democracy, rather than improved economic circumstances and opportunity (Sambanis 2001: 267). To this end, Sambanis argues that more democratic regimes provided greater opportunities to ameliorate the risk of civil war by preserving rights and institutionally accommodating grievances.

Beyond greed and grievance, the impact of globalization has also been identified as a key ingredient in the outbreak of civil war, particularly since the end of the Cold War. For Kaldor, such wars need to be understood in the context of globalization, which has brought about a greater military, cultural, political and economic interconnectedness. Indeed, the collapse of the Eastern Bloc and the Soviet Union was very much a product of these regions succumbing to 'the inevitable encroachment of globalization' (Kaldor 2006: 4). New wars largely revolve around 'identity politics' – the claiming of power on the basis of a 'national, clan, religious or linguistic' identity. Often such identities were 'reinvented in the failure or the corrosion of other forms of political legitimacy' (Kaldor 2006: 6). Pressures of globalization not only encroached on old forms of legitimacy, but also influenced the character of the conflicts, which were commonly transnational in character. The greater ease of travel and communication meant that diaspora communities could have an enhanced influence in the conflict, and provide 'ideas, funds and techniques' from their bases in wealthier countries (Kaldor 2006: 7). Such pressures also changed the way war was waged. New wars involved guerrilla and counterinsurgency tactics, which avoided military advances characteristic of conventional war and incorporated greater control over the civilian population. Civilians were also targeted in much greater numbers through the commission of such atrocities as ethnic cleansing, massacres and systematic sexual assault (Kaldor 2006: 7–8, 52–54). While opportunities for rebellion and identity-based competition were also a factor, it was the upheaval of global change (for example, that which accompanied the end of the Cold War) that amplified these conditions, making civil war a much more likely prospect.

Another assertion is that civil wars are far more complex than much of the research claims. Kalyvas, for example, posits that such conflicts are by nature ambiguous, containing dynamics that are 'overlooked by macro-level studies of civil war, both descriptive and theoretical – with very few exceptions' (Kalyvas 2003: 480). He argues that a difference exists in motivation between the sources of power at the centre of a state and the peripheral actors at the local level. This creates a 'joint production' of action that was complex and 'not easily systematized' (Kalyvas 2003: 476). Although civil wars may emanate from the decisions and actions of a centre of power, the nature of violence on the ground is often more related to local or private issues than to the war's driving (or 'master') cleavage (Kalyvas 2003: 475–76). Civil war also provides a pretext for local actors to settle old conflicts that often have 'no relation to the causes of the war or the goals of the belligerents' (Kalyvas 2003: 476). This, argues Kalyvas, accounts for 'why civil wars produce violence that tends to assume simultaneously a highly brutal and a deeply intimate character' (Kalyvas 2006: 388). An understanding, therefore, of the broader political dynamics within a state, as well as patterns of social relations at a local level, is necessary to appreciate the complex factors that contribute to the onset of war, as well as the ensuing violence and mass atrocities.

These theories of civil war vary with regard to root causes, in particular between the salience of identity, economic opportunity and globalization. While all studies highlight a range of factors that contribute to the onset of civil war, some are limited by pre-determining the objects that they measure. Sambanis, for example, points out that the same data set could yield different conclusions if different proxies were used. By creating a different model to incorporate a distinction between identity and non-identity wars, he generated conclusions that differed from other quantitative studies. This contrast does not negate any particular project. Rather, it highlights the complexity of the risk factors and underlying causes. Kalyvas's incorporation of the interaction between local and national motivations and dynamics cautions against any generalized explanations for civil war. The variation of dynamics among locations, as well as the interactions among local and national actors, have major implications for devising structural prevention programmes.

Genocide and mass atrocities as distinct phenomena

As with the research into the root causes of ethnic conflict, since the early 1990s, scholarship on genocide and genocide-like violence has expanded considerably (Straus 2007: 476–77). This has yielded diverse views in comparative genocide studies as to what in fact constitutes genocide. Some chose the definition outlined in the Genocide Convention, while others proposed new interpretations of genocide (see, for example, Jones 2006: 15–18; Semelin 2007: 322–24; Straus 2007: 478–79). Some researchers positioned their point of reference in broader terms, such as 'mass killing' (Valentino 2004), 'murderous ethnic cleansing' (Mann 2005), 'massacre' (Semelin 2007), or 'mass political murder' (Chirot and McCauley 2006). Because of the range of disciplinary approaches to the study of genocide and related violence, and a variety of conceptual frameworks, conclusions on the causes of such violence vary somewhat. Nevertheless, one can point to some common themes in the research. They include the existence of a pluralistic society, the experience of upheaval or loss, and the impact of regime type.

A common root cause or risk factor identified by many scholars is the presence of a pluralistic society. Kuper posits that genocides 'are particularly a phenomenon of the plural or divided society' (Kuper 1981: 17). 'The source of genocide', he argued, 'is to be found in the social conditions of man's existence' (Kuper 1981: 53). Similarly, in his account of the common elements in genocides across time, Kiernan emphasizes 'social forces' arising from difference, particularly dynamics that were a product of racism. He argues that racism is an example of 'idealized conceptions of the world' that are 'imposed on reality' (Kiernan 2007: 21). These social conditions or forces are shaped by the way that collective differences are perceived and categorized. For Fein, the root causes (or preconditions, as she referred to them) of genocide can be understood as a process by which victim groups are 'defined outside the universe of obligation of the dominant group' (Fein 1979: 17). The classification of groups represents the first stage (of eight) toward genocide that Stanton identifies. The foundation upon which further discrimination and persecution is based – whether racial, ethnic or religious – determines how collective difference within a nation is classified. More racist societies display stricter classification schemes and little or no mixing (Stanton 1996). Adding a psychological perspective to these differences, Semelin traces social forces back to the *imaginaire* of the individual. From the beginnings of social interactions, the construction of 'us and them' unfolds in processes of scapegoating and bullying. This process, he claims, 'always lurked as a possibility in man's future and his possible end' (Semelin 2007: 10).

However, the causal link between such pluralistic societies and mass violence is a tenuous one. Most scholars identify 'social conditions' or 'social forces' as necessary (but insufficient) conditions for such violence. While mass atrocities rarely occur in the absence of these social forces, these forces do not themselves directly cause such violence. Chirot and McCauley (2006: 19) point out that there are far greater social divisions in societies than there were instances of genocide or ethnic cleansing. Appreciating how identity-based distinctions become a basis for prejudice and discrimination is important to understanding mass atrocities. However, the ambiguous causal link between these conditions and mass atrocities creates a predicament for practitioners and policy makers. If mass atrocities are unlikely to occur, then preventive strategies might not be needed. Indeed, it would be virtually impossible to prove that the absence of mass violence results from investments in prevention. Furthermore, given that there is a greater tendency for such divisions *not* to result in atrocities, understanding why this is the case should yield insight into how risk is managed locally.

The second major root cause identified by scholars is the experience of upheaval and loss, often blamed by elites on groups that have already been defined as potential victims. Upheaval can take the form of an economic, natural or political crisis, or decline in the prosperity and power of a regime over time. Loss of territory, or political or economic power is often linked with such upheaval, although the sense of loss may reflect perceived threat rather than tangible change. Melson points out that the genocides of Armenia and the Holocaust were preceded by upheaval and the weakening of a formerly powerful regime in societies already characterized by social division. This was accompanied by the swift advancement of a minority group assigned an inferior status in the broader community, generating a perception that such groups constitute a threat (Melson 1992: 17). This sense of threat is then articulated by newly emerging organizations propounding extreme ideologies of 'revolutionary transformation', and proclaiming the growing threat to the broader community or its elites. Similarly, Midlarsky (2005: 83) argues that loss could increase a state's sense of vulnerability, making threats more salient. Those who had the potential to perpetrate genocide commonly blamed or scapegoated a minority group for the loss. A response that sought to eliminate this threat, even if the loss was perceived rather than real, could potentially spawn genocidal policies. Using the Holocaust among other examples to illustrate this process, Midlarsky identified Germany's defeat in the First World War, and its subsequent punishment by the victors at the Treaty of Versailles, as central to the Nazis' genocidal policies. The Jews were primarily blamed for Germany's loss in the war, and promises of revenge were levelled as early as 1919. As the Nazis consolidated power in the 1930s, such promises were starkly realized through a wide range of policies which weakened, isolated and sought to eliminate the Jews (Midlarsky 2005: 133–57). The loss of power and prosperity that Germans experienced in the 1920s resulted in loss compensation in the form of the Nazi Party and its extreme brand of nationalism.

Some scholars point out that the underlying social divisions in a society, when provoked by changing circumstances, often further strengthen a group's perception of inferiority. It also underscores an incompatibility with the utopian ideas that political elites often propagate. For Chirot and McCauley (2006: 20–34), the motives for mass murder or ethnic cleansing can arise not only from fear, but also from a desire for revenge, or mere expediency. In his comparative analysis of the genocides committed by Nazi Germany, the Khmer Rouge, the Soviet Union under both Stalin and Lenin, and Milosevic's Serbia, Weitz (2003: 237) observes that all of these regimes 'envisaged distinct utopias' that sought to transform their societies completely. This was accompanied by revolutionary changes characterized by visions of a 'new man' and 'new woman' (Weitz 2003: 237). Embedded in this was the belief that certain categories of people were 'incapable of improvement and constituted a drag on the well-being of the population as a whole' (Weitz 2003: 237). Thus, for these regimes, moving toward utopia meant protecting people regarded as valuable from the 'negative influences of dissolute and degenerate ones' (Weitz 2003: 237). What distinguished the valuable from the degenerate was bound up in identities of race and nation that 'commingled with the great intellectual advances of the Scientific Revolution and the Enlightenment of the seventeenth and eighteenth centuries, which forged new ways of categorizing human beings' (Weitz 2003: 49). Semelin articulates this incompatibility with the goals of such regimes as reflecting a desire for purity. A perceived 'need for security' lent greater urgency to the process, and promoted violent methods (Semelin 2007: 49). The risk of genocide grows more acute when social divisions intersect with upheaval and change.

This combination of social division, upheaval and perceived threat clearly figures in many past genocides, but there are many examples where such factors do not lead to genocide or other mass atrocities. The contrasting examples of Malaysia and Indonesia during the 1998 financial crisis illustrate this. In Indonesia, the crisis triggered riots in Jakarta and other large cities, with those involved casting blame on the Chinese minority. Hundreds of Chinese Indonesian citizens were injured and killed (see, for example, Human Rights Watch 1998). However, in Malaysia, which also contained a significant Chinese minority, and where the effects of the crisis were equally felt, there was no rioting and no scapegoating. The collapse of communism in the late 1980s and early 1990s precipitated many ethnic conflicts, with widespread atrocities in Georgia, Azerbaijan, Russia (Chechnya), Croatia and Bosnia. Yet other countries avoided such violence. In Czechoslovakia, divisions resulted in the peaceful 'velvet divorce', and in ethnically diverse Kazakhstan, the transition to independence provoked no instability. Zambia experienced major political and economic upheaval in the late 1980s, but this instability became a clarion call for reform, to which the government responded constructively. Like the relationship between social division and mass atrocities, questions remain about why upheaval and loss lead to mass atrocities in some cases, yet not in others.

The most significant actor in the causal path to genocide and mass atrocities is the regime. In most cases, those who orchestrate and plan mass atrocities are governments or other national political elites (Fein 1979: 8; Kressel 2002: 171; Kuper 1981: 49; Valentino 2004: 1). With regard to which kinds of regime are more likely to commit atrocities, two main arguments emerge from the literature. One is that the lack of democracy is a strong risk factor, while another is that democracy itself can increase risk, particularly in countries undergoing democratic transition.

There is no doubt that in the twentieth century, the mass atrocities that caused the highest casualties were committed by non-democratic states. Rummel claims that all instances of major (and minor) political mass murder, such as the Soviet Union, communist China, nationalist China and Nazi Germany, featured a totalitarian regime in common (Rummel 1994: 4). He argues: 'the more power a government has, the more it can act arbitrarily according to the whims and desires of the elite, and the more it will make war on others and murder its foreign and domestic subjects' (Rummel 1994: 1–2). In authoritarian regimes, 'interests become polarized, a culture of violence develops, and war and democide follow' (Rummel 1994: 23–24). This is peculiar to regimes that held 'absolute power', as they lack 'cross pressures' and the moderating 'political culture' of democracy. These social forces, he claims, restrain the regime, and prevent it from acting arbitrarily. Similarly, Harff found that although autocracies might remain stable for prolonged periods, when they experienced upheaval or collapse they were far more likely to commit mass atrocities than other regimes (Harff 2003: 66). There is no doubt that autocratic states committed extensive atrocities in the twentieth century, but other findings reveal that democracy does not always provide protection from such violent outbreaks.

The relationship between democracy and mass atrocities is sometimes intimate. According to Mann, 'murderous ethnic cleansing' is especially characteristic of the twentieth and twenty-first centuries, and 'a hazard in the age of democracy', as it tends to link the *demos* inseparably with a country's numerically dominant *ethnos*. This then prompts moves to marginalize and exclude groups lying outside the dominant demographic (Mann 2005: 2–3). When ethnicity becomes the defining point of social division, ethnic hostility is likely to escalate. If the state itself is radicalized by such ethnic division, then it is likely to tip 'over the brink into the perpetration of murderous cleansing', even if this was not its original intent (Mann 2005: 6). This symbiosis of *demos* and *ethnos* is also identified by the Political Instability Task Force (PITF) as a destabilizing characteristic of countries undergoing democratic transition. According to their findings, partial democracies 'with factionalism and dominant executives' exhibited by far the greatest risk of political instability (Goldstone and Ulfelder 2004: 13). Factional division is particularly problematic if the polarizing element is ethnic or religious.

While there is no doubt that the character and behaviour of regimes shape the risk of mass atrocities, the precise nature of this risk is complex and contextually specific. Some countries evince risk without a record of atrocity. The autocratic regime of Kazakhstan, for example, has remained stable for 20 years, enjoying economic growth and increasing wealth. The country's president, Nursultan Nazarbayev, pre-empted the possible aggravating of ethnic divisions amidst the 2008 financial crisis by establishing a coalition of the major social groups. This assisted in maintaining channels of communication and resolving tensions (see, for example, Lillis 2009). In Africa, both Zambia and mainland Tanzania supply examples of socially diverse countries that to date have managed the transition from autocracy to democracy with only limited violence. Given that there are exceptions to claims and findings in the literature, more research is needed regarding the precise constraints that manage risk in various types of regimes.

Scholars who have theorized about the root causes of genocide and other mass atrocities display a variety of perspectives informed by varied disciplinary backgrounds. Nevertheless, an overview of their research reveals some common themes, particularly with regard to root causes and long-term preconditions. Most identify propitious 'social conditions' and extreme 'social forces' as necessary (but insufficient) conditions for violence at this scale. Such forces arise from the social classification of diverse groups within national borders, and their subsequent negative treatment of designated victim groups. It can also trigger perceptions of threat, and articulations of what is idealized in and excluded by particular utopian worldviews. Many perspectives on genocide and mass atrocities, such as Kaufman's 'Modern Hatreds' approach, examine the way in which long-term social classification is employed by political extremists for destructive purposes. In short, the various theories of genocide and mass atrocities share a view that the root causes of such violence stem from the management and mismanagement of diversity within states and societies.

Summary

Examining the causes of mass atrocities through any theoretical lens will never fully account for the multi-faceted and deeply contextual circumstances that combine to steer a path towards such a violent outcome. As Kalyvas demonstrates, the dynamics of violence at a local level tends to differ from a conflict's 'master cleavage'. In fact, variation is often evident, not only between local and national levels, but also among localities (Kalyvas 2003: 475). One example cited by Kalyvas is Guatemala in the 1980s, where hundreds of villages were destroyed, and tens of thousands killed. Yet amidst this destruction, some localities remained untouched. Similar trends are found in other wars, such as the Spanish and Colombian civil wars (Kalyvas 2006: 2).

Two broad themes do emerge from the literature. The first is that root causes of violence are predominantly local in character. They are rooted in identity, social relations, and elite actions and institutions. Poverty and inequality also play a powerful role. Second, scholars stress that such root causes and structural factors do not directly cause atrocities or make mass violence inevitable. Some claim they are necessary but insufficient factors, while others point out their correlation with future violence. Still others argue that these structural factors make it easier for elites with exclusionary ideologies to gain power, often after crises or upheavals. Clearly, understanding these local and national dynamics is crucial for effective long-term prevention. With sufficient political will, international direct preventive strategies might halt escalation or rising violence, but they will not address the underlying structural conditions that provoke division in the first place (see, for example, Ban 2008: 14).

Given that these scholars generally point to the root causes of mass atrocities as emanating from local national dynamics, it is logical that structural prevention strategies should also arise principally from governments and communities within states. After all, this is what the various UN reports on prevention have repeatedly stressed (Annan 2001, 2003, 2006; Ban 2008, 2009a). However, as with the academic literature on conflict and atrocities prevention,[2] the prevention strategies recommended by most scholars prioritize or simply assume the role of international actors. The following section provides an overview of these recommendations, and also points out that successful structural prevention derives from the insights of a small number of these sources, principally those prioritizing local and national actors.

Scholarly prescriptions for prevention

Scholarly prescriptions for prevention can be categorized in three broad areas: punishment, direct prevention and diagnoses of root causes. First, some scholars regard the punishment of genocide and other atrocities as an effective deterrent to future mass violence. Weitz states that 'those rushing to commit genocide might think twice because of the courtrooms and verdicts that might await them' (Weitz 2003: 53). Mann speculated that criminal courts have the potential to be part of a 'broader interventionist regime' that could pull 'ethnic conflicts back from the brink' (Mann 2005: 529). However, there are currently limits to the effect that punishment can have on prevention. The International Criminal Court is not recognized by all countries,[3] and many, including the United States, have actively sought to weaken it (Bellamy 2009: 123).

Second, and most commonly, strategies of direct prevention are recommended. Mann identifies a number of 'powerful geopolitical restraining influences' that require broad application, including greater arms control and 'an international regime more sensitive to regional conflicts ...' (Mann 2005: 525–26). Kuper's focus is the development, largely under UN auspices, of the practical implementation of the institution's 'ceaseless manufacture of normative documents' (Kuper 1985: 210). The 1982 agreement on the mandate of a High Commissioner for Human Rights was a positive development, and provided a formal means by which the UN could pressure offending governments (Kuper 1985: 214). Fein encourages the international censure of states where genocide seems likely, citing the response to Iran's treatment of its Bahá'í minority in the early 1980s as an example of success (Fein 1993: 102). Contrasting this, Midlarsky emphasizes 'loss compensation', arguing that such compensation could be introduced earlier, 'instead of taking the form of genocide' (Midlarsky 2005: 382). This holds value for both inter-state and inter-communal relations. For example, if the Arusha Accords had included an international guarantee of 'continued Hutu political influence in Rwanda in proportion to their number', this might have precipitated a different outcome in 1994 (Midlarsky 2005: 383). None of these recommendations effectively addresses the complex array of root causes and risk factors that these scholars have identified. Rather, they do little more than offer various strategies to stall escalating tensions or violence. With regard to root causes such as pluralistic societies, discrimination and lack of democracy, there is little discussion about how long-term measures can manage the risk these factors pose.

The third area is related to structural prevention. However, those who focus on underlying causes are ambiguous about how this can help to build effective structural preventive mechanisms. For example, both Kiernan and Melson argue that the most important step in long-term prevention is identifying the causes of such mass violence. For Kiernan (2007: 606), the 'cure' for genocide lies in diagnosing its causes. Melson (1992: 257) suggests that identifying the causes of genocide and other atrocities 'might help in laying the groundwork for more informed philosophical and normative discussions'. This, according to Semelin (2007: 372), is the responsibility of social scientists, who have a 'responsibility to know and to make known'. Where such philosophical discussion and knowledge might lead is unclear.

However, not all scholarly recommendations for prevention assume the primacy of international actors. A small number of scholars have argued that prevention is a broad concept that needs to reflect the context-specific, interactive complexity of factors that are associated with the risk of mass atrocities. Both Kaldor and Kaufman stress the importance of local actors in driving prevention. Although Kaldor emphasizes the impact of globalization on the causes and character of 'new wars', she cautions that such responses often are not underpinned by a sufficient grasp of case dynamics (Kaldor 2006: 10). For her, the long-term solution lies in 'the restoration of legitimacy, the reconstruction of the control of organized violence, by public authorities, whether local, national or global' (Kaldor 2006: 10). In other words, what is central to long-term prevention is to maintain or re-establish legitimacy through good governance and the rule of law. This is an intrinsically national process, and while the breakdown of legitimacy and control clearly requires international assistance post-conflict, the process principally concerns national actors. For Kaufman, 'the most important measures for avoiding ethnic war must be those taken to recast nationalist myths and erode the bases of ethnic hostility over the long run'. Such measures, he argued, would be most effective when undertaken by leaders of the groups in question (Kaufman 2001: 216). He also recognized the role that regional organizations could play in fostering reconciliation between different ethnic groups, and in promoting 'non-chauvinistic' national mythologies (Kaufman 2001: 217). This process cannot be controlled by external actors; Kaufman rightly acknowledges that it must be driven by local elites.

Another reason why long-term prevention must prioritize local and national actors is the complex and interconnected array of local national dynamics that determine the nature of violence in civil wars. Kalyvas contends that in these complex environments, the main protective factors against violence are 'state sanctions and mechanisms of social control [that] prevent translation into violence and provide ways of managing tension' (Kalyvas 2003: 485). The primary responsibility for prevention, therefore, lies with national and local actors and processes. Kalyvas does not explicitly address the issue of the prevention of civil war. Nevertheless, his 'mechanisms of social control' provide a fresh angle on prevention, one that Woodward astutely identifies. Acknowledging Kalyvas's research, she argues that the policy focus for prevention 'should not be on causes as conventionally understood, but on how mechanisms that keep limits on the use of violence as a means to political ends are destabilized or restored' (Woodward 2007: 158). In other words, prevention is not simply a matter of ameliorating root causes, but of developing effective mechanisms to limit people's capacity to use violence to pursue their political goals.

Kalyvas's analysis of civil war highlights two important insights for structural prevention. First, effective preventive strategies must be informed by an understanding of a country's complex and contextual dynamics. This does not simply involve identifying and ameliorating root causes. As Kalyvas points out, the 'local grudges' that could contribute to a rise in violence existed in most places, and did not necessarily produce violent outcomes (Kalyvas 2003: 485). Also necessary for prevention, Woodward notes, is appreciating how certain mechanisms within a country serve to manage or 'limit' the use of violence for political purposes. The task, in other words, is to gauge the extent to which institutions and structures, both formal and informal, foster the non-violent resolution of conflict. This suggests that structural prevention strategies should do more than simply identify and ameliorate root causes. They should, instead, work to recognize and utilize existing processes that help to prevent and limit violence.

Premising prevention on such an understanding is a novel approach, and clearly a departure from the common method of addressing root causes. It focuses on what local and national actors already do to mitigate risk, rather than devising strategies to be implemented by external actors. Pioneering such a consideration are Chirot and McCauley, who recommend strategies that incorporate a wide variety of actors, all contingent on context. They suggest four broad categories of preventive strategies. The first set is directed at government leaders, incorporating policies and structures to limit ethnic conflict.

They examine a number of ethnically diverse countries that have had success in managing ethnic and religious diversity, although none has been free of tensions and discrimination, and violence has characterized some. Switzerland's semi-autonomous cantons, Canada's bilingual system, and India's ethnic and religious diversity with its plural array of provinces all provide examples of approaches in which democracy has allowed minorities to articulate their grievances and govern themselves with a measure of autonomy. While India, in particular, has not been free of ethnic and religious violence, the country has, as the authors point out, 'managed to create a sense of nationhood' (Chirot and McCauley 2006: 150–63). The second set of preventive strategies comprises those imposed internationally to bring perpetrators of mass violence to justice. This involves intervention on one hand, and establishing legal tribunals on the other. While both measures involve a reaction to violence already committed, or are instigated after violence has ceased, the value of tribunals lies in the distinction they draw between 'what is internationally acceptable or not' (Chirot and McCauley 2006: 176). International interventions, though rare, have the potential to secure justice and deter future tragedies (Chirot and McCauley 2006: 177). International intervention thus has a place, but it is not the sole strategy.

The third broad strategy incorporates local approaches to tensions arising from diversity. Examples included developing relationships between groups, bolstering civil society, and strengthening democracy. Whether such approaches involve local actors exclusively, or also feature international agents, the authors point out that long-term success is premised on strong local institutions (Chirot and McCauley 2006: 187–195). Chirot and McCauley contend that a 'mythologized history of the past full of resentment' against another social group, defined as enemies, accompanies many violent conflicts punctuated by atrocities (Chirot and McCauley 2006: 204). One suggestion to mitigate the risk that such ideologies sustain is the educating of 'substantial numbers of young potential elites' about the dangers of exclusionary ideologies (Chirot and McCauley 2006: 210). These recommendations incorporate the strategies of local and national actors, together with international processes that punish past crimes. The emphasis is clearly on domestic processes and capacity.

Summary

Many scholars conducting research into the causes of mass atrocities regard prevention as primarily a process enacted by international actors. They identify international tribunals, direct prevention and ascertaining root causes as measures that can impede outbreaks of mass violence. Although ending impunity for perpetrators of mass violence is an important goal, the International Criminal Court still encounters limitations. Direct preventive strategies, such as military intervention, can halt escalating tensions and violence when the political will exists. Recent interventions have prevented further atrocities in Libya and Côte d'Ivoire. They demonstrate that some situations require such an assertive international response, although they do little to change the structural problems at the heart of such conflicts. Long-term strategies such as economic aid are important long-term mitigators of risk, given that most countries experiencing civil war and atrocities are poor (see Collier *et al.* 2003; Feron and Laitin 2003; Sambanis 2001). However, it can also contribute to further violence and marginalization. The Oil for Food campaign in Iraq in the 1990s gave the genocidal Baathist regime the resources that allowed it to remain in power (Marr 2004: 282–83). Economic aid was diverted into the personal bank accounts of African leaders on both sides of the Cold War divide, such as Mobutu Sese Seko, Idi Amin, Samuel Doe and Mengistu Haile Miriam, all notorious for committing atrocities against their own citizens (Moyo 2009: 23). International involvement in both structural and direct prevention thus may be both necessary and desirable, especially with regard to structural prevention, but assigning such a role to outside actors is both controversial and one-dimensional.

Conclusion

Many countries display root causes of mass atrocities – without enduring such atrocities. Poor countries are more likely to experience mass violence and conflict, but many poor countries have been free of such violence. In many instances, the risk of mass atrocities exists, but it does not escalate to the point where international intervention is needed. As many scholars point out, underlying or 'root causes' are necessary but insufficient conditions for the perpetration of mass atrocities. In other words, they do not directly cause mass atrocities; rather, they are commonly antecedents of such violence. Rarely acknowledged (with the exception of Chirot and McCauley, Woodward and Kalyvas) is that such antecedents also exist in many places that have *not* experienced mass atrocities. As Levene (1999: 19) emphasizes, 'ethnic and cultural antipathies may exist without ever leading to massacre'.[4] Thus, an accurate measure of prevention is not simply the identification and amelioration of such causes and risk factors, but the skill of governments and communities in managing diversity and mitigating inequalities. As pointed out in Chapter 1, this approach is promoted by the UN Special Adviser on the Prevention of Genocide. It is also championed by Gareth Evans (1993: 50), who argues that prevention must include not only fixing what is wrong, but fortifying what is right and positive. By contrast, the research into the causes of intra-state conflict and mass atrocities tends to investigate only what goes wrong, and to prioritize external actors in atrocity prevention and conflict resolution.

Research has generally overlooked what goes right and why to prevent conflict and preserve stability. Lost in the process is a wealth of insights shedding light on how countries confront challenges, maintain stability and bolster social cohesion. Recently in comparative genocide studies, a few scholars have followed Chirot and McCauley's important lead. Mayersen and McLoughlin (2011) compared positive and negative cases in their analysis of Rwanda and Botswana. Both Straus and Verdeja argue for the need to incorporate negative cases in order to advance our understanding of genocide and related violence: Straus's (2012) comparative analysis of Côte d'Ivoire and Rwanda sought to explain why the violence in the former was 'restrained' compared to the genocide in Rwanda, while Verdeja (2012: 315) argues that an understanding of genocidal causes must incorporate not only places where such violence has occurred, but also those where it has not. Such assessments are, for the most part, overlooked by researchers and policy makers concerned with prevention. Research into mass atrocities needs to move beyond an understanding of root causes, to incorporate factors and policies that promote resilience and stability.

Notes

1 The same as Collier and Hoeffler, and Fearon and Laitin.
2 See Chapter 1.
3 Currently 120 countries have ratified the Rome Statute.
4 Recently, a few publications exploring negative cases (or non-events) have emerged. In relation to genocide, see Mayersen and McLoughlin 2011; and Straus 2012. In relation to civil war, see Mucha 2013.

3 Understanding risk and resilience

The previous two chapters pointed out some key oversights in the literatures on both structural prevention and the causes of mass atrocities. Both areas neglect to consider the impact of local and national sources of resilience in the long-term mitigation of risk associated with such violence. In comparative genocide studies, as well as the broader scholarship on intra-state conflict, the tendency has been to focus on positive cases for the purpose of identifying common antecedents. In the academic and policy literature on structural prevention, the tendency has been toward external diagnosis and prognosis. To redress these limitations, the concept of prevention needs to be broadened to incorporate not only an understanding of root causes, but also an understanding of sources of resilience. I seek to detail the experiences of states and communities that already have had success at mitigating the risk inherent in such root causes. This would enable researchers and practitioners better to understand how vulnerable countries manage risk through policies and processes that build resilience and accommodate diversity.

This chapter presents a fresh framework for understanding the structural prevention of mass atrocities. It points to three things: first, the existence of risk factors; second, the existence of sources of resilience; and third, the relationship between the two. Such processes and dynamics are highly complex and deeply contextual. Therefore, this model is intended to serve as a general guide only. Furthermore, the tendency for researchers to focus on root causes has had two consequences – one positive and one negative. On the positive side, our knowledge of the long-term structural factors that make countries and communities more vulnerable to violence has increased dramatically over the last few decades. A negative consequence is that we have little knowledge of what mitigates risk in the long term, in particular what local actors do to build resilience in spite of high levels of political, social and cultural diversity. Little information is available on the factors promoting stability, or as the Human Security Report expressed, the 'causes of peace' (Human Security Report Project 2011: 65). Given the paucity of research in this area, the second part of this framework is informed by a much smaller pool of research. However, the framework provides a sufficient basis to begin to understand the relationship between risk and resilience, and how this can inform the structural prevention of mass atrocities.

The chapter is structured as follows: the first section proposes a definition of resilience. The second section identifies eight key factors that demonstrate long-term risk in relation to the commission of mass atrocities. These risk factors are a synthesis of research into the causes of genocide and mass atrocities. Also referred to as 'root causes' or 'underlying causes', I refer to them as risk factors because they lack a direct causal link with mass atrocities (see, for example, Chirot and McCauley 2006; Fein 1979; Harff 1998, 2003; Kiernan 2007; Kuper 1981; Melson 1992). In other words, their presence does not indicate a causal inevitability. Rather, I assert that mass atrocities rarely occur in the absence of some of these risk factors. The third section provides a synthesis of research into the various sources of resilience, by identifying seven broad factors. Finally, I explain how the framework will be used as an analytical tool throughout the three case studies that follow. The framework is not intended to identify specific mitigators for each precondition. Rather it allows for any kind or combination of factors to be exploited in managing risk, as these dynamics are largely contingent on specific local dynamics. In addition, the framework is sufficiently broad to include a wide range of processes, some of which may not necessarily correspond with the research hitherto undertaken on sources of resilience.

Understanding resilience

An approach to prevention that incorporates resilience begins with the idea that in states displaying a risk of mass atrocities, local and national actors have the capacity to develop risk-management strategies. Although external support may be needed to promote structural prevention, such support is best utilized to facilitate processes initiated by domestic actors. In this sense, understanding how domestic sources of resilience mitigate the risk of mass atrocities becomes a valuable element of structural prevention (see, for example, Bellamy 2011: 11). In order to incorporate resilience into a framework for long-term prevention, I draw on disaster management, psychology and ecological systems theory to examine three key questions:

1   What coping and support mechanisms exist to manage the risk of mass atrocities in societies?
2   How do political and social institutions absorb crises?
3   How do these institutions adapt and improve their management of diversity and mitigation of risk over time, so that stability is enhanced?

In relation to the first question, the incorporation and understanding of internal coping and support mechanisms is a logical starting point in understanding what states at risk already do to mitigate the risk of mass atrocities. In contrast to the preventive paradigm in public health, it draws on an approach developed by cognitive behavioural therapy (CBT) as a response to post-traumatic stress disorder and depression, which encourages patients to develop their own coping and support mechanisms (see, for example, Murphy and Cohn 2008; O' Malley 2010; and Southwick *et al.* 2005). The UN International Strategy for Disaster Reduction employs a similar definition: 'the ability of a system, community or society exposed to hazards to resist, absorb, accommodate and to recover from the effects of a hazard in a timely and efficient manner' (Kindra 2013).

The second question borrows an approach to resilience currently used in ecological systems thinking. Here, resilience is defined by one source as 'the capacity of a system to absorb shocks and disturbance and still maintain function' (Berkes and Folke 1998: 12). Given that a key turning point in the causal path to mass atrocities is the experience of upheaval, understanding how vulnerable states have avoided escalating tension and violence following upheaval is worth investigating. As such, an important dimension of resilient societies, where they have been established, is how effectively they have absorbed the 'shock and disturbance' of upheavals, including economic and political crises.

The third question also draws on ecological systems thinking, which has defined resilience as 'the capacity of a social-ecological system to adapt to change through self-organization and learning' (Berkes *et al.* 2003: 14). The long-term resilience of states is premised not only on how well they absorb the shocks of upheaval, but also how well they adapt, and promote stability in a regional and global environment subject to constant change. These questions are designed to underscore the various ways in which sources of resilience in states mitigate the long-term risk of mass atrocities. The framework in Table 3.1 synthesizes the research on key structural risk factors and root causes on the one hand, and key mitigating factors on the other.

Risk factors associated with mass atrocities

This section outlines the structural conditions – or risk factors – that make a country more susceptible to the perpetration of mass atrocities. It uses, as its starting point, theoretical perspectives on genocide. The sketch of risk factors for mass atrocities incorporates research into the causes of genocide and related violence, such as political mass murder, ethnic cleansing and massacre.

As noted, although these risk factors do not directly cause genocide, mass violence and atrocities rarely occur in their absence. Leo Kuper – a pioneer of comparative genocide studies – argued that while genocide is a crime committed by political elites, a number of structural conditions are conducive to allowing elites with extreme exclusionary ideologies to exert control. He acknowledged that such conditions do not automatically result in genocide, but heighten the risk of other forms of mass violence, referred to here as mass atrocity crimes. Kuper saw genocide as 'an extreme manifestation of a broader phenomenon – of violence, of destructiveness, or aggression' (Kuper 1981: 52). Such factors include social divisions (religious, ethnic or political) that involve various forms of discrimination and a history of past atrocities;

Table 3.1 Framework for understanding the prevention of mass atrocities

Risk factors of mass atrocities	Factors that mitigate the risk of mass atrocities
Social divisions	*Social cohesion*
1 Religious, ethnic division	1 Religious, ethnic cohesion
2 Social, economic or political	2 Social, economic and political inclusion
3 History of genocide and/or mass atrocities	*Good governance*
	3 Strong rule of law
4 Human rights violations	4 A transparent and functioning democratic system
Weak or abusive regime	
5 Limited rule of law	5 Constraints on the power of the chief executive
6 Limited democracy	
Economic weakness	*Economic strength*
7 Poverty and economic stagnation	6 Trade openness
8 Inequality of wealth and opportunities	7 Equality of economic opportunity
9 Low economic interdependence	8 Sustained economic growth

issues of governance, including widespread and systemic human rights abuses and weak rule of law; and finally, a low degree of integration into the world economy, together with profound inequality of opportunity.

Because these risk factors are broad indicators rather than specific causes, they share many of the same characteristics of the conditions that precede political instability. As Goldstone *et al.* argued, 'genocides do not strike out of the blue, instead they nearly always occur in the context of an ongoing episode of instability' (Goldstone *et al.* 2005: 29). The best way to decrease the risk of genocide is to decrease the risk of instability in general (Goldstone *et al.* 2005: 28). This is even more pertinent in preventing not only genocide but other mass atrocity crimes, such as war crimes, crimes against humanity and ethnic cleansing, as such crimes occur most commonly during an outbreak of any of the four types of instability.[1] The main reason is that these preconditions/risk factors for genocide include a wide range of social, economic and political variables (see Table 3.2) that are also evident in many ethnic and other civil conflicts and situations of unrest.

Social divisions

Entrenched religious, ethnic or political division between groups is a clear risk factor for genocide or mass atrocities. Although division alone is not enough to trigger an episode of genocide or mass violence, the ability to impose collective difference is essential to inflicting social discrimination. In this sense, social differences, if regarded negatively, can become entrenched and irreconcilable. According to Leo Kuper, 'societies with persistent and pervasive cleavages' between existing ethnic and/or religious groups have social conditions conducive to genocide (Kuper 1981: 57). Fein (1979: 9) also identified such cleavages as the first of four major preconditions for genocide. The separate identification of a victim group is important in enabling any newly

Table 3.2 Risk factors associated with mass atrocities

Social divisions	Religious, ethnic, political division
	Social, economic or political discrimination
	History of genocide and mass atrocity
	Human rights violations
Abusive or weak regime	Absence of rule of law
	Absence of democracy
Economic weakness	Low economic interdependence
	Inequality of opportunities
	Economic decline/stagnation

formed regime or political elite to introduce a novel political agenda, and to extend its power over other groups (Fein 1979: 9). Barbara Harff (2003) also pointed out the link between pre-existing social divisions and genocide/politicide, which she claimed was particularly clear when a victim group suffered discrimination. As ethnic conflict has preceded nearly two-thirds of the genocides and politicides of the last century, discrimination against a minority group is a serious cause for concern. This also applies in circumstances where the minority group holds political power. Indeed, where a political elite is represented entirely by a single minority group, the risk of genocide or politicide is two and a half times greater than in other circumstances (Harff 2003: 67). Social division has been widely recognized as a risk factor for future atrocities. Numerous genocide scholars have highlighted social divisions as an antecedent to past genocides; Stanton's stages,[2] the Minorities at Risk[3] project and the UN's OSAPG[4] identify social division as an important risk indicator. Minorities at Risk (2009b) measure political, economic, religious and language-based discrimination; Harff (2012: 54) identifies state-led discrimination as a significant indicator of risk; and the OSAPG (2009) regards 'past and present patterns of discrimination against members of any group' as an early warning indicator for genocide.

Cleavages between different ethnic and religious groups can be manifested through social, economic or political discrimination, and segregation (Kuper 1981: 58). Political inequality takes a variety of forms, but is most commonly seen in the denial of equal voting rights or under-representation in public institutions. Closely related is economic inequality, as manifested in unequal education and employment opportunities, wage differentiation according to identity, and variations in access to the means of production (Kuper 1981: 58). The extent and duration of such discrimination varies in intensity and duration. If it occurs under a repressive autocracy where the price of resistance is higher, such discrimination and inequality may continue for decades. Indeed, the nature of collective reaction to such inequalities is largely contingent upon the type of regime that fuels them.

Social cleavages characterized by entrenched discrimination were salient in Guatemala, and provoked grievances that had devastating consequences. The conflict and subsequent genocide in Guatemala in the 1980s occurred against a backdrop of decades of economic discrimination against indigenous Mayans by the landowning ruling class, which came to a head as the economy slowed in the face of an anti-government insurgency and the 1976 earthquake (Pastor and Boyce 2002: 366). Similar cleavages were apparent in El Salvador after indigenous groups were evicted from their lands in the nineteenth century, which then fell under the control of coffee-growing oligarchs. Indigenous farmers became labourers who endured wage cuts and unemployment whenever the price of coffee fell on the world market. Resistance to such conditions dates back to the Great Depression, with the formation of the Salvadoran Communist Party, but any sign of resistance was met with swift retribution by the military, including massacres of tens of thousands of people and targeted assassinations of opposition leaders. By the early 1980s, opposition to the government shifted from peaceful resistance to guerrilla warfare, which spiralled into a civil war characterized by the commission of atrocities that took the lives of 30,000–60,000 civilians, overwhelmingly at state hands (Pastor and Boyce 2002: 368–70).

Discrimination is almost universally regarded as a risk factor. Stanton's list recognizes this – his second stage, 'symbolization', emerges when symbols of difference are officially deployed to enshrine these classifications. These symbols may take the form of identity cards with an ethnic classification, in which case they become a particularly alarming indicator of the heightened risk of genocide or mass atrocities. Such classifications ease the path to 'dehumanization' – stage three (Stanton 1996).

Entrenched social cleavages are particularly dangerous if genocide or mass murder has occurred in the recent past, whether in the same country or the surrounding region. Countries with a history of genocide or other mass atrocities are at much greater risk than those without such a legacy (Harff 2003: 63). For example, in the 126 internal wars examined by Barbara Harff, 35 resulted in genocide or politicide. Ten countries experienced 'multiple genocides' and the risk of a renewed genocidal outbreak increased three-fold if a prior genocide had occurred (Harff 2003: 66). According to Midlarsky (2005: 43), the prior commission of genocide and mass atrocities makes further atrocities more likely in two ways. First, it provides a sense of continuity between earlier experiences of mass murder and the contemporary context, creating empathy with either perpetrators or victims. Second, the vulnerability of a victim group to genocidal appeals is deepened when the group identifies with the goals of the prior perpetrators or the suffering of past victims.

Long-term violations of human rights based on ethnic, religious or political difference are a significant risk factor for genocide and other mass atrocities. The promulgation and implementation of public plans, principles and policies targeting the rights of a particular group are an urgent cause for alarm. They can be manifested in various actions, including denial of employment, education and political representation, lasting years or even decades. In many cases, such violations trigger resistance by the targeted group. Whether that resistance is violent or not, a common state reaction is violent repression. If the victim group has managed to turn the tables of power, such violence may be inflicted against the original perpetrator group.

Three case examples illustrate this risk. In the second half of the nineteenth century, Armenian communities in Anatolia endured extensive violations of human rights under increasingly oppressive Ottoman rule. They had no political influence within the Empire, being barred from service in the government and army (Fein 1979: 10). Periodically, they were the victims of violence instigated by Kurdish chieftains and imperial authorities. When various Armenian groups began to organize and resist, acts of retribution by state-sanctioned Kurdish militias escalated into major massacres between 1894 and 1896 (Jones 2006: 104).

Likewise, the decade preceding the Holocaust was characterized by a steady increase in the frequency and scope of human rights violations against Jews. Hilberg identified these violations as a form of expropriation, by which the Jewish community in Germany was reduced from a wealthy and skilled group 'to a band of starving forced labourers asking for their meagre meal at the end of the day' (Hilberg 1985: 83). This process, extending over a period of years, was executed through various policies that deprived the Jews of their possessions, businesses, wages, savings and investments, access to food, and even personal belongings (Hilberg 1985: 83).

The relationship between long-term human rights violations and mass atrocities was clearly evident in Burundi. Colonial rule prior to 1962 independence saw the assertive implementation of policies that opened cleavages between Hutus and Tutsis by favouring Tutsis for positions of power and privilege, while denying Hutus a wide range of human and civil rights. Hutu representation in the king's court decreased, and Hutus were denied educational opportunities (Lemarchand 1997: 321). This under-representation reached breaking point after the 1965 elections, when the king refused to appoint a Hutu prime minister, prompting a violent reaction by some prosperous Hutus, followed by disproportionate acts of retribution by the Tutsi-led authorities (Lemarchand 1997: 322). This set the tone for a more widespread exclusion of Hutus from the government, civil service and army, leading eventually to the genocide of 1972, in which Tutsis systematically massacred some 200,000 Hutus (Lemarchand 1997: 323).

These examples illustrate the connection between ongoing human rights violations and the risk of future atrocities. In addition, the OSAPG (2009) identified a pattern of serious human rights violations as an early warning sign of future genocide. The Political Terror Scale likewise charts increasing levels of violent human rights abuses on a scale of one to five (one being zero violations of human rights, and five being violations against an entire population) (Political Terror Scale 2011).

Social division on its own does not substantially increase the risk of mass atrocities, but when inequality and discrimination are imposed along ethnic, religious or political lines, then the risk of instability and the perpetration of mass atrocities more than doubles. Social discrimination sanctioned by a government or other political elite can turn divisions that were previously benign into entrenched cleavages that breed mistrust and hatred. Collectively, such conditions create contexts within which the commission of mass atrocities becomes more likely. This reflects the vulnerabilities of the 'plural societies' that Kuper (1981: 14) claimed experienced most twentieth century mass violence.

Weak or abusive regime

Two risk factors related to regime type and behaviour significantly raise the risk of mass atrocities. The first is an absence of or limitation on democracy; the second is a limited rule of law. As noted, state-led discrimination resulting in the denial of opportunities, human rights abuses and social inequalities marks a regime as fundamentally abusive. The role of the state in carrying out such policies (or openly permitting discrimination) is key to identifying risk of instability and mass atrocities.

Two types of regimes hold significant risk for the future commission of mass atrocities. They are autocracies and regimes undergoing a democratic transition featuring factional division and an excessive concentration of power in the executive branch.[5] The PITF concluded that regime type was the most significant factor bearing on political instability (Goldstone *et al.* 2005: 2). An overwhelming consensus exists among scholars that the crime of genocide is committed by regimes or other political elites in a pre-meditated and calculated fashion (see, for example, Fein 1979: 9; Harff 2003: 58; Kuper 1981; Rummel 1994: 1–2; Valentino 2004).

Such extremely violent policies are, according to Harff, commonly imposed by autocracies. While most episodes of political instability between 1955 and 1996 did not result in genocide and politicide, a factor that decisively heightened their risk of doing so was a non-democratic political elite with an 'exclusionary ideology' (Harff 2003: 63). Over the twentieth century, democracies have killed far fewer of their own citizens than non-democracies – 160,000 as opposed to nearly 170,000,000, according to Rummel (1994: 1–27). The reasoning is that a democratic system of government contains institutional and ideational deterrents that impede political elites from attacking their own populations. Krain pointed out that 'power diffusion' of the kind that exists in most liberal democracies reduces the possibility of state failure, and thus the chances of 'state sponsored mass murder' (Krain 2000: 45). Although the transition to democracy often results in greater political instability, when autocratic states do fail they are three and a half times more likely to commit genocide than are failed democratic or semi-democratic states (Harff 2003: 64).

Many former autocracies undergoing a transition to democracy also display a high risk of political instability and mass violence. Krain argues that

regimes with some democratic characteristics may still be prone to the commission of mass atrocities if too much power is placed in the hands of one
individual or party (Krain 2000: 44). The PITF echoes this, concluding that
countries undergoing transition are at particular risk of political instability
when the executive has a surfeit of power, which they claim encourages a
'winner-take-all' struggle for hegemony. Risk is further exacerbated if political
competition is characterized by factional division (Goldstone and Ulfelder
2004: 13; Snyder 2000: 352–53). In such situations, entire collectives may be
marginalized within a country, and victors rewarded with immense power.
Mann (2005: 2) argues that this creates 'the possibility that the majority
might tyrannize minorities'. Therefore, while democracy is regarded by the
PITF as a key protective factor against political instability and ensuing mass
atrocities, the process of democratization can be profoundly destabilizing. As
Snyder argues, 'nations are not simply freed or awakened by democratization;
they are formed by the experiences they undergo during that process' (Snyder
2000: 36). For the PITF, if the process includes factionally driven competition
and a lack of constraint on the authority of the executive, then it is fraught
with risk:

> Yet, as dictators age, or as populations grow richer and more anxious to
> share in political power, autocracies often slip into allowing some poli-
> tical competition, ostensibly to appease regime opponents. Unless steps
> are truly taken toward strong partial or full democracy, the result is
> sometimes the opposite of appeasement; autocracies with some political
> competition create the promise without the reality of sharing power, and
> this awkward combination can unleash factional divisions and encourage
> radical responses.
>
> (Goldstone *et al.* 2005: 29)

'Rollback' in new democracies is also not uncommon. A number of state-
sponsored mass killings have occurred when former or fledgling democracies
have reverted to autocracy, usually during political or economic upheavals.
Rwanda in 1994, Nazi Germany and Chile under Pinochet are three such
examples (Krain 2000: 40–48).

Regime is central to understanding the risk of future atrocities. The
OSAPG regards regime character as a significant warning sign for potential
genocide if it promotes 'an exclusionary ideology' and publicly vilifies a target
group (OSAPG 2009). Harff's (2012: 54) measure of risk rates autocracies
highest, followed by partial autocracies. Regime is also a risk factor in the
'Peoples Under Threat' (PUT) list, if 'factionalized elites' are discernible
(Minority Rights Group International 2010a).

Human rights, political stability and economic prosperity all are premised
on the rule of law. When a weakening or abusive regime disregards the rule of
law, particularly where democratic checks and balances are absent, a population is far more vulnerable to deprivation and discrimination. The lack of an

impartial judiciary allows impunity for acts of discrimination and violence against vulnerable groups (Smith 2008: 85). When this is coupled with exclusionary policies, the extent to which the human rights, personal security and property rights of civilians are under threat is much greater. Such countries then resort to violence as the most common strategy to maintain order. Conversely, as Kaldor argued, 'the internal pacification of modern states was achieved not by violence, but by the extension of the rule of law ...' (Kaldor 2006: 115). The rule of law ensures that the recourse to violence is obstructed and re-channelled.

Likewise, the absence of a capable and impartial law-enforcement body to protect populations from violence, as well as from social and economic discrimination, allows conditions that heighten risk to fester. The incitement of violent acts against such minority groups such as the ethnic Chinese in Indonesia (Human Rights Watch 1998) and Jews in Germany (see, for example, Hilberg 1985), to name just two, requires a climate of impunity and the breakdown of the rule of law. Likewise, the government and other elite policies that exclude and marginalize minority groups can more easily occur when there is no independent judiciary. Absence of the rule of law is a risk indicator on the PUT list (Minority Rights Group International 2010a). The OSAPG (2009) identifies an independent judiciary as protecting a population, and its absence as an early warning sign, particularly if the legal recourse of vulnerable groups is restricted. Impunity for past crimes is also a warning sign. The rule of law thus points to both risk and resilience. When it is weak, the risk of mass atrocities is higher. When it is strong, the risk is diminished.

Economic weakness

Three risk factors of mass atrocities relate to economic weakness or inequality: a combination of poverty and economic stagnation, inequality of economic opportunity, and low economic interdependence.[6]

Economic stagnation and negative growth in poor countries are strong indicators of political instability and mass atrocities. Most countries experiencing instability and mass atrocity are relatively poor (Collier 2007: 19; Nafziger and Auvinen 2000: 102–3; Stewart 2008: 4). Although such violence is not limited to poorer countries, the incidence in poor countries is higher. Yet on its own, this is an insufficient risk factor. Stewart (2008: 4) points out that violent conflict is not exclusively waged in poor countries; nor do all poor countries experience such violence.[7] Nevertheless, as Nafziger and Auvinen (2000: 98) point out, most countries that have experienced violent conflict have also endured 'negative or stagnant growth'. While economic stagnation is not uncommon in wealthy countries, 'widespread negative growth among populations where a majority is close to levels of subsistence increases the vulnerability to humanitarian disasters' (Nafziger and Auvinen 2000: 98). One example is the economic decline of Somalia under Siad Barre between 1969 and 1991. This decline precipitated the collapse of the Barre regime, and was then further escalated once inter-factional fighting took hold in the immediate aftermath of this collapse (Nafziger and Auvinen 2000: 99). Similarly, Rwanda experienced a sharp downturn in the mid-1980s due to a collapse in global coffee prices, directly preceding and exacerbating the civil conflict which finally led to full-scale genocide. While this was not the only factor provoking tension, the economic decline certainly underscored Rwanda's growing instability, manifested in a growing scapegoating of Tutsis (Hintjens 1999: 256–57; Mayersen and McLoughlin 2011: 260). Such decline can best be measured by growing unemployment rates and drops in real income. Both become more salient when they are concentrated among particular identity groups.

Inequality of economic opportunity between minority groups, also known as horizontal inequality (see Stewart 2000: 15–18), can increase the risk of atrocities in two ways. First, such inequalities can be the product of regimes with exclusionary ideologies that deliberately marginalize particular groups. Activities aimed at depriving a particular ethnic, religious or political group of equal access to employment, education, wealth attainment or property ownership represent a clear warning of genocide or mass atrocities. Hilberg, tracing the gradual accumulation of policies in the decade that preceded the Holocaust, pointed to Jews being 'deprived of their professions, their enterprises, their financial reserves, their wages …' (Hilberg 1985: 83). This was implemented through a number of specific policies, from the liquidation of Jewish enterprises and the freezing of Jewish capital, to a reduction of wages and increased taxes for Jewish labourers (Hilberg 1985: 95, 139, 146).

Horizontal inequality can also be among the long-term conditions that increase the vulnerability of a country to humanitarian emergencies (Stewart 2000: 2), within which atrocities are commonly committed (Vayrynen 2000: 81). Stewart contends that economies with slow growth are more 'violence prone' than economies growing quickly, particularly if inequalities are high. This often results in deprivation for a portion of the population in contrast to others whose advantages become more apparent in the presence of such deprivation (Stewart 2008: 21–22). An example is the 1971 genocide in Bangladesh (formerly East Pakistan), which was preceded by two and a half decades of economic exploitation by Pakistan. This was part of a greater transfer of wealth resulting in substantial economic inequality between East and West, to the extent that many Bengalis felt that they had simply replaced one colonial ruler (the UK) for another (Pakistan) (Jahan 1997: 293). This wealth discrepancy between East and West grew more pronounced over time. In 1947, per capita income in West Pakistan was 10 per cent higher; in 1969, it was 60 per cent higher (Kuper 1981: 76). This growing inequality of wealth precipitated support for political moves to secure autonomy from the West. Subsequent pro-independence mobilizations were met with a crushing military reaction, resulting in the deaths of anywhere between half a million and 3 million Bangladeshis (Kuper 1981: 78). In this case, profound economic inequality created grievances that eventually took the shape of political opposition movements.

Despite this, the inclusion of horizontal inequality as a precondition is not without controversy. Its effect on the risk of genocide was found by at least one scholar to be 'ambiguous' (Besançon 2005: 393). However, Stewart highlighted the risk it carried in more general terms: it increased the likelihood of humanitarian emergencies, where atrocities are commonly committed, although she also cautioned, 'we should not expect an automatic relationship between horizontal inequalities and conflict' (Stewart 2008: 22). However, such inequalities also often reflect patterns of discrimination. The wealth gap between black and white communities in apartheid South Africa was clearly a product of entrenched discrimination on a broad scale. The poverty of the San in modern Botswana is partly a product of discriminatory land policies. While controversy swirls about this risk factor, when the inequality of economic opportunity exists alongside other risk factors such as discrimination, it is, as Stewart shows, an important measure of risk.

Low economic interdependence has been identified as a risk factor for genocide, as well as political instability in general. Countries with low economic interdependence are more likely to experience genocide or mass atrocities than those exhibiting higher levels of interdependence. Leaders from states that are relatively isolated from international trade are more likely to calculate that internal policies of elimination can be implemented without evoking a strong reaction from the international community (Harff 2003: 65). The PITF also concludes that countries with lower trade openness are two to three times more likely to experience instability (Goldstone *et al.* 2005: 23). For Harff, a measure of interdependence can be gleaned from the extent of a country's membership in regional and international organizations. The premise is that a higher number of memberships indicates the extent to which a country is influenced by, and accountable to, the international community (Harff 2003: 65). Harff also found that trade openness is a good indicator of 'state and elite willingness to maintain the rule of law and fair practices in the economic sphere' (Harff 2003: 65). Countries with the lowest levels of trade openness (and thus low economic interdependency) have a higher risk of genocide. For all these reasons, low economic independence is a strong risk factor for future atrocities (Harff 2012).

Summary

These risk factors for mass atrocity crimes are characterized by entrenched social divisions and increased political and economic weakness. Most importantly, such conditions result either from a complete lack of democracy, or from profound limitations on the democratic process. By themselves, the presence of these risk factors does not automatically produce genocide and mass atrocities. However, they heighten the risk of instability, and intensify social division and discrimination, making the perpetration of mass atrocities far more likely in the advent of instability. However, the presence of some or many of these risk factors does not chart an inevitable path to mass atrocities. What also needs considering is how these risk factors interact with each other, and how they are mitigated by factors that promote stability.

Resilience: factors mitigating the risk of mass atrocities

In examining states that display risk without having committed mass atrocities, we must also examine what they are doing *right*. Which policies and structures have these states put in place to avoid the kind of instability that might produce mass atrocities? Broadening the focus to incorporate an understanding of what goes right, alongside what goes wrong, challenges the commonly accepted notion of structural prevention as centred on the identification and amelioration of root causes by international actors. For Evans (1993: 39), this broader focus means questioning whether and how the core needs of security, living standards and existential identity and worth are met. Evans emphasizes the general applicability of such an approach:

> To a large extent, peace-building involves doing exactly the sorts of things that a civilized international community, and the states that make it up, should be doing anyway – i.e., putting in place effective international rules-systems, dispute resolution mechanisms and cooperative arrangements; meeting basic economic, social, cultural and humanitarian needs; and rebuilding societies that have been shattered by war or other major crises.
>
> (Evans 1993: 40)

Wolter also highlights the importance of analysing positive forces as well as negative ones. In his view, the biggest problem with premising prevention on addressing negatives was the 'restrictiveness' of such an approach, and its failure 'to explain the causes of conflict without looking at the often more important issues of developing the right strategies to deal with conflicts' (Wolter 2007: 50). Overlooking what strategies work in managing conflicts, especially before they turn violent, inevitably limits effective prevention.

The over-emphasis on the 'negatives' is reflected in the paucity of research on the conditions of peace and stability (Human Security Report Project 2011: 61). There are a few exceptions. The most comprehensive and significant research into what factors promote stability was conducted by the PITF, and developed in its Phase III, Phase IV and Phase V findings. The Phase III report measured state capacity and its role in maintaining political stability by conducting a survey of country experts who measured a government's effectiveness and legitimacy (Goldstone *et al.* 2000). Findings from Phase IV yielded a number of factors contributing to stability, most importantly the presence of democratic institutions fostering open competition, avoiding factionalism and placing constraints on executive power. This, the Task Force contends, sees free and open elections as merely part of a democratic system, founded on 'the necessary institutions to constrain executive authority, which generally rest on the effectiveness and independence of a country's legislative and judiciary branches, media, local governance, and civil associations ...' (Goldstone and Ulfelder 2004: 18). The Phase V findings reiterated the principal importance of democratic regimes in providing a combination of open political representation and 'fully institutionalized and functional political competition'. This dramatically decreases the probability of 'ethnic wars, revolutions, and genocides' (Goldstone *et al.* 2005: 31). States with lower infant mortality also proved more resilient to instability, suggesting that economic development exerts some influence. While infant mortality was less significant in Africa, other factors dominated. These included trade openness and the absence of state-led discrimination (Goldstone *et al.* 2005: 26).

A second major source on the sources of stability was produced by the Carnegie Commission. Its report, *Preventing Deadly Conflict*, equates structural prevention with meeting needs in three broad areas: security, well-being and justice. Yet it does little more than assume that the presence of these conditions automatically prevents deadly conflict. Providing for such needs, it claims, creates an environment free from violence or the fear of violence, with institutions that ensure the equitable provision of rights (Hamburg and Vance 1997: 69). What this model does not explain, however, is how meeting these needs combines with attention to 'root causes'. Rather, an assumption prevails that meeting needs automatically ameliorates 'root causes'. Moreover, often such ideals of security, well-being and justice are beyond the practical reach of many countries, yet many still experience success in managing risk associated with diversity. What the report neglects to examine is how countries mitigate risk despite often profound constraints. Meeting needs should be understood in terms of the broad risk factors that can lead to instability, upheaval and consequent mass atrocity.

Two points require further elaboration. First, the measures that a domestic government implements to ensure stability need to be examined, rather than only focusing on international actors. Second, the assumption that providing for such needs automatically addresses root causes can be challenged. Although certain types of economic development can fan the flames of tension rather than reduce it, more space is needed to negotiate need provision in environments characterized by profound constraints and risks.

The Human Security Report also conducted extensive research into the causes of peace. They framed this research by accounting for the decline in the number of civil wars occurring following the end of the Cold War. Most of this research is focused on the factors and processes that have aided in stopping war and preventing future outbreaks of conflict. They attribute this positive trend to improvements and greater investment in preventive diplomacy, peace making, peace keeping and peace building, and sanctions (Human Security Report Project 2011: 65–75). While less attention was paid to domestic sources of resilience, the report did identify two important domestic processes as contributing to political stability: improvements in democracy and rising national income (Human Security Report Project 2011: 76–77). Greater democracy and a more prosperous economy bolster a regime's strength and legitimacy (Goldstone and Ulfelder 2004: 19).

The 'buffer' theme is taken up (albeit briefly) by both Woodward and Kalyvas. Woodward, in questioning whether addressing root causes can prevent conflict, argued that a more effective approach was to develop strategies limiting the use of violence. Often, she claims, it is the local nature of violence that shapes ethnic conflict equally with the broader political dynamics (Woodward 2007: 156). She argues that 'civil wars are the outcome of long-developing processes of decay in the socio-cultural and official institutional mechanisms that normally keep limits on the use of violence in a particular locality or country' (Woodward 2007: 158). This is also articulated by Kalyvas: 'State sanctions and mechanisms of social control prevent translation into violence and provide ways of managing social tension' (Kalyvas 2003: 485). From this perspective, it makes sense to identify what mechanisms work well, and why some localities or states do not descend into violent conflict. In addition, if such a 'breakdown' is in progress, it needs to be identified as contributing to the conditions that make mass violence more likely.

Other scholars have also explored the factors that influence political stability and instability, but in the narrower framework of regime change engineered through *coups d'état*. Feng, for instance, concludes that democracy promotes stability. The flexibility that democracies offered (in terms of government change through election) offsets the chances of a government being overthrown in a coup, and positively affects economic growth (Feng 1997: 392). Londregan and Poole argue that low economic growth commonly precedes and facilitates coups. This significantly raises the possibility of further coups (Londregan and Poole 1990: 175). A small pool of comparative research has been conducted on states that have avoided war. Ware and Ogunmola, for example, conducted a comparative analysis of four West African states, including Ghana. They argue that Ghana benefited from a strong leader in Jerry Rawlings, who despite his flaws transcended ethnic difference, had a genuine interest in the welfare of all the country's citizens, and succeeded in bringing about sustained economic growth (Ware and Ogunmola 2010: 83–84). Ghana's civil war avoidance is also the subject of Langer's comparative analysis with Côte d'Ivoire. He argues that Ghana successfully managed the social divide between north and south, employing a raft of strategies over time to balance political representation, with policies to redistribute wealth to economically deprived northern regions (Langer 2008: 187–88). Policies aimed at offsetting potential social cleavages and managing diversity within political structures are also identified by Chirot and McCauley (2006: 55–70), who analyse a range of approaches in contexts including India, Malaysia and Switzerland.

As already stated, the most comprehensive and evidence-based research on stability promotion was conducted by the PITF (see Goldstone and Ulfelder 2004). It identifies regime type as pivotal, as does Feng (1997). The Carnegie

Commission, for its part, identifies justice or 'adherence to the rule of law' as one of three key elements that prevent violent conflict. Democratic institutions, including checks on executive power, bolster social inclusiveness. This is reflected in the Task Force's findings, and in the Carnegie Commission's conclusions. The Task Force recognizes that democratic institutions penetrated to all levels of society, and the absence of state-led discrimination was an influential factor in the promotion of stability. For the Carnegie Commission, 'the social accommodation of diverse groups, and equitable economic opportunity' reflected a functioning justice system and the rule of law (Hamburg and Vance 1997: xxxiv). Trade openness, as both Harff and the Task Force observe, mitigates against genocide and instability in general. These key factors, like the risk factors for mass atrocities, can be classed in three main categories: social cohesion, good governance and economic strength. Social cohesion considers the way a society accommodates identity groups, avoids discrimination and encourages participation. Good governance focuses on democracy, the rule of law and constraints on executive power. Economic strength, trade openness and equality of economic opportunity are also used as measurements of stability in Table 3.3.

This framework is not without its limitations. Because it synthesizes a limited pool of research, its list of risk factors is not exhaustive. Inevitably, we confront gaps in our knowledge about the factors that mitigate the risk of mass atrocities. Therefore, the framework is better utilized as a guide rather than a restrictive lens. Nevertheless, the breadth of the categories allows for the examination of diverse dynamics and processes that buttress stability and resilience over time. As such, they are sufficient to begin thinking about positive measures to promote resilience.[8]

Social cohesion

Most states are composed of more than one religious, ethnic or social group. Such diversity is not in itself a cause of instability. Rather, as Table 3.2 highlights, it becomes a risk only if it forms the basis of discriminatory policies. By contrast, where such diversity exists, the policies that foster cohesion and

Table 3.3 Factors that mitigate the risk of mass atrocities

Social cohesion	Religious, ethnic cohesion Social, economic and political inclusion
Good governance	Transparent and functioning democratic system Strong rule of law Constraints on the power of the chief executive
Economic strength	Trade openness Equality of economic opportunity Sustained economic growth

inclusion in practice serve as a good indicator of the country's level of stability. If its history is defined by harmony and cooperation rather than mass atrocities, or if tangible attempts at redress have been made for a past that included discrimination and exclusion, then greater stability will be fostered. This fosters, in turn, a sense of well-being and justice, two key factors that the Carnegie Commission identifies as crucial to structural prevention.

Stanton (1996) and Goldstone and Ulfelder (2004) both argue that religious and ethnic diversity in a society is not problematic in itself – discriminatory government policies create cleavages that can be exploited and exacerbated. However, policies that promote cohesion and coexistence are also worth examining. Policies that allow for the expression of religious and ethnic identity attest to a country's cohesion and stability. As the Carnegie report states, 'freedom of religion' and 'freedom to preserve important cultural practices including the opportunity for education in a different language' (Hamburg and Vance 1997: 98) are prerequisites for developing 'a sense of national cohesion' (Hamburg and Vance 1997: 100). Examples include policies recognizing minority languages, as with the 1993 Welsh Language Act in the UK, which placed Welsh on equal footing with English in Wales. Many multi-ethnic states officially recognize diverse languages: 11 in South Africa and 18 in India (Hamburg and Vance 1997: 98). Freedom of religion is another measure of social cohesion. Policies protecting the right of all religions to worship publicly, and encouraging interaction and exchange among religious traditions, provide a solid basis for religious cohesion. Education, particularly at the primary and secondary levels, which promotes an appreciation of and curiosity about other cultures and avoids sowing prejudice and division, is instrumental in fostering harmony and cohesion (Hamburg and Vance 1997: 120).

Such policies need to move beyond mere tolerance to ensure that there is no discrimination in terms of economic and political participation. Social, economic and political inclusion means that in a country with diverse social groups, no laws or policies favour one group over another. The aim is to prevent any group from being marginalized, and hence accumulating grievances. Policies that prohibit discrimination on the basis of ethnicity, religion or other social differences in relation to employment, access to education and the acquiring of private property can foster inclusion. Policies that help to redress past inequalities are also important indicators of inclusion. Examples include educational assistance for marginalized groups, as well as investment in previously neglected areas inhabited primarily by a particular identity group, such as northern Ghana (Langer 2008: 76–86).

Social, economic and political inclusion is also strengthened by active participation from civil society groups. The extent of activity, and the amount of support that such groups receive from their government, are indications of the level of inclusion at a grassroots level (Schnabel 2004: 123). Organizations as varied as unions, human rights groups, religious organizations and welfare groups all play a valuable role in campaigning against injustices and in favour of providing support to those in need. In Zambia, for example, a coalition of civil society organizations formed a new political movement that challenged the authority of the longstanding authoritarian government, and became a leading player in the burgeoning era of multi-party democracy in the early 1990s (Larmer 2009: 118–19). Civil society organizations play a vital role in fostering a tolerant and democratic public (Schnabel 2004: 123).

Implementing policies that ensure cohesion and promoting the benefits of diversity can create a base from which a history of coexistence, rather than a history of violence is formed. The occurrence of past mass violence can increase risk in two ways. First, it can fan the flames of unresolved grievances aimed at a particular group. Second, events in a more distant past can be resurrected by elites to create the perception of grievance, which can then legitimize the perpetration of new atrocities. In this sense, in divided societies, the challenge is to promote a culture of inclusiveness. One example is the approach adopted by Kazakhstan. President Nursultan Nazarbayev emphasized that all ethnic groups were equal, and frequently extolled the achievements of various groups at international sports competitions and other forums. In addition, he sanctioned the activities of the Assembly of the People of Kazakhstan, a multi-ethnic organization with the goal to promote inter-ethnic harmony (Lillis 2009). Although Kazakhstan is a democracy only in name, the inclusive message from political elites (as well as the elites of various ethnic groups) was deliberately aimed at countering the possibility of separatist movements emerging. In particular, it was a response to other events in the region, especially the recent momentum afforded the breakaway regions of Abkhazia and South Ossetia.[9] While this is not a panacea, even limited democracies that promote such policies are far more stable than those that promote divisive policies. As Harff points out, it is the combination of an autocratic regime with an exclusionary ideology that creates a high risk of genocide and politicide (Harff 2003: 62–63).

The implementation of policies that respect difference and cultural/religious freedom clearly demonstrates a respect for human rights. While instability in many cases is preceded by years or even decades of human rights violations, the absence of such violations also merits analysis. Such an absence usually points to efforts to foster rights, the rule of law, and equality of opportunity in the social, economic and political arenas. Specific laws (like the Racial Vilification Act in Australia) seek to prevent discrimination, while services such as education, health and infrastructural development can alleviate the disadvantage of some groups.

Good governance

Good governance includes the rule of law, and a democratic system that avoids factionalism and places limitations on the power of the chief executive. The test of a transparent and stable democracy is not simply frequent multi-party elections, but the extent to which the voters' will is respected and implemented through a 'competent and accountable' police and civil service (Hamburg and Vance 1997: 94). If national elections are simply a vehicle for attaining the spoils of government, then the longevity and legitimacy of government becomes limited. The symbiotic relationship between democracy and strong public institutions is evident (by its absence) in Sierra Leone, both before and after the conflict of the 1990s. In the previous decade, in a climate of International Monetary Fund (IMF)-instigated policies, funds allocated to education decreased by 85 per cent. Teachers were denied an income, and an entire generation of youths was left without skills or literacy, providing rich recruitment opportunities for the Revolutionary United Front (RUF) (Hanlon 2005: 460). While post-conflict reconstruction has been hailed as a success due to two successive free elections, the hasty return to democratic elections, without an institutional capacity that would allow elected governments to provide basic services to citizens, risks exacerbating the original causes of the conflict. Hanlon argues that elections did not create stable governance in Sierra Leone. Rather, they produced a 'weak, corrupt and partisan government' (Hanlon 2005: 461).

Good governance is premised on rule of law, which protects individual rights, property rights, cultural expression and religious freedom (Hamburg and Vance 1997: 90). Bearing in mind that no state is entirely free of discrimination, an independent judiciary gives citizens the chance to seek justice non-violently and to redress perceived wrongs. Fair laws that do not advantage some groups over others reduce the need to look outside the system for justice. Adherence to the rule of law provides accountability even in the face of discriminatory government policies. It also ensures that institutions of public service and protection are under civilian control, and are 'competent, honest and accountable' (Hamburg and Vance 1997: 94). One example of an independent judiciary protecting a marginalized group from government discrimination was a landmark ruling in 2006 by Botswana's High Court. It declared illegal a 2002 government order to evict the San Bushmen people from their ancestral land (BBC News 2006a). An independent judiciary provides a forum for justice and human rights grievances that transcend a governmental or other elite agenda, allowing for conditions to be addressed which, if left unchecked, could license human rights violations against minority groups.

Although the rule of law is broad and incorporates all areas of governance, a measure of its efficacy is the extent to which the legislative branch of government is constrained by the judiciary, and individual and collective rights are protected by the legislature, the judiciary and law enforcement. If judicial decisions are independent of ruling-party agendas, and if they are consistently adhered to by the legislative branch, then this indicates that the rule of law is strong. A judiciary that does the bidding of the government, or a military used to enforce partisan decisions based on an exclusionary ideology, are clear indications of a breakdown of the rule of law. In addition, states in which democracy and the rule of law are strong, and in which property rights are respected, display a greater ability to attract international trade and investment, further bolstering economic prosperity and stability (Human Security Report Project 2011: 31). In fact, as Fine argues, there is very little that either local or international actors can do to prevent mass atrocities 'in the absence of a political, economic and civil environment that honours at least some major rules of law and practices the rudiments of public discourse' (Fine 1996: 543). Rule of law is the foundation of strong democratic societies, enabling prosperity and fostering stability.

In addition to the rule of law, political stability is more likely to be fostered by a transparent and effective multi-party democracy. This is not because the 'myriad social, demographic, economic and environmental forces that are often cited as the causes of political instability' are miraculously absent in such regimes (Goldstone and Ulfelder 2004: 11), but because liberal democracies possess the resilience to deal with such pressures (Goldstone and Ulfelder 2004: 14). In a separate study on the relationship among regime type, degree of democracy and conflict, Hegre *et al.* (2001: 44) argued that civil peace is greater, more just and more durable in democratic societies. When political competition is fair and open, when opposition parties are robust and active, then a state's resilience and stability are much higher. According to the Carnegie Commission, a democracy 'assures all citizens the opportunity to better their circumstances while managing the inevitable clashes that arise' (Hamburg and Vance 1997: 94). In other words, a democratic state provides a space for 'accommodating competing interests', decreasing the likelihood that dissenting groups will be marginalized or seek to achieve their goals by taking up arms. A liberal democratic system has a positive effect on economic growth (Feng 1997: 413), and economic growth in turn increases political stability (Londregan and Poole 1990: 182).

Equally important are constraints on the power of the chief executive. Excessive executive power increases risk in two ways. First, it opens the possibility of leaders expanding their power and moving towards a dictatorship. Second, if competition in the state is factionalized, the chief executive's office becomes a prize that one side takes at the expense of the others, in a 'winner-takes-all' scenario (Goldstone and Ulfelder 2004: 16).

Resilient democracies create greater stability by limiting the power of the chief executive, encouraging fair and open competition among political forces, limiting corruption, and guaranteeing political rights and civil liberties. To this end, free and fair democratic elections must be supported by strong political institutions that strengthen democracy. This involves much more than simply holding free and fair elections (Goldstone and Ulfelder 2004: 10). Other key elements may include an independent judiciary, free media, local governance strategies that encourage equitable participation and representation, and active civil associations. The healthy functioning of such institutions helps to constrain power elites and underpin the development of a 'democratic culture', featuring greater public participation in decision making through 'debate, demonstrations, and protests as well as negotiation, compromise, and tolerance' (Rummel 1994: 23).

The existence of a liberal-democratic system of power is central to political resilience and to stability. A democracy that promotes open competition free from factionalism and constrains the power of the chief executive positively influences all other aspects of this framework. In such a system there is less chance of state-led discrimination. Where such discrimination does exist, an independent judiciary provides a forum for the non-violent airing and redressing of grievances. Such a system of equitable representation at all levels of society also promotes economic growth, a factor to which I turn next.

Economic strength

Economic strength does not simply measure a country's wealth, but rather its stability and cohesion. Three main indicators are the extent of trade openness, the equality of economic opportunities and sustained economic growth.

A state that trades openly, both within its region and globally, is more likely to conform to international trade agreements and to play a positive role in other international forums. As Harff notes, 'the greater the degree to which a country is interdependent with others, the less likely its leaders are to attempt geno-/politicides' (Harff 2003: 65). The PITF also identifies trade openness as one of the ingredients of political stability, particularly in Africa (Goldstone *et al.* 2005). Harff (2012: 54) claims that trade openness provides an indication of 'state and elite willingness to maintain the rules of law and fair practices in the economic sphere'.

Equality of economic opportunity is closely related to the factors that contribute to social cohesion, and is a product of good governance characterized by the rule of law and a liberal democracy with appropriate checks and balances. The Carnegie Commission argues that prosperity alone is not enough to avoid violent conflict, because if prosperity is characterized by imbalance and inequality, the benefits of growth are likely to be undermined by resentment and unrest (Hamburg and Vance 1997: 84). According to Stewart, marked economic differences among groups have a strong bearing on group mobilization, increasing the risk of violent conflict (Stewart 2000: 9). Conversely, the Carnegie report argues that access to employment and the development of human skills and capacity promotes greater well-being and stability, and mitigates the resentment that is associated with a perception of economic inequalities (Hamburg and Vance 1997: 89).

The final economic factor that promotes stability is sustained growth. The Human Security Report concludes that as a state's per capita income rises, conflict decreases. An example is the economic transformation of Southeast Asia in the post-Vietnam War period, from the late 1970s to the 1990s. During this time, average incomes increased by almost 100 per cent, while regional conflicts decreased by nearly half (Human Security Report Project 2011: 52). The report's authors also point out that the economic costs of joining a rebellion or fighting a war are considerably higher in wealthier states where there is much more to lose (Human Security Report Project

2011: 52). As Collier (2007: 20) argues, becoming part of a rebellion may offer a possibility of economic gain for young men who might otherwise have no prospects.

Conclusion: buttressing resilience

This chapter has sought to explore why some states located in vulnerable regions do *not* experience mass atrocity crimes, such as genocide, crimes against humanity, ethnic cleansing and war crimes. A focus on the relationship between risk and resilience over time generates insights into how structural prevention is carried out by local and national actors, and how it can be facilitated, if and when needed, by international actors. Understanding how domestic processes mitigate risk broadens the long-term preventive focus beyond root causes, to incorporate the constructive management of diversity. As argued in the first two chapters, the commonly accepted concept of structural prevention has limitations, with regard to violent conflict in general and mass atrocity crimes in particular. Framing structural prevention in terms of addressing root causes assumes a linear approach to conflict, in which a conflict will inevitably occur if these causes are not ameliorated. Such an assumption is limited and potentially inaccurate.

This book's framework, by contrast, seeks to overcome these limitations in two main ways. First, it moves the analysis away from notions of causal inevitability to emphasize instead risk factors – structural factors that are antecedents of genocide and mass atrocities, but are not directly causally related to such violence (see, for example, Fein 1979; Harff 2003). While such factors do not directly *cause* mass violence, atrocities rarely occur in their absence. Their presence, therefore, indicates a degree of risk that makes a country more vulnerable to instability and mass atrocities. The framework also identifies key factors that promote resilience, stability and social inclusion.

The next step is to apply the framework to states located in regions characterized by violent conflict and mass atrocities, and to understand how and why some states have managed to maintain stability against the odds. I turn now to consider the cases of Botswana, Zambia and Tanzania.

Notes

1 The Political Instability Task Force has identified four types of instability: revolutionary wars, ethnic wars, adverse regime changes, and genocides and politicides.
2 Stage one, 'classification'.
3 Group characteristics that denote distinctiveness, including language, custom, religion and race.
4 The OSAPG identifies a pattern of tense relations between groups as a risk factor.
5 Polity IV refers to regimes with such characteristics as 'anocracies'.
6 A high proportion of young, unemployed men has also been identified as a factor that correlates with the likelihood of civil war, although this has not been identified in the research into the risk factors of mass atrocities. See Collier 2009: 130.

7 Two of the case studies in this thesis – Zambia and Tanzania – are among the poorest countries in the world, yet have avoided such violence.

8 Moreover, the framework itself was not based on specific findings from the three case studies. Rather, it synthesized existing research into both the preconditions and the mitigating factors. That factors identified in the case studies were absent from the framework highlights the need for more study into resilience building. However, to add to the framework based on this single study would be to generalize from only three cases. I have identified patterns, such as strong inaugural leaders, but further study is needed to investigate their broader relevance.

9 The separatist war in Abkhazia in 1992/03 was triggered by strong rhetoric from Georgian political elites advocating 'Georgia for the Georgians', which allowed little space for a separate Abkhaz identity.

4 Botswana
Managing scarcity and abundance

In 2006 Botswana's High Court issued an historic ruling. In the case of the First Peoples of the Kalahari against the Government of Botswana, it declared illegal the government's policy of forcibly evicting groups of San Bushmen from the Central Kalahari Game Reserve (CKGR). This was followed by a ruling from the Court of Appeal in 2011, which gave the San Bushmen the right to re-open a borehole on the CKGR, previously closed by government authorities, as well as to drill further boreholes for the necessary provision of fresh water. The San Bushmen are the poorest and most marginalized minority group in Botswana, and have endured entrenched discrimination throughout (and indeed prior to) the country's independent history. Yet these rulings provide an insightful lesson in the understanding of risk and resilience in relation to the structural prevention of mass atrocities: often the very system that provokes risk can also provide the means for its mitigation and possible amelioration over time. This is especially true in the case of Botswana – a country that has enjoyed long periods of economic growth, democracy and political stability, amidst profound inequalities of wealth and power.

Unlike most of its neighbours, Botswana has not experienced violent conflict and mass atrocities in its post-independence history (see, for example, Collier 2007: 18–21). It has remained peaceful, democratic, and achieved the world's fastest economic growth figures between 1966 and 1999 while its neighbours were mired in civil war, or struggling against repressive governments.[1] This is despite the fact that Botswana has many of the risk factors associated with future atrocities. There are deep inequalities, mainly along ethnic lines, as well as human rights violations committed against a specific ethnic group. Despite the country's relative wealth, more than 30 per cent of the population still live in extreme poverty, and up to 40 per cent are not formally employed. There is a profound inequality of economic opportunity, so much so that the UNDP has warned of future instability in its most recent *Human Development Report* (UNDP 2005: 19). These preconditions and Botswana's relative stability make it a suitable case for investigating how this risk has been mitigated.

This chapter examines the potential risk of mass atrocities in Botswana, and seeks to explain why Botswana has remained immune to the atrocities experienced by most of its neighbours by demonstrating the extent to which risk has been mitigated. It makes two key arguments: first, in Botswana there exists moderate risk for the future perpetration of mass atrocities. This risk includes the preconditions of ethnic division, discrimination, human rights violations and inequality of economic opportunity (see Table 4.1).

Second, this risk has remained moderate due to a number of mitigating factors that have enhanced the resilience and stability of Botswana's governance. In particular, Botswana's rule of law and robust democracy[2] have maintained social and political stability, and provided a space for the voicing of minority grievances. In addition, some ethnic-based pressure groups have been able to use the judiciary to advance their goal of greater equality. Therefore, while Botswana experiences deep horizontal political and economic inequalities, the flexibility of its democratic institutions, the strength of its rule of law, and prudent economic management have enabled social change and improvement, albeit incremental. Importantly, the space for opposition and non-violent conflict resolution has been preserved through a variety of institutions that have enabled many marginalized groups to challenge discriminatory government policies and improve their status.

Background

Located in Southern Africa, and sharing borders with South Africa, Zimbabwe, Zambia and Namibia, Botswana gained independence in 1966. This was achieved through a smooth transition of power, ending 80 years of British colonial rule in what was formerly known as Bechuanaland (Magang 2008: 347–48). Prior to that, the territory was populated by numerous tribal groups, the strongest coming from the Tswana groups, who were among the more recent migrants from the north. There were also up to 35 other tribes and languages, and although there is some fluidity among tribes, no census of the exact population of various groups has been taken during the republic's nearly 50-year lifespan (Leith 2005: 29).

Botswana's pre-colonial history was characterized by successive waves of migration by Bantu tribes, notably the various Tswana groups that settled in the territory around the Kalahari beginning perhaps 1,000 years ago, and cohabitating with the earliest inhabitants, collectively known as the San (Tlou 1997: 34). After initial amicable encounters and equitable partnerships between the indigenous San and various Tswana groups, relations grew more

Table 4.1 Risk in Botswana

The risk factors associated with mass atrocities in Botswana
Ethnic division
Discrimination
Human rights violations
Inequality of economic opportunity

unequal. According to Miers and Crowder, this initial cooperation saw the San helping the Tswanas to hunt. However, with the rapid expansion of hunting in the 1840s as a result of a greater presence of European traders, the larger Tswana groups[3] began to profit, and assumed greater political control of the land. They then expanded their trade by increasing cattle grazing, establishing wells and cattle posts on traditional San hunting grounds. With diminished game, the San and other established groups like the Bakgalagadi and the Wayeyei were forced either to forage for survival, or to work for these cattle-owning tribes, becoming dependent on cattle outposts for sources of water, milk and occasionally meat (Miers and Crowder 1988: 175). This dependency evolved into total submission. The San in particular were referred to by their Tswana masters as *malata* (meaning slave), and were treated as another form of private property, to be bought and sold (Parsons 1977: 119). In his journey through Bechuanaland between 1859 and 1869, the English missionary, John Mackenzie, wrote extensively about the enslavement of both the San and the Bakgalagadi[4] and the contempt that their Tswana masters had for them (Mackenzie 1969 [1883]: 57–58). Slavery continued until the British declared it illegal in 1936, yet the San's dependency on remote cattle posts owned by Tswana tribes continued (Miers and Crowder 1988: 191–92).

Although not all non-Tswana groups were enslaved, a rigid hierarchy appeared to determine the status of various groups. Datta and Murray (1989: 59) contend that those groups that were '[a]bsorbed by conquest, were acephalous and lacked a corporate identity, lived close to the capital, and were alien in language and culture to their new masters would be forced into the class of serfs and would be exploited for the benefit of other classes'.

Other groups more closely related to the Tswana tribes, culturally and linguistically, would be regarded more favourably as 'commoners' or 'foreigners' (Datta and Murray 1989: 59). These complex distinctions determined economic and political opportunity, and although there was some flexibility with status,[5] wealth and political power were reserved for the Tswana aristocracy alone. Moreover, it was this relationship that enabled the larger chiefdoms to consolidate and expand their power. It freed up more Tswana men to participate in politics, seek education and engage in the cash economy by working in the mines in South Africa, knowing that their cattle were being tended at little cost. Miers and Crowder (1988: 177) argue that this system of slavery and servitude '[l]ay at the very roots of the highly successful Tswana pastoral economy, allowing the masters to build up large herds while freeing them from pastoral, agricultural, and domestic chores and enabling them to engage in politics, herd management, trade and wage labour'.

The consolidation of territory and power in the hands of a few Tswana tribes was further entrenched following the creation of Bechuanaland as a British protectorate in 1885. The British colonial administration recognized the political legitimacy of eight Tswana tribes, and arranged their system of rule around these tribal boundaries. This entrenched in law the Tswana tribes' rigid social hierarchy and dominance, gained through centuries of dispossession and expropriation. Opting to leave these tribal structures intact, the British ruled from neighbouring South Africa, allowing the chieftaincies to rule with minimal external interference (Stevens 1967: 113). This consolidation of Tswana dominance, referred to as 'Tswanadom', underscored the path to independence, apparent in Botswana's nascent democracy in 1966, where most MPs were from wealthy Tswana cattle-owning families (Nyati-Ramahobo 2002: 686; Parsons 1985: 29–39). Consequently, the Tswana devised economic policies that primarily protected the traditional pastoral economy, and further limited economic opportunities for those formerly indentured groups. The link between wealth and subordination is thus quite clear in Botswana, and has served to elevate the Tswana aristocracy at the expense of dispossessed non-Tswana groups, especially the San.

Nevertheless, the path to independence was a comparatively smooth one, notably lacking acrimony towards the British. As independence approached, a new and sophisticated constitution was forged. It preserved the traditional structures of the chieftaincies, but vested power firmly in a constituency-based multi-party democratic system (Parsons *et al.* 1995: 108–9). Spearheading this form of governance was Seretse Khama, a former heir to the largest chieftaincy, the Bamangwato. The co-founder of the Botswana Democratic Party (BDP), Khama relinquished his traditional title and advocated for inclusive democratic rule following decolonization. In the absence of the kind of anti-colonial rhetoric that issued from the territory's other major party, the Botswana People's Party (BPP), Khama and the BDP preserved good relations with the resident commissioner, Peter Fawcus.[6] In this way, the path to independence was approached as a partnership with the colonial rulers, rather than an antagonistic break with the past. Commissioner Fawcus was also instrumental in convincing both the white community and the chiefs to accept a common voters' roll rather than one that would elevate particular communal groups (Parsons *et al.* 1995: 211). This provided a strong foundation of equitable democratic participation, achieving a delicate balance between traditional rule and a modern centralized democracy (Fawcus and Tilbury 2000: 130–34).

The approach, however, has had negative impacts on Botswana. The wealthy and well-positioned elite of the eight Tswana tribes played the greatest role in shaping the independence process, and have continued to influence government policies substantially (see, for example, Schapera 1970: 3; Stevens 1967: 113). Tswana elites supply the vast majority of candidates in competing parties in elections to this day, and retain the largest portion of the nation's wealth and power. Perhaps most damagingly, it allowed for the illusion of a largely mono-ethnic population. The political and economic marginalization of non-Tswana ethnic minorities, evident in colonial Bechuanaland, continued into modern Botswana.

Despite very modest beginnings, Botswana has developed into a middle-income country. At independence, it was one of the poorest countries in the world, or as Good and Taylor (2008: 751) explain, 'amongst the poorest of the world's least developed countries'. It has since experienced rapid and solid economic growth, and maintained a multi-party democracy with regular elections. It is an active member of the Southern African Development Community (SADC), and is regarded as one of the most successful African states, in terms of economic growth and democratic resilience. However, a number of scholars and journalists have challenged the idea that Botswana is an 'African miracle', pointing out the high percentage of unemployed (18 per cent), the number of people living in extreme poverty (31 per cent), and the continuing denial of rights and opportunities for many of the country's ethnic minorities (see, for example, Gall 2001; Good 1993, 2008; Good and Taylor 2008; Hillbom 2008; Taylor 2006). Although independent Botswana has enabled the Tswana elite to take advantage of the new political system, the constitution underpinning the multi-party system has also provided a legal basis for equal rights amongst the country's many marginalized groups. These groups have, on numerous occasions, invoked the constitution in the High Court to redress historical and contemporary grievances. Thus, while Botswana clearly provided advantages for the Tswana elite at the expense of traditionally marginalized ethnic minority groups, the robust democratic system created at independence established, as Solway argues, 'the conditions for its own challenge and provided an orderly means by which dissenting parties could proceed' (Solway 2002: 711). The co-existence of disadvantage and inequality along historical social and ethnic lines, and the presence of institutions capable of confronting these inequalities, makes Botswana an ideal case with which to analyse the relationship between risk and resilience in relation to potential mass atrocities.

Botswana and the risk factors for mass atrocities

Botswana is located in a region notorious for violent conflict, repression and atrocities, yet it has avoided this fate. Four major risk factors are present in Botswana – ethnic division, discrimination, human rights violations and economic inequality. Despite Botswana's reputation as Africa's success story, the country has appeared on a recent Genocide Watch watchlist as exhibiting a moderate risk of future genocide (Genocide Prevention Advisory Network 2009). It has also been identified by the Center for International Development and Conflict Management (CIDCM) as having a high risk of future instability (Hewitt *et al.* 2010). Nevertheless, this risk has remained steady.

Social division

Ethnic division

Many scholars have identified the existence of deep social cleavages as a significant structural precondition for genocide (see, for example, Fein 1979; Harff 2003; Kuper 1981). Such cleavages certainly exist in Botswana. The country's ethnic composition is diverse, with up to 35 different language groups of varying sizes, not to mention even greater tribal complexity (RETENG 2006: 26). Such diversity is not in itself indicative of risk. Stanton points out that it is 'bipolar' societies – that is, those characterized by two dominant identity groups – that are most at risk of genocide and mass atrocities (Stanton 1996). However, amidst this diversity, there exists in Botswana 'persistent and pervasive cleavages', as Kuper (1981: 57) called them. Botswana's national identity is based on the numerically dominant Tswanas, who constitute approximately 70 per cent of the population (Good 2008: 85). Unlike Rwanda and neighbouring South Africa, where ethnic and racial groups were formally classified and marked on identity cards, in Botswana tensions and inequality have arisen partly due to a *denial* of ethnic difference, and consequently a reluctance to acknowledge cultural, economic and political points of distinction.

It is difficult to find reliable data on the precise breakdown of ethnic groups – as noted, the government in Botswana does not collect information on ethnicity. The last time such information was collected was by the British in 1946 (Leith 2005: 29; RETENG 2006: 26). Leith argues that the question of ethnic identity was stripped from censuses in the years leading up to independence, and thereafter, as part of government efforts to promote national unity (Leith 2005: 30). Nevertheless, some approximations have been attempted, and have generally concluded that most of the population, upwards of 70 per cent, hails from one of the eight officially recognized Tswana tribes. The rest of the population comprises 37 different minority groups, including the San Bushmen, the Wayeyi, the Bakgalagadi, the Kalanga, as well as white Afrikaners (see, for example, Good 2008: 85; RETENG 2006: 26).[7] This diversity is the product of waves of migration over two millennia. Prior to this, the territory was inhabited by various groups of San Bushmen – or *Basarwa*, in the country's official language, Setswana. As others (mostly Bantu groups, including the eight major Tswana chieftaincies, from Central and Eastern Africa) settled around the Kalahari, competition for resources in the arid landscape increased tensions between these groups, although most managed to coexist peacefully. Eventually the larger cattle-grazing tribes became the most dominant. Smaller groups such as the Wayeyi, the Bakgalagadi and the San were dispossessed of their traditional hunting and grazing land and incorporated into the lowest rungs of the rigid hierarchies that characterized the more powerful Tswana chieftaincies. Most became servants, or even slaves, looking after cattle on remote outposts in return for food and shelter. The San were rarely incorporated fully into these societies, being classified as 'foreigners' by the Tswana chieftaincies. In most cases, this prohibited them from interacting with chiefs and other aristocrats, an inherent right of all Tswana 'citizens' (Miers 1988: 175). The marginalization of non-Tswana groups has a long history, dating back centuries.

This historical background of inter-ethnic relations is important, as it provides a context for the patterns of discrimination and human rights violations that have mounted in Botswana since the mid-1990s. The groups most discriminated against are those who were at the lowest levels in the pre-colonial tribal hierarchy, especially the San Bushmen. As noted, when the territory became a British protectorate in 1885, the colonial administration recognized the tribal sovereignty of eight Tswana chieftaincies, and allowed them to continue to exercise control over most areas of governance (Stevens 1967: 113). This advantaged the larger Tswana chieftaincies both politically and economically, while the use of *malata* to tend to cattle grazing and other forms of labour freed up the wealthier members of the chieftaincy to pursue educational opportunities, granting them an advantaged position in the years leading up to independence. For example, Seretse Khama, educated in England, was one of many members of the Tswana elites who shaped the direction of the newly independent country in the 1960s.

Consequently, Botswana's national identity was formed by and around the dominant Tswana. Botswana literally means 'land of the Tswana', and all citizens of Botswana are *Batswana*, which has two meanings – citizen of Botswana, and member of the Setswana-speaking group. National identity is based on the dominant ethnic group, and it is the denial or neglect of other identities that has defined discrimination in Botswana (Cullis and Watson 2005: 21). The dominance of the Tswana tribal elite continued as the most powerful leaders, both politically and economically, came from this group. As a consequence, their power was consolidated in the constitution and in many precedent-setting policies,[8] leading some scholars to argue that Botswana's democracy extends little beyond the conducting of elections every five years (du Toit 1995: 25; Good 2009: 1). A system of governance that favoured the dominance of the old ruling elite permeates much of the culture of the modern state. The status and even the existence of other ethno-linguistic groups were denied.

Discrimination

There are many examples of discrimination against minority groups in Botswana, reflecting government policies and, in some cases, constitutional provisions. These have, to varying degrees, excluded minority groups politically and disadvantaged them socially and economically. This discrimination can be seen in the spheres of political representation, land distribution, and education and culture. Cumulatively, it poses a risk of mass atrocities.

With regard to language, Botswana officially recognizes English and Setswana. The exclusion of other languages is most acutely felt in the education sector, especially in areas where the native language of the majority of residents is not recognized. Although Setswana and English are widely spoken in the country as second and third languages, there is evidence that literacy and completion of schooling is lower in the more remote areas where the native language is more likely to be a minority one, and where poverty and destitution are already widespread, along with a tendency to leave school early in search of work (Good 2008: 94). The denial of education in other languages runs counter to the policy in the decades leading up to independence, when other languages were also taught in schools (Nyati-Ramahobo 2000: 265). Moreover, in an effort to attract support from all constituencies in the months approaching the country's first election in 1965, the BDP printed 'how to vote' instructions in a number of languages that were subsequently excluded from official publications and communications (Solway and Nyati-Ramahobo 2004: 606). Those who speak non-Tswana languages as their native language have thus been disadvantaged culturally and economically.

Politically, only the eight Tswana chiefs are recognized in the House of Chiefs, Botswana's upper house. Indeed, this was a prudent measure at the advent of independent statehood. Acknowledgement of the country's eight recognized traditional rulers[9] in the new multi-democratic structure – and one which limited their power by giving them an advisory capacity only, without the power of veto – ensured continuity in the transition to a centralized democratic system (Beaulier and Subrick 2006: 108). Although the Chieftaincy Act was later amended in response to a legal challenge by one minority group (the Wayeyei), the amendment did not provide equal recognition for other traditional leaders. In the new House of Chiefs, consisting of 37 members, the dominant position of the eight Tswana chiefs remains intact. These leaders maintain permanent positions in the House, while the other leaders are appointed by the government on a non-permanent basis (RETENG 2006: 7, 28). This has perpetuated the political and economic marginalization of non-Tswana ethnic minorities.

In economic terms, two policies in particular have crystallized this marginalization: the Tribal Territories Act and the Tribal Grazing Land Policy (TGLP). The Tribal Territories Act[10] of 1968 precipitated the creation of land boards to take over the administration of customary land that had until that time been administered by the eight major chieftaincies (Cullis and Watson 2005: 8). Although the act ostensibly withdrew the tribal chiefs' power of land allocation, the land boards set up to assume this responsibility are chaired by members from the same tribes (Somolekae 1998: 194). In theory, all decisions are made in the interests of the eight Setswana-speaking tribes, excluding all other language groups and cultures. Under such administration, non-Setswana-speaking tribes have at times been moved from their ancestral land, mostly without consultation or compensation (Cullis and Watson 2005: 21; Good 2008: 115). This occurred especially in the aftermath of the land privatization process spurred by the TGLP.

The TGLP, established in 1975, institutionalized what became known as the enclosure movement: privatizing and fencing land that was formerly owned communally, under the administrative control of the eight Tswana tribes (Fidzani 1998: 237). This process was supported by the World Bank in the so-called 'Livestock Development Project – 1' (LDP1), which encouraged ranching of the kind conducted by white settlers, on the assumption that communal grazing had degraded the land (Cullis and Watson 2005: 8). Guided by the World Bank's advisers, the TGLP adopted a new system of land management under which the land board divided land into four categories: commercial land (for private use), communal land (a continuation of the traditional approach to property, but managed differently), reserved areas (land set aside for future use), and wildlife management areas (Cullis and Watson 2005: 8).

The Policy created three main problems in its implementation. First, much land set aside for commercial use was deemed empty and unused, when in fact it was inhabited by people who used it for practices that had been 'overlooked'. In particular, the San had traditionally used large tracts of such 'commercial' land for hunting and gathering as well as small-scale herding (Cullis and Watson 2005: 9). Following from this, the second problem was that the Policy disadvantaged small-scale cattle herders. The land boards allocated commercial land to those who most effectively argued that they would put the land to good use. In keeping with the ranch model supported by the World Bank, most private plots were allocated to large cattle owners (Cullis and Watson 2005: 21). The third problem was that poorer grazers were denied access to traditional water sources. Some communal land was reserved for those who owned just a few head of cattle, but the TGLP rendered such grazing virtually impossible, mainly because boreholes were no longer accessible to communal land users.

Privatization under the TGLP further decreased the economic options of small-scale herders. This meant that the poorest and non-Setswana-speaking groups (very often the same people) were unable to support themselves on the land (Good 1993: 216). These policies were a catalyst for the increased destitution of ethnic minorities, and improved the wealth and standing of the large cattle owners – the same people who were educated, ran the land boards and had a greater stake in the new regime (Cullis and Watson 2005: 17). Moreover, in the process of privatization and land allocation, large tracts in the west of the country were officially deemed empty, despite the presence of San and Kgalagadi communities (Good 2008: 114). These populations were relocated to government settlements or nearby towns, where traditional patterns of life and meaningful employment were largely unattainable. Thus, the pattern of dispossession from colonial and pre-colonial times was reinforced by the laws and policies of independent Botswana. This ongoing discrimination has entrenched ethnic division in Botswana, and clearly limited the economic opportunities of many remote San communities. Such state-led discrimination is recognized by Harff, the OSAPG and Minorities at Risk as a significant risk factor in mass atrocities (Harff 2012: 54; Minorities at Risk 2009a; DSAPG 2009). Economic, social and political discrimination in Botswana have all spurred this risk.

Human rights violations

Contemporary patterns of dispossession had their most acute expression in the forced government evictions of San Bushmen from the CKGR, a process that occurred between 1997 and 2002. Reminiscent of the uprooting of indigenous populations in colonial Australia, South Africa and Algeria, Good notes, 'Historically, relocation exists as an icon of the absence of human rights and the fate of indigenous peoples under specific political conditions of a colonial or quasi-colonial kind' (Good 2008: 124). Such forceful relocation not only violated Article 13 of the Universal Declaration of Human Rights, guaranteeing the rights of citizens to move and reside freely within the borders of their own country (United Nations 1948b: Res 217 A(iii)), but also Botswana's own constitution, as those coerced into relocation were denied basic liberties (see, for example, Dow 2006; Phumaphi 2006).

The relocations were initially presented as optional. Many residents from various small communities within the reserve opted to move to a new settlement just outside the territory's borders, called New Xade, to gain better access to government services like education, water, shelter and welfare provisions where needed. In the following years, many returned to the CKGR and continued to pursue their traditional means of hunting, gathering and goat herding, at least for part of each year. When the 'voluntary' resettlement programme of 1997 failed to empty the settlements within the CKGR, the government announced a complete withdrawal of all services by January 2002 (Good 2008: 126–33). No one was allowed to return without official permission, and those caught hunting without a permit were arrested and fined. The downgrading of existing services in the reserve was accompanied by coercive negotiations that eventually led to the eviction and relocation the last groups of San Bushmen. These evictions were carried out by police and other government officials; all water tanks and boreholes were destroyed to prevent any San from returning. Although this process was not novel – many other indigenous groups had been dispossessed and marginalized prior to and during colonialism – this episode was unique in Botswana, as it was planned and executed by a post-colonial democratic government. While the land boards in the territories managed the privatization of land based on commercial interests monopolized by Tswana elites, the CKGR was also exceptional. It was set up specifically for the last San groups still living on their ancestral lands, in the heart of the Kalahari Desert where large-scale cattle grazing was not viable. Thus it was overlooked by Tswana cattle owners (see, for example, Silberbauer 1981). The deep historical inequality in Botswana resulted in a Tswana-dominated government passing judgement on the way of life of the most marginalized groups: the government regarded the traditions of the San as 'outdated', and resettled them on that basis (Gall 2001: 200).

The denial of settlement in the CKGR continued even after a 2006 High Court ruling that the evictions were 'unlawful and unconstitutional' (BBC News 2006a; Dow 2006; Phumaphi 2006). The government had denied the San the right to re-open one of the boreholes that had been closed down (Survival International 2009). After unsuccessfully challenging this action in the High Court in 2010, the residents, represented by the First Peoples of the Kalahari, won the right to access water in a Court of Appeal decision in January 2011 (BBC News 2011a). This abuse of human rights, though confined to a relatively small population in the CKGR, is indicative of the conflict of interest in terms of land use that has been enshrined in the Tribal Territories Act. Moreover, it is the government's treatment of the San Bushmen, particularly in this instance, that prompted Genocide Watch to declare a risk of mass atrocities there.[11] Government evictions and the denial of return likewise drew the attention of the UN Human Rights Council (UNHRC), which criticized the Botswana government for not allowing most San to return to the CKGR, even after the High Court ruling in 2006 (Nieuwoudt 2008).

Inequality of economic opportunity

Discriminatory policies have also increased inequality of economic opportunity in Botswana. Such inequality has remained high, in an environment that both marginalizes poor rural dwellers and produces consistently high unemployment in urban centres as well. Botswana has the world's fourth highest income gap between rich and poor, according to the Gini coefficient (Good 2008: 89). According to the UNDP's 2005 *Human Development Report*, 47 per cent of all farming households had no cattle, and a further 24 per cent had between one and 11 heads, while the richest 2.5 per cent of households owned 40 per cent of all cattle (UNDP 2005: 17). According to Leith, the proportion of rural households owning ten or fewer (or no) head of cattle increased from 50 to 60 percent during the first 20 years of independence, indicating that the process of land enclosure and privatization significantly exacerbated wealth inequality in rural areas (home to 50 per cent of the population) (Leith 2005: 65; see also Gall 2001; Good 1993, 2008; Mackenzie 1969 [1883]; Miers 1988; Silberbauer 1981; Wilmsen 1990). With consistently high unemployment over decades, mostly due to a failure of economic diversification, the urban migration induced by rural marginalization has spawned destitution and widespread poverty, despite Botswana achieving the world's highest rate of GDP growth from the 1970s to the 1990s (Leith 2005: 4). Such growth, the result of diamond export revenues, has further deepened inequality and entrenched ethnic divisions.

Assessing risk in Botswana

Four factors associated with the long-term risk of mass atrocity exist in Botswana. Clearly, there are 'deep and persistent cleavages'. There is also clear evidence of discrimination based on ethnicity. Such patterns of discrimination have led to forced evictions of the San with ancestral ties in the CKGR – a clear violation of human rights. Furthermore, there are patterns of political exclusion and one of the most unequal distributions of wealth anywhere in the world. These are recognized as atrocity risk factors by organizations including Genocide Watch (Genocide Prevention Advisory Network 2009), the CIDCM (Hewitt *et al.* 2010: 21) and Minorities at Risk (2009a).

However, this assessment of risk in Botswana fails to explain why such risk has not escalated, and why it has not led to the commission of mass atrocities.

The Minorities at Risk analysis of Botswana argues that the repression of the San is mitigated by the existence of a democratic regime (Minorities at Risk 2009a). Indeed, Botswana's multi-party democratic system is rare in Africa – only one of three that have continued uninterrupted since independence. Its strong rule of law has provided an avenue for marginalized groups to challenge discriminatory government policies. In addition, the country's export-oriented economy and longstanding membership of the World Trade Organization (WTO), among other features, demonstrate its integration in the global economy. Furthermore, the government's equitable provision of services has ensured that even the most marginalized have access to health services and education. These mitigating factors are significant for two reasons. First, an absence of democracy is a key predictor of future political instability. Second, even when a democratic country discriminates against certain ethnic, religious or political groups, the rule of law, particularly a robust and independent judiciary, can provide a safety net. That Botswana has both a democratic regime and the rule of law, at least in some significant degree, indicates that there is a measure of constraint on discrimination and inequality. Deploying the framework from Chapter 3, the next section demonstrates how Botswana's strengths have effectively mitigated the risk posed by entrenched discrimination and inequality.

Resilience in Botswana

The combination of a robust multi-party democracy, rule of law, the equitable provision of services and trade openness has mitigated the risk posed by discrimination, inequality, human rights abuses and ethnic cleavage. This can be seen in two ways. First, there is the political space for opposition and the advocacy of greater equality conducted without fear in a democratic space allowing for public expression of dissent and debate, through a free press and numerous organizations advocating for political and economic change. Second, and related, embedded in this opposition is a respect for due process. Since independence, all expressions of opposition have been articulated within the provisions of a constitution that sets out the boundaries of political contestation. This has seen challenges to established elites in the form of opposition political parties, High Court challenges and ongoing dialogue with the government. To date, there has been no attempt to use violent resistance or guerrilla warfare, nor have there been attempts at secession. All opposition and pressure for change has taken place within the mechanisms of due process.

Social cohesion

Ethnic inclusion through access to services

Policies certainly marginalized some minority groups, but a counterweight was Seretse Khama's insistence that the public sector – the country's largest employer – recruit and promote solely according to merit. In situations in which Botswana has been unable to find appropriate technical expertise domestically, particularly in the early post-independence period, it has not hesitated to utilize foreign expertise. At the same time, it strove to strengthen domestic expertise through local and international educational institutions (see, for example, Leith 2005: 57; Masire 2006: 99; Samatar 1999: 8). Over time, this has ensured that ethnicity does not factor in appointments and promotions. Nor is it a consideration for location of employment. Staff and students are often relocated to different parts of the country, regardless of ethnic affiliation, offsetting the possibility of tribal or ethnic homogeneity developing within key sectors in each region (du Toit 1995: 59). Although the inherent poverty of some groups, like the San, is accompanied by a dis- proportionately low rate of literacy and secondary school representation, other groups have flourished under this system. The urban-based Kalanga, for example, enjoy an advantaged position in Botswana society (Werbner 2004: 51). Reward based on merit, not ethnicity, has elevated many besides the traditionally powerful elite.

While land policies aggravated the country's ethnic asymmetries, the equi- table provision of education has given many members of minority groups the capacity to challenge discrimination and prejudice. Even rural-based minority groups who were previously at the lower end of Tswana tribal hierarchies 'found themselves in a position in which they could directly access the state in order to gain rights to land, education, employment, services, subsidies, and the courts, instead of having to rely, as in the past, upon the patronage of an ethnic intermediary' (Solway 2002: 717). Access to education, as Solway argues, has had 'an empowering impact on minority groups and has led some members to reflect and re-evaluate their place in Botswana society' (Solway 2002: 717). In other words, the state provision of education prompted many to question the constructions of national identity, and this led to activism by a number of groups that emerged in the 1990s. RETENG, Kamanakao, First Peoples of the Kalahari and the Society for the Preservation of the Kalanga Language are examples. The academic and University of Botswana deputy vice-chancellor, Lydia Nyati-Ramahobo, has worked to advance political representation for a minority group, the Wayeyei. A founding member of Kamanakao, she was instrumental in successfully challenging the government in the High Court case on the composition of the House of Chiefs, and has campaigned for recognition of the Wayeyei language, as well as other minor- ity languages (Nyati-Ramahobo 2000, 2002; Solway and Nyati-Ramahobo 2004). Historically one of the most marginalized minority groups, the Bak- galagadi have benefited considerably from services offered by the modern independent state. As the markers of status and success became measured by academic and financial achievement, old notions of tribal superiority[12] became less meaningful (Solway 1994: 262). Such social change brought about a rise in Kgalagadi ethnic consciousness, whereby 'the ethnic identity constructed and imposed by politically dominant peoples upon a number of subordinated and disparate peoples ... became a source of pride and a political tool ...' (Solway 1994: 255). The public provision of education has advanced political reform in Botswana by giving a voice to the very people who were the object of discrimination. It has also empowered members of minority groups to challenge the way their own identities have been constructed by the Tswana elite. Although there are clear social benefits from such action, including greater political representation, these public challenges also mitigate the risk of mass atrocities by overturning discriminatory laws and policies.

Botswana's merit-based system of employment and education has elevated many in addition to the wealthy Tswana. In raising up those who traditionally had been suppressed, it also precipitated a rise in the ethnic consciousness of many minority groups, heralding non-violent activism on many fronts. In particular, different groups have utilized the legal system to challenge specific government policies as well as parts of the constitution.[13] Likewise, despite the denial or neglect of ethnic diversity in the country, the government has never sought to prohibit the open expression of ethnic difference.[14] While the newly independent state inherited and further entrenched many of the inequalities of the Tswana chieftaincies, it also established democratic institutions that allowed such minorities – over time – to challenge these disparities. This has helped place limits on discrimination, and on occasion decrease it – the reform in relation to the House of Chiefs being an example. Thus, the risk of mass atrocities has been managed through education and respect for due process.

Good governance

Democracy

Good governance is pivotal to a country's resilience, especially in the presence of risk. As Goldstone and Ulfelder (2004: 14) state, 'political institutions and the patterns of political behaviour that evolve around them determine a country's resistance to instability'. Botswana's political institutions were established by the Tswana elite in the mid-1960s; since then, these institutions have frequently accommodated and absorbed profound challenges to the social, political and economic status quo premised by this original dominance. As Solway argues, 'In creating effective institutions, the state produced conditions for its own challenge and provided an orderly means by which dissenting parties could proceed' (Solway 2002: 711). Botswana's multi-party democratic system and strong rule of law have underscored nearly five decades of stability, characterized by free and fair elections, a relatively independent judiciary, a vocal free press and a conspicuous absence of the mass violence that has afflicted nearly all of its neighbours (see, for example, Freedom House 2011; World Bank 2011a). It has conducted elections at municipal and national levels deemed by independent bodies to be free and fair on every occasion (EISA 2010: 3). It has consistently scored high on Polity IV's measure of democracy (Marshall and Jaggers 2010). Although the BDP has won every national election, Botswana's opposition has been strong, often winning municipal elections in major urban centres, and at times winning close to 50 per cent of the national popular vote (Good and Taylor 2008: 56).

Three key factors have characterized Botswana's strong institutions, allowing over time for a more inclusive and equitable system of rule. They are a smooth transition to independence, a strong inaugural leader, and continuity between traditional and modern structures of conflict resolution. The country has been particularly successful in incorporating traditional structures of conflict resolution into the modern state, providing continuity with the past. On the eve of independence, the incorporation of the eight major chiefs into the House of Chiefs, and the continued use of a traditional forum and customary court known as the *Kgotla*, guaranteed unanimous support from the established traditional power structures. They also supplied the general public with familiar cultural markers, and forums for the airing of views and grievances during the transition to a centralized multi-party system. This also meant that the modern state inherited the inequalities and discriminatory practices entrenched in the chieftaincies (as explored in the previous section), but with a major difference: the independent multi-party state offered channels through which marginalized groups could campaign for greater inclusion and equality.

Botswana's first president, Seretse Khama, was instrumental in forging the structures of the new democratic state, as well as winning the consent of the eight major tribal chiefs. As independence approached, a new constitution provided a framework to preserve the traditional structures of the chieftaincies, but rest power firmly in a constituency-based multi-party democratic system (Parsons *et al.* 1995: 108–9). Khama gained widespread support through negotiation and persuasion, in language that was notably lacking in anti-colonial rhetoric (Masire 2006: 79). The path to independence was approached as a partnership with the colonial rulers, rather than as an antagonistic break from the past. In addition, Khama travelled extensively throughout the territory, eventually persuading all eight chieftaincies to surrender their rights to land and natural resources in the name of national unity (Masire 2006: 77–79). This created a strong foundation for equitable democratic participation, and achieved a delicate balance between traditional rule and a modern centralized democracy (Fawcus and Tilbury 2000: 130–34).

The quid pro quo was the very limited participation of the eight chiefs in government. The upper house of Botswana's parliament was established as the House of Chiefs. This gave the eight Tswana tribal chiefs, along with a number of sub-chiefs, a role in the running of the nation. However, the role of the House of Chiefs was restricted to an advisory capacity, without veto powers. The real decision-making power was centred in the (mostly) elected lower house and the office of the president. This prevented a lack of consensus among the chiefs from undermining the new state. At the same time, it was remarkably successful in preserving traditional forms of authority and preventing tribal-based factionalization during the decolonization process. It is true that this process initially excluded minority groups that had for centuries been subject to a lower status, but at the time of independence the potential for political dissent and territorial fragmentation lay in the hands of the eight Tswana chieftaincies. Without their unanimous support, Botswana's formative years as an independent state would likely have been characterized by tribal division and challenges to centralized rule. Recognizing the eight chiefs was seen as a gesture toward the status quo, while simultaneously winning the chieftaincies' support for an entirely new form of governance (Masire 2006: 74).

This incorporation did not occur without some disagreement by powerful tribal figures. In the first term of the BDP government in the late 1960s, two tribal chiefs expressed opposition – Chief Batheon II and Chief Linchwe II. Batheon, in particular, was unhappy with the way members of the governing BDP had treated the chiefs,[15] and challenged the government on this issue. Both, however, expressed their dissent within the bounds of the constitution by joining opposition parties and becoming elected representatives in parliament. Eventually Linchwe accepted the position of ambassador to the United States (du Toit 1995: 51). Batheon participated in party politics by joining the opposition Botswana National Front (BNF) (Masire 2006: 116). No calls for secession were heard. Therefore, factional division was avoided at the country's nascent stage. This was a significant achievement, given that such division is, according to the PITF, a major source of instability for emerging democracies (see Goldstone *et al.* 2005; and the discussion in Chapter 3). It provided a strong foundation for Botswana's stability.

The peaceful transition to independence meant that traditional societal systems of governance and conflict resolution continued to function effectively. The *Kgotla*, for example, has operated since pre-colonial times. It is a public forum where laws are announced, grievances heard and judgments pronounced (Masire 2006: 62). It is also, essentially, a public assembly in which any member of the community can express an opinion. Prior to independence, this process of public dissemination and gathering of information was a central pillar of political and cultural life, although all final decisions were ultimately left to the chief. Although originally a product of the *Batswana* chieftaincies, *Dikgotla* now operate throughout the country, and are instrumental in the customary courts that form one tier of the country's legal system (Ngcongco 1989: 46).

Today, members of Botswana's parliament visit the *Dikgotla*, which continue to act as a way of gauging public opinion (Seepapitso IV 1989: 212). In fact, the BDP has fostered the *Kgotla* both as one of its main avenues of communication with the general populace, and as a vehicle to enhance democratic participation (Holm 1993: 103). It was the preservation of this institution that provided a framework for the majority of citizens to relate to and support multi-party democracy following the transfer of power in 1966. As Holm argues, it 'led to the public being able to adjust easily to participation in the new liberal democratic structures established at independence' (Holm 1993: 93). At times, popular pressure expressed in the *Dikgotla* has led to major changes in government policy. In 1991, for example, villagers in the Okavango Delta prompted the government to cancel a major irrigation project following an extended *Kgotla* meeting between residents and public officials (Ayittey 2005: 359). The use of the *Kgotla* was crucial in facilitating the smooth transition to a multi-party democratic republic and nearly five decades of stable governance. Underscoring this political arrangement is Botswana's robust rule of law, characterized by a strong and independent judiciary.

Rule of law

Democratic governance in Botswana has been strengthened by the rule of law. In particular, the country's judiciary has on numerous occasions overturned policies and laws that reinforced historical inequalities, mainly along ethnic lines. In so doing, the risk of mass atrocities inherent in such discrimination has been managed and lessened.

Three examples demonstrate this accountability. The first was a 2002 ruling that found the constitutional structuring of the House of Chiefs to be unjust. This was in response to sections 77 to 79 of the Constitution, which outlined the structure and membership of the House of Chiefs. On the grounds that it neglected to represent minorities other than the eight dominant Tswana chiefs, the Kamanakao organization challenged it, along with the Chieftaincy Act. The subsequent ruling declared both the relevant section of the constitution and the Chieftaincy Act were 'discriminatory and unconstitutional', denying the Wayeyei and other minorities 'equal treatment and protection' (Nyati-Ramahobo 2002: 695). This precipitated reform that increased participation and decreased political discrimination.

The second example was a landmark ruling in 2006 by Botswana's High Court, declaring illegal a 2002 government order to evict the San Bushmen people from their ancestral land (BBC News 2006a; Dow 2006; Phumaphi 2006). The BDP government publicly acknowledged the decision, and promised to abide by it. Although there is clear evidence to suggest that they did not, in fact, respect it – that they shut down the group's borehole and blocked their only access to water (Survival International 2009) – the ruling itself showed that due process could be used to secure the legal rights of minority groups.

The third example is related: a January 2011 ruling by the Court of Appeal in a case brought by the First People of the Kalahari against the government of Botswana. The ruling declared that those who were previously judged to have the right to dwell in the CKGR also had the right to re-open the borehole in the settlement of Xade, as well as drill other boreholes in the reserve (Simpson 2011). This was in response to the government's refusal to allow residents to access water, either through drilling or transporting it from outside the reserve. The High Court challenge was a response to unanswered requests from the San, claiming that the government had prevented them from dwelling in the reserve despite the 2006 ruling.

What these examples highlight are two important protective features of Botswana's system of governance. First, the judiciary in Botswana is independent from the government, and has passed judgments that on occasion contradicted government policy and buttressed constitutional provisions against demonstration. The government also responded by setting up a commission (the Balopi Commission) to re-examine the composition of the House of Chiefs, and thus promoting debate about the national character and issues of ethnic diversity (Werbner 2004: 44). Second, these examples have highlighted a continuing trust in due process. Ethnic minority advocacy groups have often used the High Court to gain recognition of inequality or discrimination. At no time in their struggle for rights have any of these groups threatened to break away from the sovereign state, or to achieve their goal by means of armed struggle. While a sparse population and other physical constraints exert an influence here, the opportunities to advocate for change within Botswana's democratic system need to be recognized. Although the state has perpetuated discrimination, it has also provided mechanisms to challenge such discrimination. In the process, it has mitigated the risk of mass atrocities.

The successes of Botswana's governance

In Botswana, as Solway and Nyati-Ramahobo (2004: 604) point out, it is the independent state's success, not its failure, that has exacerbated and deepened ethnic cleavages. The majority of citizens in Botswana have enjoyed the fruits of this success in some way, but a few of the policies introduced by this nascent state within the first decade of its independence 'compromised ... a significant sector of the population' (Solway and Nyati-Ramahobo 2004: 603). These include, most significantly, the Tribal Territories Act, the TGLP and the Chieftaincy Act. In aggravating division and discrimination, these policies have increased the risk of mass atrocities. However, other policies have provided essential services for all. The state's institutions (especially the judiciary) have also provided a means for marginalized groups to redress these inequalities. Although these gains have not eliminated inequality – indeed, Botswana has one of the highest gaps between rich and poor of any country in the world – they have limited government discrimination and provided a safety net for historically excluded groups.

Economic inclusion

Equitable provision of services, trade openness and economic growth

Botswana's economic management has helped to mitigate the risk of mass atrocities. With the revenues from diamond exports, the government has provided extensive public services and infrastructure. Such provisions include universal primary education, universal health coverage, an effective drought prevention programme and extensive investment in roads – from 50 km in 1966 to more than 10,000 km some five decades later (Beaulier and Subrick 2006: 104). While some policies have advantaged the already powerful, there are many examples where the government has provided equitable services for nearly all citizens. Such programmes and services have bolstered the Botswana government's legitimacy. Until the late 1990s, when HIV/AIDS started to show great negative effects on the general population, life expectancy and living standards had gradually improved, and although the gap between rich and poor continually widened, the poor had become slightly better off (Leith 2005: 17). Life expectancy approached 70 years by the mid- to late 1990s – a substantial increase from 20 years earlier (Leith 2005: 13). This suggests that even though the gap between rich and poor was widening, the poorest were living longer as well.

This provision of social services was made possible by export revenue from diamond mining. This of course is not a virtue in itself – mineral wealth on the African continent has more often been a curse than a blessing. Trade openness, however, gave the country the means to improve services. Botswana's trade openness and level of economic freedom is one of the highest in the region (Heritage Foundation 2013). A democratic system provided the impetus. So, trade openness and good management of the terms of trade contributed to the stability of Botswana, and the subsequent equitable provision of services provided greater legitimacy to the BDP government (Beaulier and Subrick 2006: 112).

While Botswana's trade openness is indeed an important dimension of the country's stability, it is the government's prudent management of diamond revenues that gives great insight into how an initially desperately poor country managed consistent and steady growth for nearly five decades. Under Seretse Khama's leadership, the government negotiated a partnership with De Beers for the extraction of diamonds. This resulted in the creation of a joint venture, Debswana, which ensured that almost three-quarters of all diamond revenue would be obtained by the government, through dividends, tax and royalties (Masire 2006: 206). The government carefully managed these revenues through a measured and restrained approach to spending during boom periods. Similar resource windfalls in other African countries have led to increased instability – the result of spending binges, followed by financial crises in leaner years (Ayittey 2005: 358). By contrast, economic management has deliberately avoided such reckless swings in Botswana. Since the late 1960s, when revenues started to accumulate, the government has been building up its foreign currency reserves. This has enabled Botswana to maintain a consistent level of spending on public services (especially in education and primary health), regardless of international price fluctuations and global economic swings (Leith 2005: 107).

Botswana's consistently high economic growth also fostered stability. The economy grew by an average of 7 per cent between 1966 and 1999 – the highest of any country in the world during that period. The country's trade openness and its prudent economic management have been instrumental in buffering economic challenges and maintaining economic stability.

Risk mitigation in practice

Mass atrocities almost always occur during or in the aftermath of upheaval, whether war (Bellamy 2011: 2), political or economic crisis (Fein 1979: 9; Midlarsky 2005: 85), or natural disaster (Jonassohn 1998: 44; Keen 1994). Botswana's management of three key crises since the 1980s offers insight into the ways that this combination of good governance, prudent economic management and equitable service provision have mitigated the effects of serious natural, political and economic challenges.

The first crisis was a major drought. In the early 1980s, Botswana experienced the most profound economic crisis of its short life as an independent nation. The drought almost put a halt to all agricultural production, and placed over half the population at risk of starvation. Depletion of food stocks was greater than in the Ethiopian famine of 1984, when over 1 million people died of starvation.[16] By contrast, Botswana 'avoided significant famine-related loss of life' (Belbase and Morgan 1994: 286). This was principally due to the country's drought relief programme, established in the previous decade. The programme outlined a process for comprehensive coordination between local and national institutions, through the District Drought Committee, which included members from local councils, tribal administrations and national ministries. The committee regularly assessed drought conditions, and made prompt recommendations. A second body, the Inter-Ministerial Drought Committee (IMDC), then made direct recommendations to the Cabinet concerning the funds and interventions needed (Belbase and Morgan 1994: 290). This system operated effectively throughout the drought, and relief was timely, owing both to the well-established rural infrastructure and the country's substantial foreign exchange reserves (Belbase and Morgan 1994: 286). Food relief was provided to remote area dwellers (RADs) unable to feed themselves; funds were given to small-scale farmers to dig boreholes; and stockfeed was subsidized to allow the pastoral industry to continue functioning (Jacques 1995: 46–47). The readiness to gather information, consult and review policies on a regular basis, particularly with regard to the most vulnerable rural groups, made the country 'exemplary' in its ability to provide drought relief and prevent the onset of famine (Jacques 1995: 43). In short, good governance, prioritizing large foreign exchange reserves in the long term, and multi-level coordination for the duration of the crisis, provided effective relief (Jacques 1995: 43; Vogel 1993: 96). In doing so, upheaval and possible political instability were avoided.

A second and simultaneous crisis compounded these challenges. For a six-month period during the 1980s, not a single diamond was sold on the international market (Leith 2005: 10). For a country dependent on a single resource for 80 per cent of its export revenue, this was potentially disastrous. Once again, however, foreign exchange reserves acted as a 'shock absorber' (Leith 2005: 10). Neither the sudden drop in export revenues nor the drought affected the trajectory of the country's rapid economic growth. Indeed, throughout fluctuations in revenue over the decades, the Botswana government maintained a consistent spending regime, ensuring a constant provision of public services. In a country with very little public infrastructure at independence, this prudent management of resources has been instrumental to economic and social stability.

The third crisis was caused by the HIV/AIDS epidemic. By the late 1990s, Botswana had the world's second highest rate of HIV infection per capita, at nearly 36 per cent of the population (Policy Project for Bureau for Africa 2001: 8). Life expectancy dropped from 67 to 46 during this decade (Leith 2005: 126). No family or workplace was unaffected. While initially slow to confront the problem, the Botswana government seized upon the advent of generic anti-retroviral drugs to provide this treatment, free of charge, to all citizens with HIV (Dow and Essex 2010: 180–87). This substantially cut the number of people dying from the disease, and although the rate of HIV is still high, available treatment has enabled people to remain active and relatively healthy. The Botswana government's rapid and comprehensive response to the challenge has surpassed that of all other African states. Once again, the government's commitment to maintaining foreign reserves, combined with the equitable provision of services, positioned it to respond effectively to the HIV crisis.[17]

These three cases illustrate how Botswana's democratic and legal institutions have allowed the country to confront challenges and accommodate diversity. As a result, it has so far avoided major upheaval of the kind that can provoke political instability and precipitate mass atrocities.

Conclusion

While Botswana is often hailed as an 'African success story', and even the 'Switzerland of Africa', it is certainly not without the risks associated with genocide and other mass atrocities. The economic, political and social marginalization of non-Tswana minority groups including the San, the Bakgalagadi and the Wayeyei has further entrenched historical patterns of wealth and poverty, power and submission. In light of these factors, especially with regard to the San, Genocide Watch identified Botswana as a country with moderate risk of future genocide.

Confronted with such risk, the case of Botswana has demonstrated that long-term prevention is a broad and complex process founded on effective domestic institutions, laws and policies. Botswana's democratic institutions have fostered stability through equitable service provision, prudent economic management and disaster mitigation schemes. The country's judicial system has provided a safety net for the most marginalized groups, even in the face of discriminatory government policies, and this has lent credence to the efficacy of due process when injustice occurs. The public sector's system of recruitment and promotion based on merit has given many non-Tswana citizens the chance to rise to key executive positions, a policy that has particularly benefited the minority Kalanga group. Under Seretse Khama's presidency, Botswana's government invested in universal primary education and the provision of primary health. Further investment was put into the University of Botswana, in order to elevate the skills of citizens in order to compete for public-sector employment on the basis of merit. The government's development of a comprehensive drought response plan, coupled with the accumulation of foreign reserves, ensured that the country was resilient enough to absorb the shock of a five-year drought and periods of low diamond sales. This enabled the country to withstand profound challenges without making major changes to public spending. Consequently, such crises did not provoke political upheaval.

In examining risk mitigation in Botswana, however, processes and complex dynamics are evident that are not so prominent in the framework outlined in Chapter 3. For example, good governance was grounded in the country's history, particularly the nature of its decolonization. Two processes were instrumental here: the smooth transition to independence, and the vision and charisma of the country's first leader, Seretse Khama. Botswana's positive relations with the colonial administrators allowed for a large pool of expatriate civil servants to stay on in the first decade of independence, offering expertise in governance when the new country had few human resources on which to draw. Seretse Khama – with the help of Quett Masire – was influential in winning the consent of all major Tswana chiefs to the new centralized multi-party system of governance. Without this, the likelihood of deep political divisions and competing contentions of power would have been much greater.

An ability to accommodate change also lies at the heart of effective risk mitigation. The establishment of Tswana inter-tribal consent on the eve of independence provided a solid foundation for national unity. However, recent circumstances indicate that such consent is often open to question and reconsideration. The 2010 High Court challenge by Chief Kgafela – a dispute over the distinction between traditional and statutory law – demonstrated that the relationship between old and new remains unresolved, and is once again subject to debate. However, this challenge has been articulated through the country's legal institutions. As Botswana matures as a state, its ability to absorb and accommodate the possibility of structural change like this is another sign of the country's resilience.

There was one further observation that challenged the framework: the distinction between factors that created risk and those that fostered stability was often very thin. In Botswana, many policies and structures that contributed to national unity and stability also yielded negative consequences. For example, the incorporation of the eight major chieftaincies into the House of Chiefs fostered national unity, but also marginalized the non-Tswana tribal groups. This exclusion further entrenched ethnic division in the country. However, Botswana's democratic institutions provided the means by which this marginalization could be redressed. The judiciary, opposition parties and the country's free press have all provided channels to articulate and challenge discriminatory government policies. Thus, the relationship between risk and resilience is not always a matter of distinct risk factors and mitigating factors. Often the same factors that generate risk also provide opportunities for its mitigation.

Notes

1 According to IMF data, over a 33-year period from independence in 1966, no other country in the world had a faster growth rate of gross domestic product (GDP) per capita. Some countries exceeded Botswana's growth rate in the 1990s, but not even Singapore, South Korea or Taiwan surpassed Botswana's growth rate for this extended period. See, for example, Leith 2005.
2 It has the longest enduring multi-party democratic system in Africa.
3 The Bamangwato tribe in particular.
4 A distinct language group that inhabited the region around Ghanzi, in the west of modern-day Botswana.
5 Some groups moved from serfs/slaves to commoners or foreigners, and within the same group there could be a mix of serfs, commoners and foreigners.
6 In 1963 he was promoted to queen's commissioner.
7 RETENG has identified a total of 45 tribal groups in Botswana – 34 Bantu (including eight Tswana) and 11 San.
8 In particular, policies related to the privatization of land that was formerly in the possession of the chieftaincies clearly gave an advantage to wealthy Tswana cattle owners. This will be discussed in the following section, on 'discrimination'.
9 These eight chieftains were recognized during British colonial rule.
10 Also referred to as the Tribal Land Act.
11 See Genocide Prevention Advisory Network (www.gpanet.org/content/genocides-politicides-and-other-mass-murder-1945-stages-2008).
12 They were traditionally subordinate to the Bakwena tribe, where they were given the status of servant and 'foreigner'.
13 For specific examples, see the rule of law section that follows.
14 This is in stark contrast to Turkey, another country whose national identity was premised on a single national identity, but whose authorities (until recently) outlawed the use of language and other intrinsic forms of cultural expression. One consequence of this is the decades-long separatist conflict between the Kurdish Workers' Party (PKK) and the Turkish military.
15 Linchwe, on the other hand, differed from the BDP on ideological grounds, preferring instead to support the pan-Africanist BPP.
16 The Ethiopian drought of 1984 affected Tigray, in the country's north. In the country as a whole, ample food stocks existed to feed everyone.
17 Although the high rates of HIV did not increase the risk of mass atrocities (in Botswana as elsewhere, the virus did not discriminate between social groups), the effective management of the crisis is an example of good governance, which itself offers protection against mass atrocities.

5 Zambia
Resilience through trial and error

In the early years of its independence, Zambia appeared to be a country doomed to fail. Landlocked and poor, its economic fortunes were firmly in the hands of three minority-white-ruled countries – Rhodesia, South Africa and Mozambique. By contrast, Zambia's 'non-racialist' democratic regime left no room for regional complacency, and soon it was supporting guerrilla movements in Rhodesia and Portuguese Africa, inviting an uncertain economic path already made precarious by dependence on a single resource commodity, copper. Domestically, Zambia's challenges were no less stark. Calls for secession came from the traditional elite of Barotseland, a territory that had been treated differently under British colonial rule. In addition, divisions based on ethno-linguistic difference began to destabilize democratic competition. Ethnicity was emerging as the key distinguishing feature, not only between political parties, but between the factional groups within the ruling United National Independence Party (UNIP). This had a knock-on effect in the burgeoning public sector, with ministers recruiting members of their own groups to head government departments and take control of the spoils of governance. This then threatened to entrench ethno-linguistic division in a region where similar divides have provoked repeated atrocities, including genocide. Zambia fared no better in ensuing decades, which witnessed a shift to authoritarian rule in 1973, persistent economic decline throughout the 1970s and 1980s, growing internal dissent and no fewer than five wars in neighbouring countries. How Zambia avoided the perpetration of atrocities committed around its borders is a story well worth relating.

Despite these challenges – or perhaps because of them – Zambia, like Botswana, has been regarded as an African success story. In 1991, after a peaceful transition from a one-party system to a multi-party democracy, Zambia became known as a 'model for Africa' (Bratton 1992: 81; Rakner 2003: 12). It was one of the first one-party African states to make such a transition, and it provided proof that popular opposition to an authoritarian regime need not culminate in mass violence. This is just one instance in which independent Zambia has demonstrated resilience in the face of risk of violent conflict and mass atrocities. Like Botswana, Zambia features a number of risk factors for such violence. This risk has been recognized by the CIDCM, which ranked Zambia tenth in the world for estimated risk of instability between 2008 and 2010 (Hewitt *et al.* 2010: 13). The intersection of political vulnerability, ethnic cleavages and profound economic inequality highlights some of the key interactive factors that have appeared in many states prior to an outbreak of such atrocities (see, for example, Harff 2003).

This chapter provides an analysis of the risk factors that exist (and have existed) in Zambia, and explores the ways in which the risk of mass atrocities has been, and continues to be, mitigated. Zambia has four identifiable risk factors: the existence of ethnic division, limited democracy, limited rule of law and inequality of economic opportunity (see Table 5.1).

For all the risk inherent in these conditions, Zambia has avoided the fate of many of its neighbours: it has avoided civil war as well as the perpetration of mass atrocities. Its resilience is manifested in a variety of ways, but two significant factors can be observed: the legacy of the country's first president, Kenneth Kaunda's efforts to manage ethnic divisions and foster national unity, and the ongoing work of civil society organizations to ensure that the current transition to democracy and greater accountability in economic management continues to progress, albeit very slowly.

Background

Located in Southern Africa, Zambia borders with Zimbabwe, Malawi, the Democratic Republic of the Congo, Namibia and Botswana. Formerly a British colony, after a mainly peaceful struggle for self-rule, independence was nominally granted in 1962, then absolutely in 1964. Prior to British colonial rule, the territory of modern-day Zambia consisted of around 73 independent chieftaincies of varying sizes and structures of rule and organization (Roberts 1976: 82). All had their own distinct dialects (Posner 2005: 56), the largest of which were the Kazembe and Lozi Kingdoms, occupying the northwest and west of the territory, respectively (Roberts 1976: 94–99). It was the Lozi Kingdom that initially sold mineral rights to Cecil Rhodes's British South African Company in 1888. Rhodes' company then made treaties with Mambwe, Lungu and Tabwe chiefs in the east, with both regions then securing British 'protection' (Roberts 1976: 156–57). These two regions merged in 1911, although the British Colony of Northern Rhodesia was not officially controlled by the British government until 1924, when it established a Legislative Council (Roberts 1976: 182). Under the rule of the Legislative Council,

Table 5.1 Risk in Zambia

The risk factors associated with mass atrocities in Zambia
Ethnic division
Limited democracy
Limited rule of law
Inequality of economic opportunity

laws were formalized to exclude Africans from representation, owning property and running businesses. European immigration was encouraged, and the most favourable land was reserved for them, uprooting about 60,000 locals in the process (Roberts 1976: 182–83). At the same time, mission schools increased in number, and missionaries selected four major languages (representing four different regions of the protectorate) for instruction: Bemba, Lozi, Tonga and Nyanga. Although the Legislative Council initially had no African representation, in the late 1930s this began to change slowly, as a number of African organizations emerged in the larger urban areas and the Copperbelt.[1] Through increased political activity, both officially through the Legislative Council and informally through a range of civil-society organizations, an independence movement emerged. Leading the movement was the Zambian African National Congress (ZANC), which was headed by Kenneth Kaunda from 1953. He advocated for an independent country, which at its heart would be committed to 'uniting Africans, and any Europeans who cared to listen, in a sense of belonging to a new nation called Zambia' (Roberts 1976: 211–12, 219–20). In 1959 the ZANC was banned, and Kaunda imprisoned. Along with many other leaders, he was charged with the possession of banned publications (Macpherson 1974: 171). Upon his release in 1960, Kaunda joined and then became the leader of the UNIP, which became instrumental in negotiating majority African representation in the Legislative Council (Roberts 1976: 220–21; Rotberg 1965: 308). This advanced a move toward full independence, which was achieved in 1964.

Zambia's 50 years of history as an independent state have brought it fluctuating fortunes, both politically and economically. Scholars generally divide Zambia's independent history into three main phases, or 'republics', reflecting the nature of the regime in power. The three republics in modern Zambia are delineated by two major regime shifts. The First Republic, spanning ten years from independence in 1964, marks the first period of multi-party democracy. In the Second Republic – from 1973 to 1991 – Zambia was a one-party state, led by the country's inaugural President Kaunda. 1991 to the present marks the Third Republic – a period of ongoing democratization with Zambia's shift back to multi-party democracy, dominated by the Movement for Multi-party Democracy (MMD).

The First Republic experienced many challenges in administration and governance. Dominated at the time by UNIP, with Kaunda as party leader and national president, political competition was increasingly marked by ethnic competition among the four major language groups (Posner 2005: 57). At this time the country enjoyed high revenues from a booming copper industry, and attempted to direct it to establishing essential infrastructure throughout the country, most parts having been neglected by the British colonial administration. Despite a booming mining sector, British sanctions against white-minority-led Rhodesia severely affected Zambia, limiting its ability to diversify its economy (Roberts 1976: 226). A massive expansion of education and health services ensued, demanding a dramatic rise in the appointment of local ministry secretaries among other positions, a recruitment drive that saw increasing demand outstrip existing expertise (Burdette 1988: 66). It was during this period of rapid public service expansion that recruitment and political competition came to be dominated by ethno-linguistic affiliation (Molteno 1974: 63). This caused tensions not only between parties, but also within the dominant UNIP. In an attempt to mitigate these tensions, Kaunda engaged in constant reshuffling of executive appointments, a process that contributed towards inefficiency within all levels of administration and governance (Burdette 1988: 69–70). He also developed 'humanism' – a philosophy that attempted to combine Christian, socialist and pre-capitalist Zambian values as a unifying national idea, in further efforts to foster national unity and counter ethno-linguistic tensions (Burdette 1988: 77; Hall 1969: 48–50). Contending that the multi-party democratic system encouraged such ethnic contestation, Kaunda eventually banned opposition parties and changed the constitution to establish a 'one party participatory democracy', a move he anticipated would calm tensions and improve cooperation (Pettman 1974: 237). While tensions did indeed decrease, Kaunda's economic management was disastrous, hindering economic development at a time when the country could no longer rely on mining revenues.

The Second Republic of one-party rule began in 1973. While Kaunda publicly encouraged political participation within UNIP, in reality all dissent was frowned upon, and the expression of opposing views commonly resulted in the loss of position and employment (Phiri 2006: 164). This was particularly significant in an economy increasingly dominated by the public sector. The office of the president gradually acquired more ministries until it became virtually the sole seat of power, with parliament being pushed increasingly to the periphery of decision making. At the same time, the state, wanting to profit further from lucrative mining revenues, began nationalizing all major industries. This process commenced just as the copper industry was to experience a dramatic decline in prices, from which it would not recover for 30 years. Given Zambia's dependence on copper sales for government revenues, this decline in the industry triggered a widespread downturn in the national economy (McCulloch *et al.* 2000: 3).

By the 1980s, Zambia was highly dependent on international aid to cover basic expenses. With the introduction of a Structural Adjustment Programme (SAP), Kaunda's government was compelled to accept a number of reforms, such as the privatization of industries and enterprises, including the banks and the mines. He was also required to remove food subsidies, a move which saw the price of staples double overnight. The nearly two decades of authoritarian government, as well as the political fallout from the removal of food subsidies, provided a significant catalyst for change, both politically and economically (Phiri 2006: 165–67; Tordoff and Young 2005: 409).

Pressure for political liberalization grew throughout the 1980s, with former politicians, unions and other civil society groups forming a loose coalition called the MMD. Increased economic hardship, particularly the increase in the price of food, triggered large popular demonstrations, which escalated into widespread riots. These riots were initially suppressed violently, but they increased the pressure for Kaunda to respond to the growing dissatisfaction. This period also saw a growing number of government MPs within UNIP pushing for change (Larmer 2009: 118). Eventually Kaunda relented, and agreed to stage multi-party elections, held in 1991. At a time when both Kaunda and his party were deeply unpopular, UNIP suffered a decisive loss and transferred power to the MMD.

The emphatic victory of the MMD marked the beginning of the Third Republic in Zambia – a return to a multi-party system. The new president, Frederick Chiluba, initiated political and economic reform during the first three years of his tenure, but this process stalled as the next national election approached in 1996. In the meantime, Chiluba's presidency developed many similarities to Kaunda's during the Second Republic (Rakner 2003: 13). Intolerance of dissent grew, corruption increased and rules for electoral party competition became more rigid. Chiluba even attempted to amend the new constitution to allow for a third term of presidency, but in the year prior to the 2001 elections civil society groups and others opposing the move waged a successful campaign against it (Burnell 2002: 1111–12). Chiluba was then replaced by Levi Mwanawasa. Mwanawasa commissioned an investigation into allegations of corruption during Chiluba's rule. He even removed the former president's immunity, compelling him to stand trial (Larmer 2009: 123).[2] Mwanawasa's anti-corruption stance and the gradual rise in world copper prices saw Zambia's economy begin to recover and stabilize (Larmer 2009: 129). Following Mwanawasa's death in 2008, the MMD's Rupiah Banda became president and continued the party's domination of Zambian politics, despite the growing strength and organization of opposition, especially the new Patriotic Front (PF) led by Michael Sata. The PF won both the parliamentary and presidential elections of 2011, which marked the first democratic change of regime since the shift to multi-party competition in 1991.

Zambia remains an extremely poor country with a multi-party democratic system that has not entirely detached itself from the centralized institutions of power left over from the Second Republic. In addition, the return to a multi-party system of political competition has brought back to the fore coalition building based on ethno-linguistic distinctions, especially during election campaigns. This has aggravated factionalism, and regularly spilled over into violence. Limited democracy, ethnic and social cleavages, acute poverty and inequality of economic opportunity all indicate that some preconditions for the commission of future mass atrocities exist in Zambia. Nevertheless, as this risk has fluctuated over the last five decades, the country has avoided outbreaks of mass atrocities. In fact, what makes Zambia remarkable amongst most of its neighbours is the way it has managed crises. Contrary to many genocide scholars who argue that mass violence follows major upheaval (see, for example, Harff 1987; Krain 1997; Melson 1989; Midlarsky 2005), in Zambia crises have been opportunities for reform and improvement.

Risk factors in Zambia

Zambia has four identifiable risk factors that are associated with mass atrocities. These are: the existence of ethnic division, limited democracy, limited rule of law and inequality of economic opportunity. Although the country's democratic situation has improved since the re-introduction of a multi-party electoral system in 1991,[3] limitations – factional division based on ethnicity, as well as a chief executive with excessive power – continue to impede the country's democratic transition. Rule of law is limited – this is evident in both the judiciary's limitations of independence and the arbitrary use of power by the country's police force. After decades of economic stagnation, Zambia's recent growth has further exacerbated the divide between rich and poor; wealth inequality remains among the highest in the world.

Social division

Ethnic cleavages

Like Botswana, Zambia has a diverse population, with up to 73 tribal groups, each with distinct territories and dialects. Unlike Botswana, four dominant language groups emerged from these tribal groups, a development which was the result of missionary encouragement and colonial policy. Bemba, Lozi, Tonga and Nyanga became widespread, with most of the population speaking one of these either as a first or second language (Posner 2005: 57). According to Burnell, 40 per cent of the population use Bemba as their first or second language, 30 per cent used Nyanga, 12 per cent spoke Tonga and 10 per cent employed Lozi (Burnell 2005: 9). These ethno-linguistic distinctions became more salient as a marker of identity following independence, when Zambia became highly urbanized and original tribal languages had little influence or use beyond their limited rural boundaries. In contrast to Botswana's long history of dominance of minority groups by the Tswana chieftains, Zambia's four groups do not have a legacy of asymmetrical relations. Therefore, Zambia's diversity is not indicative of Kuper's 'societies with persistent and pervasive cleavages' that characterize risk of mass atrocities (Kuper 1981: 57). However, there are two areas where ethnic difference and risk of mass atrocities have coincided in Zambia. One is the threat of secession by the Lozi, and the second is the pattern of alliances based on ethno-linguistic difference that has been prominent during both periods of multi-party democracy in the country.

The emergence of the four main language groups in the twentieth century has shaped social divisions and influenced political competition in Zambia. Prior to the 1800s, each of the four main ethno-linguistic groups merely spoke one of the scores of tribal dialects that existed throughout the territory. Their relatively recent elevation in political terms was the product of colonial practices and policies, as well as missionary activity. These policies reified boundaries between ethno-linguistic groups (Molteno 1974: 69; Posner 2005: 56–69). Three factors, in particular, were instrumental in the emergence of these four languages: their initial selection and use by missionary schools (who were unable to use all tribal languages), colonial policy adopting these four languages in their administration, and emergence of these languages as lingua francas, through the migration of labour across the territory, particularly to the Copperbelt in the north and other major urban centres (Lindemann 2010: 10). Most dialects in the country are related, but these four languages rose to prominence as the provision of education expanded and urbanization intensified (Posner 2005: 65). Although each language emanates from specific regions in the territory, their widespread use, particularly in the cities, has, with the exception of Lozi, distanced the language groups from their regional origins.[4] In independent Zambia, therefore, these ethno-linguistic identities are associated with literacy and work – for the majority of the population, these identities have little meaning in relation to traditions and places of origin. Regional affiliation is quite broad, representing urban centres rather than specific tribal boundaries. As such, the possibility of any elite group instrumentalizing such identities through the use of historical myths to mobilize populations (see, for example, Kaufman 2001) is very low, if not non-existent. With the exception of the Lozi in the Western Province, claims to territories traditionally associated with these languages are rare, as most language users do not share the same territorial heritage (see, for example, Toft 2003).[5] Rather, such affiliations have been used in larger urban areas to mobilize support for political parties or factions.

Ethno-linguistic cleavages have become more prominent in the most recent period of multi-party democratic competition. Since the shift from one-party rule to the current multi-party system in 1991, there has been a growing emphasis on ethno-linguistic affiliation in terms of electoral competition. Political parties often use these ethno-linguistic identities as a means to gain electoral support, although they often do so discreetly (Posner 2005: 114). As a consequence, ethnic identity forms a strong part of electoral competition, and in election campaigns tension between these different groups tends to escalate. In addition to electoral competition, ethnicity also influences the nature of job recruitment and the prospects of promotion, and can even have a bearing on gaining approval for bank loans (Posner 2005: 95). According to Posner, these cleavages arise because there is a perception that being represented politically by members of their ethnic group is a way of facilitating the provision of state resources. In order to place someone in power, the best course of action is to form or be a member of a political coalition of members of the same ethnie. In this way, ethnic identity, or choosing to identify in terms of ethnicity, becomes a political tool when associated with such coalition building (Posner 2005: 91). This means of mobilizing political support has not resulted in the distinct advantage of any particular group at the expense of others, due to the fact that no group is large enough to hold power on its own. However, the actual or perceived preference for any group at the expense of another risks exacerbating factional division.[6] In 2001, former

MMD deputy Michael Sata established the PF in response to the MMD's preference of other groups over the Bemba. Courting the Bemba vote, the PF has steadily grown in popularity, winning the most recent election in September 2011. This is the first time that a party largely associated with one ethno-linguistic group has held government in Zambia (Lindemann 2010: 46). Since the election, Sata has come under criticism in the Zambian as well as international press for favouring Bembas in the cabinet, and prioritizing the recruitment of Bembas in the public sector (see Bandow 2013; CDDR 2013; Redvers 2013).

Zambia has been subject to repeated calls for secession by its Western Province. The Lozi speakers of this province are exceptional in that they inhabit a territory where one major language and a single region coincide. The region was formerly the territory of the Lozi Kingdom (known also as Barotseland), and under the British had been given greater autonomy than the rest of Northern Rhodesia, which allowed them to preserve their structures of traditional rule with little interference throughout the colonial period (Gertzel 1984: 206; Lindemann 2010: 12). While the struggle for independence grew in the 1950s, the Lozi ruling class campaigned for secession, but failed (Lindemann 2010: 12; Sichone and Simutanyi 1996: 178). In consolation, the Barotseland Agreement of 1964 gave special status to the Lozi Kingdom (Western Province), allowing them to preserve their traditional structures, although in practice many of these were dismantled by 1970 (Lindemann 2010: 12, 15). In the multi-party system of the First Republic, the Lozi established their own party, the United Party (UP), which gained much support in the Western Province, but was banned in 1968 (Lindemann 2010: 13; Minorities at Risk 2006b). Throughout the 1960s and into the 1970s, Lozi traditional rulers called for secession, but this was counterbalanced by Lozi nationalists who actively supported the integrity of the Zambian state. In the Third Republic, the Lozi-based National Party (NP) was formed, but did not attract a large following, as many Lozis preferred to support the ruling MMD. Nevertheless, the NP called for greater autonomy, as promised under the Barotseland Agreement.

In the 1990s, members of the ruling class recommenced calls for secession. The Chiluba government categorically rejected demands, but at the same time increased the representation of Lozi speakers in government. In short, while these repeated demands for secession have not disappeared, nor have they been widely supported within the Lozi-dominated Western Province. However, tensions continue. Since 1999 there have been reports that Lozi were crossing over the border to Namibia to give assistance to a secessionist struggle there. There have also been reports that in the late 1990s, the Lozi ruling class engaged in moves for the Western Province to secede and become part of Namibia. While these reports appear contradictory, and may reflect the lack of unity within the province for a united separatist policy, they are indications of the ongoing tension between the former Lozi Kingdom and the state of Zambia, emanating from ethnic difference. Such social distinctions have been recognized by both Minorities at Risk and Minority Rights International as provoking the risk of future ethnic violence. According to Minorities at Risk, the Lozi have a moderate risk of rebellion (Minorities at Risk 2006b). The risk associated with the Lozi also reflects the tendency for the two major political parties (the incumbent MMD and the opposition PF) to court the vote of the numerically dominant Bemba,[7] which sees members of this group gain the most advantage (Minorities at Risk 2006a; Minority Rights Group International 2010b). These dynamics suggest that political competition and political advantage has had an impact on social division.

In summary, ethnic division exists in Zambia. It is apparent in the courting of support in electoral competition, particularly in the Third Republic. The Lozi ruling class in the Western Province has also called for secession from the republic. Preferential treatment given to Bemba speakers since the 2011 election of the PF increases the risk of aggravating this division. However, such social differences have not been formalized through identity cards, systematic discrimination or geographic territory. Therefore, while ethno-linguistic difference has been instrumentalized by political elites and public-sector executives, inter-marriage, shared neighbourhoods and many other commonalities have combined to prevent such social divisions from becoming acute. Why such divisions are not more acute is a question that is considered in the final section of this chapter. The act of courting support based on ethnicity carries with it a risk of political instability which may lead to mass atrocities, as the Political Instability Task Force points out. They argue that factional division is a destabilizing characteristic in states undergoing democratic transition, particularly when it is associated with ethnic or religious difference (see, for example, Goldstone *et al.* 2005; Goldstone and Ulfelder 2004).

Governance

Limitations on democracy

Zambia was one of the first African states to undergo a transition from an autocratic one-party state to a multi-party democratic state. After more than 20 years of multi-party democracy, the evolution of democratic institutions has been positive, if not complete. According to Polity IV, the last decade has seen the quality of the country's democracy improve, to reach a positive score of seven (Marshall and Jaggers 2010). However, for much of the past two decades democratic reform has been slow and inconsistent, a fact that is also reflected by Polity IV's fluctuating rating since 1991. Such inconsistencies led the Human Security Report to categorize the country as an anocracy – neither autocratic nor democratic – a judgement consistent with the country's current state of ongoing political tensions amidst slow political reform (Human Security Report Project 2010). More specifically, there is evidence that excessive power resides in the office of the president, and that multi-party electoral competition has been characterized by factional division, based on ethno-linguistic difference (Freedom House 2010a). The change of government in 2011 was a positive democratic development, yet recent observations on the new PF government noted efforts to consolidate its incumbency at the expense of democratization (Redvers 2013).

Although the power of the office of the chief executive has become less centralized since the transition in 1991, some scholars noted that the presidency is still overbearing. In fact two years after the first multi-party elections, the momentum of reform slowed to a standstill (Phiri 2006: 182; Rakner 2003: 105–6). Chiluba left intact the centralized presidential power that sustained nearly two decades of one-party rule. In addition, Chiluba used the reform process not to broaden democracy, but to consolidate the power of the MMD. Most crucially, he made a key change to the constitution requiring that presidential candidates be Zambian citizens, with parents who were also born in Zambia. This excluded Kenneth Kaunda, whose parents were born in Nyasaland.[8] Seen as a deliberate strategy to undermine the most popular opposition leader, the new constitution also excluded traditional leaders from the presidential race, ruling out Kaunda's deputy (Nzongola-Ntalaja 2004: 403; Simon 2005: 202). Chiluba and the MMD won the 1996 election by an emphatic margin, having undermined UNIP, the only party that could have challenged the incumbent government. Although no international groups monitored this election, three major local groups noted irregularities, citing disagreement over the adoption of the constitution, a biased media in favour of the MMD, and problems with the registration process (EISA 2002). In particular, the law that presidential candidates had to be born of Zambian parents ruled out a challenge from Kaunda, effectively blocking the one party (UNIP) that had a possibility of challenging the incumbent government in the 1996 elections. Attempts were also made to extend the tenure of the presidency beyond two terms, but they were unsuccessful (Burnell 2003: 51). Most significantly, the MMD maintained a constitution that preserved many of the characteristics of the one-party system, leading many to claim that Chiluba simply presided over a '*de facto* one party state' (Phiri 2006: 236). For example, the disproportionate powers of presidency that characterized the Second Republic remained during the Third Republic. These advantages enabled the MMD to remain in government for 20 years, only recently losing power (BBC News 2011b).

In addition to a dominant chief executive, Zambia's multi-party democracy continues to be constrained by factional divisions. According to the PITF, 'factionalized political competition' in states undergoing democratic transition poses a very high risk for political instability and mass atrocities (Goldstone and Ulfelder 2004: 15). The convergence of ethnic competition and violence has occurred in many elections, and although at times the link between the two has been tenuous, it seems the return to multi-party democracy has coincided with a renewed increase in ethnic tensions. Posner argues that ethnicity has been the most important factor in the voting choices of the Zambian public. Such choices are not based on perceived grievances or overt discrimination. Rather, it acts as a means of forming coalitions that are perceived as a way to gain material advantage (Posner 2007: 1310; Posner and Simon 2002: 313). What is clear is that both major parties, the MMD and the newly incumbent PF, have been associated with the Bemba vote, regarded as the largest voting group (Larmer and Fraser 2007: 623; Posner 2005: 108). While the MMD were originally the base for Bemba support, recently this has shifted to the PF. The PF's founder and leader, Michael Sata, was formerly in line for leadership of the MMD, but he left the party after Chiluba's retirement, arguing that the new president, Mwanawasa, had not provided sufficient representation for Bembas. For the first time in the Third Republic, there emerged a major political party known for mobilizing Bemba support, thus giving ethnicity greater salience in electoral competition. In the 2006 elections, Sata was criticized by other political leaders, who accused him of 'stirring up tribalism' (Minority Rights Group International 2008). Although election-related violence is not comparable to the levels of Kenya in 2008, Zambia's two decades of democratic transition have seen an escalation of tensions based on ethnicity, along with greater violence, prior to and following national elections. Violence was particularly serious after the 2006 elections, when rioting broke out around Lusaka and the Copperbelt (see, for example, BBC News 2006b; Minority Rights Group International 2007). The Third Republic has indeed seen a return to a close connection between political support and ethnic identity, and although this is frowned upon, it is a pattern of campaigning that rewarded the PF, winning the 2011 presidential and parliamentary elections. Such a victory is positive in that it marks the first regime change in 20 years, and a peaceful one. This risks a further entrenchment of factional political competition. However, while some scholars have signalled such a possibility, they also point out that the PF's recent electoral success is due to its growing support base, which no longer relies exclusively on the Bemba vote (see, for example, Larmer and Fraser 2007: 632; Lindemann 2010: 33).

Despite a disproportionate concentration of power in the president's office, frequent harassment of the opposition, and the MMD's two decades of incumbency, the victory of the opposition PF in 2011 heralded the country's first peaceful democratic change of government in the Third Republic since the victory of the MMD in 1991 (Remy 2011). This victory was the culmination of a decade of rising support for the PF, as reflected in the 2006 election, which saw the party trim the MMD's legislative majority to a narrow margin (Larmer 2009: 130). In 2008, following the death of President Mwanawasa, the presidential election yielded equally close results, with MMD President Banda defeating Sata by just 2 per cent (Electoral Commission of Zambia 2008). Although the 2011 election results were a positive development for the country's democratization, ethnicity continues to be a prominent characteristic of the multi-party system's factional divisions. Given the risk that such division holds for political instability,[9] these divisions, coupled with a failure to reform the constitution to remove the legacy of Zambia's authoritarian past, indicate that the country's political institutions still contain a volatile mix of politicized ethnic divisions and a top-heavy regime.

Zambia's mixed record of reform has resulted in its incomplete consolidation as a multi-party democratic regime. A disproportionately powerful chief executive, electoral competition displaying characteristics of factional division based on ethnic difference, and a culture of intimidation of opposition groups are evidence of the fact that the country is still in the midst of an incomplete political transition, with the legacy of one-party rule still evident in the constitution. Although the country has made much progress since the period of the Second Republic, political circumstances make the country vulnerable to political instability. Chapter 3 pointed out that regime type, particularly with Zambia's characteristics, is a significant risk indicator. The office of the presidency has changed little since the days of one-party autocracy in the Second Republic, and factional division based on ethnicity has a greater presence in election campaigning and party mobilization.

Rule of law

Rule of law is weak in Zambia, with a lack of impartiality in both the judiciary and police. Freedom House alleged that during the MMD's time in government, some Supreme Court judges were known to be deferential to it (Freedom House 2010a). Similar biases are also emerging with the new PF government, amidst claims that the government is manipulating the legal system to punish MMD members and persecute dissenters (Freedom House 2013). Sporadic evidence has accrued of police deliberately targeting protesters who non-violently oppose the government. Neither the judiciary nor the police in Zambia is impartial, with a history of acquiescent judges, police brutality and corruption at all levels. In its 2010 report on Zambia, Freedom House noted undue executive-branch influence over the judiciary (Freedom House 2010a). Its 2013 report observed similar behaviour by the current PF government (Freedom House 2013). Such influence suggests an arbitrary use of power within the government, and an absence of the checks and balances needed to ensure democratic accountability and political stability.

Zambia's judiciary has long been subject to government interference. It suffered under Kaunda, particularly in the Second Republic, when decisions against the government commonly resulted in the replacement of High Court judges. This continued until the judiciary was stacked with those known to favour the government. Although Kaunda had the power to appoint judges, he could not dismiss them without an investigation by a tribunal (Burdette 1988: 332). However, Kaunda's appointment of sympathetic judges to the bench saw a gradual decrease in judicial autonomy.

This trend continued in the Third Republic. Freedom House noted a number of questionable decisions in 2009, in particular the ruling of the High Court acquitting former President Chiluba of corruption charges.[10] In the same year, the government passed new legislation that allowed the president to increase the number of judges sitting in both the High Court and Supreme Courts (Freedom House 2010a). In the majority of cases since the re-establishment of multi-party democracy in 1991, it has been rare for Zambian courts to issue decisions that limit or compromise the power of the government (Gloppen 2003: 118). A glimpse of this was seen with the forced resignation of Chief Justice Matthew Ngulube, after a newspaper exposed secret payments he had received from the government, amounting to US$184,000 (Gloppen 2003: 119). Ngulube had frequently been regarded as weak on cases that affected the government. His biased approach to such cases had implications for the 2001 elections. The Electoral Commission did not report the frequently observed cases of electoral malpractice, and it was known that the High Court simply deferred to the president's office in such matters (Burnell 2002: 1113). In 2012, President Sata suspended three highly ranked judges for misconduct, in an act widely regarded as retaliation for an unfavourable judgment (Freedom House 2013).

Such malpractice also extended to the police, who were known to do the government's bidding, and on many occasions ignored violence instigated by MMD officials. Burnell contends that it was 'well known that police are subject to government interference' (Burnell 2002: 1113). Harassment of opposition figures has been common, and police impunity in such matters has prompted an escalation of violence particularly in the lead-up to national elections. This has contributed to the politicization of ethnic cleavages that are often instrumentalized during election campaigns. Opposition leader Michael Sata was arrested on numerous occasions, charged with a wide range of offences including sedition. Police brutality and torture are common, and the security forces have frequently acted with impunity (Freedom House 2010a). Just as Sata was targeted by police while in opposition, he now uses the police to target those opposed to his government. One recent example was the targeting of Lozi-speakers in prison – this after he broke a promise to grant greater autonomy to the Western Promise by honouring the 1964 Barotseland Agreement. The governing council of the Western Province immediately declared independence. Subsequently, prison guards and paramilitary police inflicted severe beatings on imprisoned Barotse activists (Freedom House 2013).

The weakness of Zambia's rule of law is a legacy of the country's period of one-party rule, when all power was concentrated in the office of the president. This incapacity, highlighted by both Freedom House (2010a, 2013) and Polity IV (2008a), still exists because of the slow pace of constitutional reform in the country. This has resulted in the perpetuation of a range of institutions that are a legacy of the Second Republic, an era of one-party statehood in which the office of the president was ubiquitous in all aspects of national governance and administration. This legacy of one-party rule has permeated the Third Republic, and impeded the democratic functioning of institutions including the judiciary and police.

Economic weakness

Inequality of economic opportunity

Zambia's poverty and economic inequality have been sources of social tension both in the past (particularly during the sharp decline of the 1980s) and the present (with calls for secession in the Western Province influenced by the higher levels of poverty there). The evidence of horizontal inequality between the Western Province and the rest of the country has heightened the risk of instability and mass atrocities. Given that Zambia has both 'slow growth' and ethnically determined inequalities, it is at greater risk of violence (see, for example, Stewart 2008: 21–22). The combination of poverty and inequality increases the risk of future mass violence. Analysing civil wars, Paul Collier has outlined the correlation between states that experience such wars, and the level of poverty that exists. He concludes that the risk of civil war is linked to low income levels, as well as 'slow growth, or worse, stagnation and decline' (Collier 2007: 20). A weak economy (which he associates with a weak state), and moreover one with a high degree of dependence on resource extraction, makes a state especially prone to such conflict (Collier 2007: 21).

Collier could have been describing Zambia. Nearly two-thirds of the population lives in poverty, although moderate improvements have been evident over the last 20 years. While the country experienced fluctuating fortunes in the 1990s, since 1991 the level of poverty has decreased nationally from 73 per cent to 64 per cent (Central Statistics Office, Zambia 2006). This pattern has been consistent over the last decade, consistent with Zambia's steady GDP growth. However, despite these improvements, in 2005 the majority of Zambians continued to be unable to meet basic needs.[11] Moreover, this decrease in poverty has not been consistent throughout the provinces. Some have experienced sharp declines in poverty, while levels have remained the same in others. In line with the level of poverty, 65 per cent of households did not earn enough to meet basic needs of nutrition and shelter. More than half of all infants in the country are malnourished and regarded as stunted (Central Statistics Office, Zambia 2006). Despite the reduction in poverty over the last decade in particular, no corresponding decline has been evident in the number of children found to be stunted (UNDP 2003: ii). Although unemployment levels are relatively low (14 per cent in 2006), so are wages. What needs to be emphasized is the high level of unemployment in Lusaka (40 per cent) and the Copperbelt (41 per cent) – two of the most urbanized areas of Africa's most urbanized country (Central Statistics Office, Zambia 2006). Given that the rural–urban shift continues at a rapid rate, these figures in urban areas are cause for concern, as high concentrations of urban poor are found in two areas with the worst political violence.

One of the reasons underlying high levels of poverty is the pervasiveness of food insecurity in the country. Inefficiencies in agricultural production and distribution can be traced back to Kaunda's regime and the profound lack of infrastructural development in rural areas. Competing and overlapping distribution agencies also caused great confusion, and at times were largely responsible for a lack of coordination that often left bumper crops rotting in the fields or in co-op sheds. Such inefficiencies can be attributed to Kaunda's management of the public sector, and his constant reshuffling of executives. Good (1986) details the government's inability to reap bumper harvests in the mid-1980s due to overlapping and poorly functioning departments, and a lack of infrastructure and resources. While Kaunda claimed such measures were necessary to prevent 'ethnic stacking', the inefficiencies can be observed most acutely in the agricultural sector, and in the widespread malnutrition that still plagues a country with an abundance of highly fertile agricultural land.

Compounding the country's poverty is its long period of economic stagnation and decline. Since the early 1970s, Zambia has suffered from low or negative growth, following the drop in global copper prices. This economic decline was exacerbated by the nationalization of banks and major industries shortly prior to the copper slump; as a consequence, government revenue was profoundly affected. As Zambia's economy declined in the 1980s, poor infrastructure and poor management exacerbated poverty and spawned food shortages, a situation that became increasingly difficult to counter. These circumstances contributed to the country's decline in the Human Development Index (HDI), to the extent that Zambia was the only country in the world to have a lower HDI ranking in 1995 than in 1975 (UNDP 2003: 2). Economic decline and high levels of poverty were instrumental in sparking popular dissatisfaction with Kaunda's government at the end of the 1980s, culminating in widespread protests and riots. In the Third Republic, decline and then stagnation encouraged coalition building around ethnic division, in the hope that some political advantage could be won in a country with limited resources and widespread poverty.

Economic inequality is also very high in Zambia, and there is evidence of differences being characterized by region and ethnicity. One indicator is that the mean monthly income is nearly double the poverty-datum line, while 65 per cent of the population lives below it (Central Statistics Office, Zambia 2006). Another is the Gini coefficient measure of family income, which ranked Zambia 19th in the world for income inequality (CIA 2010). Horizontal inequality is also evident in the Western Province, which has consistently had the highest poverty levels in the country. This province is predominantly populated by the Lozi people, whose traditional rulers have, on many occasions, called for secession from Zambia (UNHCR 2011). While poverty rates have decreased in the country since 1991, in the Western Province they have remained consistently high, at 84 per cent (Central Statistics Office, Zambia 2006). Infrastructure is also seriously lacking: only 3.5 per cent of households have electricity, contrasted with a national average of 19 per cent (UNHCR 2011). These discrepancies sparked protests in early 2011 calling for secession and independence. Clashes with the police resulted in three deaths (UNHCR 2011). Such calls for secession have been issued on numerous occasions, indeed as early as the mid-1960s. However, previous protests cited political rather than economic grievances, since the traditional rulers of the former semi-autonomous kingdom opposed centralized control of the post-colonial state (see, for example, Lindemann 2010: 36–37). While past secessionist calls by traditional Lozi leaders have been managed through the appointment of politicians and public-sector workers from the province to key government positions, the growing economic divide has seen a renewed call for independence, further aggravated by the Sata government's reneging on its promise to honour the Barotseland Agreement. This has provoked violent clashes with security forces, and prompted a poster campaign by a pro-independence group urging 'non-Lozi' inhabitants to leave the province 'or risk being hacked to death' (UNHCR 2011).

In sum, Zambia is a very poor country with enormous inequalities of wealth. It also endured two decades of economic decline, followed by prolonged stagnation. Despite a steady increase in world copper prices in recent years, providing the government with greater revenues for improved services and infrastructure, poverty remains widespread. Moreover, it is disproportionately high in the Western Province, a region that has, on numerous occasions since independence, called for secession. The framework in Chapter 3 identifies such wealth inequalities as posing a risk of mass atrocities. Indeed, greater political instability in the Western Province is in part linked to greater levels of poverty in that region.

Zambia and the risk of mass atrocities

The presence of four risk factors in Zambia indicates a moderate-to-high risk of mass atrocities. Over the last five decades, this risk has fluctuated in severity. Tensions were high in the late 1980s as Zambians grew increasingly dissatisfied with the authoritarian UNIP government amidst manifest economic decline. In the late 1990s, after nearly a decade of promise following the return to multi-party democracy, continuing economic stagnation and stalled political reform triggered fresh dissatisfaction, notably when the ruling MMD moved to allow a third presidential term. After 2000, a new party, the PF, courted the Bemba vote, raising the possibility that political competition would become divided along ethnic lines. In addition, secessionist calls for the Western Province have continued, and even intensified in recent years. According to the framework outlined in Chapter 3, such a combination of ethnic division, poor governance and inequality poses a significant risk of future atrocities. Such risk has been recognized by the CIDCM. In their 2010 report, Zambia was placed in the highest risk bracket for future political instability, principally due to its partial democracy and location in a violent neighbourhood (see Hewitt *et al.* 2010). Nevertheless, despite the convergence of ethnic division, poverty and horizontal inequality, limited democracy and rule of law, the resulting tensions have never deteriorated into mass violence. In addition, when riots broke out in the late 1980s in protest against mounting poverty, the crisis hastened political reforms heralding a return to multi-party democracy. Widespread and peaceful opposition throughout the country prevented an extension of the presidential term in 2000. How violence was avoided, and how tensions have been managed over time, is the focus of the following section.

Resilience in Zambia

While Zambia has experienced numerous crises and limited outbreaks of violence, mass atrocities have been notable by their absence. This is due to a number of factors that have enhanced the country's resilience to eruptions of mass atrocities. In particular, four key factors have strengthened Zambia's resilience: the fluid identity of its ethnic groups, an inaugural leader who premised nation building on an inclusive ideology that transcended ethnic difference, the same leader's willingness to abandon the one-party system, and a strong civil society that has been instrumental in securing key democratic reforms. A number of other factors have also come into play, and will be examined under the rubric of these four broad themes.

Recent historical processes and the current balance of forces in Zambia buttressed a peaceful transition to a more participatory multi-party system in 1991. Converging political and economic crises produced escalating riots, resulting at times in fatalities. They also imposed limits on presidential power in 2000, when the ruling MMD sought to expand it, and they have – with varying degrees of success over the last five decades – peacefully managed calls by Lozi traditional rulers to secede from the state. In a country where ethno-linguistic difference and political support have often coincided, a strong and inclusive national identity has fostered a culture of 'anti-tribalism' in political campaigning.

Social factors

Ethnic cohesion

Zambia's ethnic divisions have been instrumentalized during election campaigning, and as Posner points out, ethnicity appears to be the most influential factor in determining voting patterns in the multi-party system (Posner 2005, 2007; Posner and Simon 2002). However, these identities are not rigid. There is much intermarriage, and with the exception of the Lozis in the Western Province, ethnic groups mostly live in larger urban centres in socially diverse communities. These circumstances make it difficult for division to become entrenched. Three reasons can be cited for this. First, the ethno-linguistic distinctions in Zambia are relatively recent, and have very limited historical significance. Prior to colonization by the British, the four major groups did not exist in their contemporary form (Posner 2003). Two factors were responsible for bringing about these new distinctions: one was the choice by missionaries to select four main languages (out of a possible 70 or more) into which they could translate the Bible (Posner 2005). Education was then provided in one of these four languages. Thus, over time, a growing number of people became conversant in at least one of the languages.

The second factor was the onset of migration to the Copperbelt and to growing urban areas, where the four languages became the lingua francas. Because most people had no use for their mother tongue outside their own villages, the four languages were largely used as second languages in urban and mining regions, and along the railway line linking these areas. Over time allegiances and alliances were formed around these language groups, but for the vast majority of people language was not tied to family or place (Posner 2005). This pragmatic notion of ethnicity meant that the kind of divisions formalized and entrenched in countries like Rwanda, Burundi and South Africa failed to take hold in Zambia. Absent were the myths and narratives that have spurred ethnic mobilization and conflict in many states (see, for example, Kaufman 2001). Absent also was the instrumentalization of ethnic difference through such polarizing policies as identification cards and restricted movement. Intermarriage is common, and urban areas display no segregation according to ethno-linguistic allegiance. The irony is that it has been the urban centres, both in Lusaka and along the Copperbelt, where these four languages are most commonly spoken, but these same highly urbanized regions have also experienced the greatest inter-ethnic and inter-tribal mingling. Therefore, the places where ethnicity could most easily be instrumentalized are the very places where greater social inclusion and accommodation of diversity exist. For the most part, ethnic difference has not been associated with territory.[12]

Third, because of the relatively recent emergence of the language groups as foundations of distinct social groups, little opportunity has existed for political elites to mobilize such difference through the construction of historical myths. Such myths in themselves do not have the power to inspire violence, but elites often use them to construct grievances, or to nurture a sense of entitlement or opportunity. This has been acutely evident in many places where identity-related atrocities have occurred, including Kosovo, Bosnia, Abkhazia and Rwanda (see, for example, Kaufman 2001). In Zambia, tribal identity has a long historical lineage, but in the arena of multi-party politics, the 70-plus largely rural tribal groups have been too scattered and diffuse to be useful political tools. As a positive consequence, although ethnicity has been instrumentalized during election campaigns in recent decades, ethnic identity has not been constructed around historical grievances or other myths. Moreover, growing resistance is evident to any use of ethnicity in election campaigns, a situation reflected in the coordinated efforts of Zambia's Human Rights Commission to form an alliance of civil society groups with the goal of preventing violence in the lead-up to the 2011 election (see, for example, Kasonde 2010). Also, the Kaunda-instigated call for 'One Zambia, One Nation' – enshrined on the coat of arms – still resonates. While neither civil society campaigns nor government cautions will eliminate ethnic competition in politics, what they do encourage is public censure of such ethnic manipulation and mobilization.

Strong civil society

As noted, the role of civil society groups, including church organizations and labour groups, has been crucial to constraining presidential power and ensuring the process of democratization continues. On two occasions, pressure from civil society has pushed through democratic reform, kept the regime in check, and ensured peaceful outcomes to potentially violent situations. The first was the role of civil society in persuading Kaunda to initiate multi-party elections in 1991. The second, in 2001, was the pressure brought to bear on the government to abandon constitutional changes allowing a third presidential term for the incumbent, Chiluba.

In 1990, Zambia's authoritarian regime – intolerant to that point of any form of dissent – relented in the face of popular pressure, and lifted the ban on opposition parties. In so doing, it paved the way for its own demise. The pathway for a peaceful transition to multi-party democracy opened in 1991, when President Kaunda accepted the demands of a coalition of civil society organizations (Bratton 1992: 81). This acceptance was both 'genuine' and 'reluctant', and largely the result of organized pressure by a broad range of organizations including students, businesspeople, church groups and the labour movement (Bratton 1992: 81, 85–86). Together, they formed the National Interim Committee for Multi-Party Democracy in 1990, declaring as their principal aim a restoration of political accountability through a return to multi-party democracy. The coalition harnessed the widespread popular discontent triggered by sudden increases in food prices. By December 1990, Kaunda had repealed the constitutional provision banning other political parties, opening the field for their formation. The National Interim Committee was the first to register as a party, establishing the MMD, which under the stewardship of union leader Chiluba went on to win the Third Republic's first multi-party elections later that year (Bratton 1992: 86). What began as pressure from civil society led to profound but peaceful political change.

Civil society groups united again in an effort to prevent President Chiluba from seeking a third term in 2001. As that year's elections approached, the MMD pushed for an amendment to allow Chiluba to seek a third term in office (Burnell 2002: 1111; Simon 2005: 205). In early 2001, the MMD organized a nationwide campaign to abandon the two-term presidential limit. Such a constitutional measure required either the support of two-thirds of the National Assembly, or victory in a referendum. Throughout the year, the MMD blocked discussion of the issue in the Assembly, and worked to promote the idea through party cadres and local chiefs, as well as church elders at the provincial level. It also resorted to widespread 'bribery and intimidation' in its campaign (Burnell 2002: 1111; Burnell 2003: 51). In response, a number of organizations, including the Law Association of

Zambia, the Oasis Forum (formed by Zambia's three principal church bodies), and the Non-governmental Organization Coordinating Committee, joined the independent press and opposition politicians in advocating against a third presidential term. At the same time, suspicion of Chiluba's corruption was mounting, prompting many civil society groups to criticize his leadership openly. By mid-year, opposition to the third term had grown significantly, to the extent that the issue was never canvassed officially, and was quietly dropped (Burnell 2003: 62; Larmer 2009: 123, 127). In both 1991 and 2001, pressure from civil society brought about significant democratic reform and prevented an erosion of democratic accountability.

Civil society in Zambia grew in strength from the 1980s onward for two main reasons. First, during the one-party era, voices of opposition were banished from parliament, as were many politicians who challenged UNIP's official line. As a consequence, opposition was increasingly expressed through civil society groups, predominantly unions and church groups. Second, a coalition of such groups collectively known as the MMD pushed for political liberalization, achieving a notable victory with the shift to multi-party democracy in 1991. This established a strong precedent for calling the government to account, which, as Larmer (2009: 115) argues, triggered a 'practical deepening of democratic culture'.

The above examples do not necessarily confirm the strength of civil society in fostering a robust democratic system. Indeed, Bartlett argues that civil society in Zambia today has only a restricted voice and weak influence, following the MMD's swift return to one-party-style rule in the early 1990s, which quickly sidelined these organizations (Bartlett 2000: 429). However, the examples do highlight that at key points in Zambian political history, civil society organizations have managed to mobilize and advocate for democratic accountability. As Bartlett rightly contends, such organizations have not been influential in the general policy making of government, but they have played a crucial role in the country's democratic reform, and in preserving the basic structures of a multi-party system. Their successful prevention of the constitutional amendment on presidential term limits countered any attempt at 'democratic rollback'. As Krain argues, political violence is more likely to occur if an individual or single party maintains a hold on power (Krain 2000: 4). Seen in this light, by successfully pushing democratic reform and preventing democratic erosion, civil society coalitions have played a major role in mitigating the risk of mass atrocities in Zambia.

Good governance

A positive record of managing ethnic diversity

Zambia's record of economic management and democracy has been mixed, and this tends to overshadow factors that have given the country considerable resilience to the risk of mass atrocities. Kaunda's nation-building drive, based on an inclusive ideology, was summed up by the coat of arms' slogan, 'One Zambia, One Nation'. His vigilance in ensuring equitable representation from all major ethno-linguistic groups supplied valuable mechanisms to confront the economic and political crises of the late 1980s, and the transition to a multi-party democracy in the early 1990s. First, during the economic decline that reached its nadir at the outset of the 1990s, ethnic scapegoating was notably absent. Second, when ethnicity became more salient in the multi-party system of the Third Republic, ethnic-based campaigning remained discreet. Additionally, secessionist pressures within the Western Province have been defused through effective government policies. Kaunda's call for national unity, and his constructive engagement with the Western Province despite its calls for secession, worked to foster stability.

During Zambia's First Republic, Kaunda implemented wide-ranging measures to prevent ethnic competition, whether between parties, within UNIP, or throughout the public sector (see, for example, Molteno 1974). This relentless push to avoid ethnic division in government prevented such practices becoming entrenched. During the rapid expansion of the public sector in the decade after independence, appointments to top positions in the various ministries were embroiled in ethnic competition and disputes. In response, Kaunda made frequent changes to senior levels of bureaucracy, resulting in a rapid turnover of both 'identity and personnel' (Burdette 1988: 69). In addition, many politicians at the time increasingly used the language of ethnicity or 'tribalism' to attract support and power. Once again, Kaunda was careful to divide up important ministerial posts to people from various ethno-linguistic groups in order to maintain a power balance among these main groups (Burdette 1988: 71–72). It was these 'personal and ethnic antipathies' that Kaunda claimed prompted his decision to suspend multi-party politics in 1973, as his efforts at 'ethnic balancing' grew more time consuming, without resolving core disputes. Nonetheless, if this constant reshuffling did not end tensions, it did succeed in preventing ethnic divisions from becoming entrenched and institutionalized. Kaunda's own solution to the predicament of reshuffling – centralizing power in a one-party state – created its own problems, culminating in widespread unrest in 1990. Another consequence was that the provision of public services was riddled by inefficiencies, stalling vital infrastructural development, and leaving the country profoundly under-resourced. The collapse of copper prices in the early 1970s further eroded government capacity, and severely limited the provision of public services. Clearly, Kaunda's efforts to manage ethnic competition had negative consequences, and his use of ethnic fragmentation as a justification for one-party rule has been questioned. Still, he was successful in muting the tendency to use ethnicity as a mobilizing tool. Despite growing political instability and popular discontent during the Second Republic, only limited violence occurred, and ethnic exclusion and scapegoating has been wholly absent. Consequently, when ethnicity grew in salience during the Third Republic, such rhetoric was usually discreet, suggesting that the overall consensus was opposed to such factionalism. More recently, former President Rupiah Banda publicly denounced attempts to divide Zambian society along 'tribal' lines (State House, Zambia 2010). Kaunda's legacy of censuring division and fostering unity has limited ethnic rivalry, and avoided the destabilization that such division often engenders.

Underpinning Kaunda's efforts to manage ethnic tensions was his philosophy of 'humanism': a combination of socialism, Biblical teaching, liberalism and antiracism. Humanism was born from Kaunda's opposition to colonialism, particularly British exploitation of the local population. Also inspired by his own faith in Christianity, Kaunda regarded humanism as 'this high value of man and respect for human dignity', which he believed was inherent in traditional Africa (Venter and Olivier 1993: 26). Kaunda believed that human dignity could only be maintained in a society that fostered individual freedom and security, through a system of law which was established to 'protect inhabitants of a state against selfish individuals that act in contravention of the common good' (Venter and Olivier 1993: 26). To realize this, Kaunda declared that two things were necessary. First, the government needed to protect its citizens from violations of their dignity and freedom. Second, the individual was duty-bound to be 'loyal and obedient to the state' (Venter and Olivier 1993: 26). For this to occur, Kaunda insisted that a government should be free of violence and exploitation. Avoiding exploitation, for Kaunda and UNIP meant establishing a socialist state that mitigated inequalities of wealth distribution. This prompted the widespread nationalization of banks and major industries in the early 1970s, and inspired welfare provisions such as heavy subsidies on staple foods. However, these policies proved economically disastrous. The economic decline of the 1970s and 1980s saw the expanded public sector haemorrhage revenue, rendering such subsidies unsustainable. Nevertheless, values as universal as human dignity and human freedom became the foundation for a national (as well as pan-African) identity, one that transcended regional and tribal differences. As Kaunda himself said, 'with any luck, this generation will think of itself not in tribal terms as Bemba, Lozi or Tonga, but as Zambians. This is the only guarantee of future stability' (Kaunda 1967: 91).

Perhaps the greatest challenge to this stability over the years has been the calls by traditional Lozi leaders for the Western Province to secede. This threat existed before 1964, stemming from Barotseland's former status as a distinct protectorate that preserved its traditional ruling structure. UNIP managed this challenge in two ways. Initially, it sowed divisions in the Western Province by exploiting tensions between traditional rulers (and their supporters) and the emerging Lozi 'nationalists' (Lindemann 2010: 36). Many young and educated Lozis favoured the new Zambian state. UNIP rewarded this by allocating them a generous number of public-sector and party positions, a strategy it often used to manage ethnic competition within the nation as a whole (Lindemann 2010: 36). This ensured that the moves towards independence in the Western Province were not coordinated. From the late

1960s these appointments also included 'traditionalists', which significantly lessened calls for secession, as well as mitigating the risk of 'secessionist violence' (Lindemann 2010: 37). After the shift to multi-party democratic competition in 1991, calls for secession were again heard, this time coinciding with the sidelining of Lozi leaders in the MMD. The MMD's record of managing Western Province grievances has not been as effective as its UNIP predecessors, and the protests in late 2010 were a response to political and economic grievances – namely under-representation and economic neglect (Lindemann 2010: 39; UNHCR 2011). However, after the 2011 election, such calls once again subsided, in response to Michael Sata's open support of greater autonomy for the province, and promises to reinstate the Barotseland Agreement, which was the basis for the former protectorate of Barotseland joining the new republic at independence.[13] His subsequent reneging of this promise has seen tensions rise once again. The risk of secession and related violence has certainly fluctuated over the decades, but the UNIP government's efforts to include Lozi speakers in political and public-sector representation clearly mitigated this risk. Also, their astuteness in dividing 'traditionalists' and 'nationalists' made a united call for secession highly unlikely. How Sata manages the same issue during his tenure as president – especially given the recent spike in tensions – will determine the stability of this region in the years to come.

While humanism was flawed in that it was never applied in any practical or tangible way, it underpinned the notion of Kaunda's 'One Zambia, One Nation', which continues to be utilized today (although 'humanism' is not). This is evident in the public censure of political appeals to tribalism (see, for example, Munshya wa Munshya 2010). There is no doubt that humanism was associated with Kaunda's authoritarian rule, but it succeeded in preventing a dangerous entrenchment of ethnic division. In short, the country's leadership propagated a philosophy that encouraged national unity for the first 28 years of its independent history. Absent in Zambia was a leader and political elite that sought to instrumentalize and exploit ethnic difference.

Peaceful transition to the Third Republic

Zambia's success in absorbing upheaval and embracing reform was evident in Kaunda's peaceful response to popular pressure for multi-party elections. His decision to concede power marked a significant turning point in Zambia's independent history, opening the way for a peaceful political transition and a renewed system of multi-party democracy. The late 1980s witnessed growing political instability largely due to economic hardship. Zambia's economy was dependent on foreign aid, and the conditions that the IMF set included the removal of food subsidies, leading to an overnight doubling in the price of staples. Mass protests and riots were met by police repression. Dissatisfaction was accompanied by calls for the government to democratize. Kaunda's eventual response was to relent, rather than use force to protect his regime –

at a time when UNIP was deeply unpopular. The election results sealed an emphatic victory for the MMD. Kaunda graciously relinquished government and handed power over to his successor, Chiluba. This peaceful transition could have easily resulted in violent conflict. By 1990, there were many risk factors pointing to this possibility: an economy in deep decline, rising food prices, massive public discontent and an authoritarian government intolerant of dissent. In the midst of such factors, Zambia's president of nearly three decades agreed to major political reform that heralded his inevitable and swift political defeat. While democratic reform since has been slow and at times halting, a precedent now exists for democratization and non-violent reform. Kaunda's political legacy, therefore, includes an ideology fostering national unity, and a history of largely non-violent policies.

Zambia's political history is characterized by a mixture of authoritarian rule and hesitant democratic reform. Despite this mixed picture, ethnic division has been avoided and national unity promoted. Zambia's authoritarian regime also demonstrated the wisdom to surrender centralized power in order to foster peaceful reform, albeit in the face of considerable popular pressure. This willingness to relinquish power saw Zambia avoid the pitfalls that have marked other overstretched authoritarian governments, as in its neighbour Zimbabwe. Not only did opting for peaceful reform eliminate the violent precedent of rebellion, uprising and civil war, but it also saw the empowerment of a wide range of civil society organizations, and their intimate role in the country's ongoing democratization process. This greater and more liberal political participation helped to ensure that the Third Republic did not experience democratic 'rollback', with a significant example being the pressure that a collection of organizations successfully placed on the government to cancel the amendment on presidential term limits.

Conclusion

In Zambia, four risk factors exist that are often associated with outbreaks of mass atrocities: ethnic division, limited democracy, limited rule of law and economic inequality. In 2010, the country was recognized by the CIDCM as at high risk of future political instability.[14] The country has also experienced 'internal strife' of a kind that can precipitate mass atrocities (see, for example, Fein 1979: 9). The mass protests and rioting in the late 1980s in response to economic decline and political authoritarianism are one example, as are calls for the secession of the Western Province, which spawned protests and even the rise of a small rebel movement.

That these preconditions have not generated mass atrocities is due to a number of counterbalancing forces, which although not successful in eliminating risk entirely, have effectively managed it over time. Zambia has a long history of developing strategies to maintain ethnic cohesion. This was especially evident during Kaunda's rule – he engaged in the constant reshuffling of ministerial posts and high-level public-sector positions to prevent 'ethnic stacking'. In addition, Zambia's ethno-linguistic divisions were relatively new, and present mostly in large urban areas, where different groups cohabited and intermarried. Absent were formal policies of classification, such as identity cards or limitations of movement. Zambia's transition to a multi-party democracy in the early 1990s was also pivotal in calming growing unrest in the country. Moreover, the initiation of this transition was significantly influenced by civil society.[15] Although democratic reform has slowed, the 2011 defeat of the incumbent MMD and the smooth transition of power to Michael Sata's PF shows that Zambia is still making positive steps toward democratic consolidation.

However, like Botswana, some key mitigating factors were not explicitly reflected in the framework. The decolonization process in Zambia was instrumental in promoting national unity and avoiding division. The struggle for independence advanced principally by UNIP and its leader, Kaunda, encouraged a unified national identity that transcended tribal and ethnic division. In addition, the transition to independence from the former British colonial administration was non-violent, despite the jailing of Kaunda and other leaders. Following independence, President Kaunda embarked on a nation-building project involving a dramatic expansion of the public sector, aimed at spreading health and education services to all parts of the country. Complementing this, Kaunda's philosophy of humanism promoted unity, non-violence and compassion. This fostered a national identity, and continues to provide a strong basis for national unity, as well as encouraging public censure of tribal and ethnic division. Kaunda's humanism was apparent in his response to growing unrest in the 1980s and 1990s, when he relented to public protests and agreed to initiate democratic reform – a move that precipitated his own defeat. The early establishment of national unity and Kaunda's philosophy of humanism were essential to preserving Zambia's resilience despite the myriad challenges the state confronted. Clearly, for both Zambia and Botswana, the historical processes of decolonization and nation building played central roles in the development of resilience. For both states, these processes were primarily influenced by the inclusive ideology of their inaugural leaders. Such processes are not explicitly identified in the framework deployed in Chapter 3.

Like Botswana, the case of Zambia demonstrates the fine distinction between factors that create risk and those that foster stability. One example is Kaunda's actions in the 1960s and 1970s to prevent ethnic division in the government and public sector. His reshuffling of key positions was effective in this respect, but had two negative consequences for the country. First, the complex management of diversity prompted Kaunda to increase presidential powers, to the extent that he banned opposition parties and rendered parliament impotent. Second, the constant changing of executive positions created enormous inefficiencies. As a result, the public services expanded in the 1960s became severely hampered in the 1980s, provoking protests and riots by the decade's end. Kaunda's efforts to prevent factional division clearly came at great cost, and generated a further risk of instability. However, UNIP's inclusive ideology of Zambian unity effectively prevented ethnic division becoming dominant in the country's formative years. This set a precedent that is still largely observed today. More recently, Zambia's period of democratization yielded a new leader who, perhaps more than any of his predecessors, utilized ethnic divisions to gain and consolidate power. The relationship between factors that generate risk and factors that promote stability is complex, and changes over time.

Despite its violent neighbourhood and domestic risk factors, Zambia has avoided outbreaks of mass atrocities. The Zambian case shows that even in one of the most unstable regions and amidst widespread poverty, inequality and limited democracy, local and national policies can provide stability and greater prosperity, and effectively manage the risk of mass atrocities.

Notes

1 This is a region in the north of the country where most of the copper mines are located. It attracted a large labour force from all over the protectorate.
2 He was eventually acquitted.
3 After the 2011 elections there was a change of government for the first time since 1991, when the MMD gained power. Michael Sata's PF won a majority of seats in the National Assembly, with Sata himself winning the presidential election.
4 Nevertheless, each major urban centre in the country is dominated by one of these languages: Bemba in the Copperbelt, Nyanga in Lusaka and Tonga in Livingstone.
5 See Chapter 2 for more on the structural causes of ethnic conflict.
6 This is explained further in the next section.
7 Although the MMD has sought to include Lozi representation, the desire to court the larger contingent of Bemba voters is often seen as limiting such representation of other smaller groups.
8 Malawi.
9 As demonstrated by the PITF.
10 In 2007 Chiluba had been found guilty of corruption in a British court.
11 These are the most recent statistics available.
12 An exception to this is the Western Province, inhabited mainly by Lozis.
13 The Barotse Agreement had been excluded from the National Constitution, although Sata had made assurances that it would be re-included (see UNHCR 2011).
14 It identifies 'governance' (characterized by limited democracy with factional division and excessive executive power) as the principal factor in this risk (see Goldstone and Ulfelder 2004: 13).
15 While civil society has been observed to be a significant protective factor in the chapter of Zambia, this evidence is not enough to warrant its generalization in the broad framework that I delineated in Chapter 3. The framework is a synthesis of broad (both quantitative and qualitative) studies on both preconditions and mitigating factors. The fact that civil society is significant in Zambia is, I think, reason enough to question the salience of civil society in other places, but evidence in one country is not enough to draw a general conclusion. Therefore it does not appear in my framework in this research project.

6   Tanzania

Unity and diversity amidst poverty

Tanzania has a mixed record in managing the risk of mass atrocities. It is regarded as one of the most politically stable countries in Africa (Klugman *et al.* 1999: 75), yet it contains challenges that are typically associated with profound instability, including widespread poverty and a government with authoritarian characteristics (see, for example, Hewitt 2010: 10). Decades of political and economic reform have failed to bring either democracy or prosperity to the country. To add to this, Tanzania contains great ethnic and religious diversity, including a variety of potential social fault lines, which have led to violence in the recent past, most notably in Zanzibar. In addition, Tanzania is located in an extremely unstable neighbourhood, which for decades has witnessed numerous civil wars and widespread atrocities. Rwanda, Burundi, Kenya, Mozambique, Uganda and the Democratic Republic of the Congo have all experienced mass atrocities, and have all challenged Tanzania with mass refugee arrivals. Yet despite both internal and external vulnerabilities, Tanzania has remained relatively stable, and has avoided the commission of mass atrocities. Even when violence has erupted, as it did in Zanzibar in 2001, the semi-autonomous archipelago's government and opposition eventually managed to deflate tension by forging a power-sharing agreement.

This chapter aims to provide greater clarity as to why and how Tanzania has, since independence in 1964, maintained relative political stability and social cohesion in the presence of preconditions associated with the risk of future mass atrocities. On the mainland there are four risk factors in evidence (see Table 6.1),[1] while in Zanzibar risk has been much higher, with seven preconditions present (Table 6.2).[2]

Two distinct analyses are provided – one focusing on the mainland, the territory that comprises the largest part of the population and territory, and the second on Zanzibar. Although these two territories formed the United Republic of Tanzania in 1964, Zanzibar remains relatively autonomous and culturally distinct. They experienced different histories, which in turn have shaped the present circumstances, particularly with regard to risk.

The chapter unfolds as follows: first, some historical background is presented for Tanzania as a whole, aimed to isolate the social, political and

Table 6.1 Risk in mainland Tanzania

The risk factors associated with mass atrocities in mainland Tanzania
Ethnic and religious division
Limited democracy
Limited rule of law
Inequality of economic opportunity

Table 6.2 Risk in Zanzibar

The risk factors associated with mass atrocities in Zanzibar
Ethnic and religious division
Discrimination
Human rights violations
Prior atrocities
Limited democracy
Limited rule of law
Inequality of economic opportunity

economic factors that have contributed to both risk and resilience. Following this is an analysis of the risk factors that appear on the mainland, and the mitigating factors that have contained this risk. Specifically, these include the inclusive vision and policies of the country's inaugural president, Julius Kambarage Nyerere, the cooperation between the country's Muslim and Christian populations which underscored the secular welfare state, the use of KiSwahili as the official language, and the ability of the political regime to manage tensions in Zanzibar through reform and negotiation. This is followed by an analysis of the more acute risk that has existed in the more explosive circumstances of Zanzibar, counterbalanced with a discussion of five major mitigating factors. These included a change in the executive leader, a rebalancing of economic inequalities, a political agreement that preserved the integrity of both contending powers, their investment in an autonomous Zanzibar, and the security inherent in being part of the larger entity of the union of Tanzania.

Background

Tanzania is located in a region that has experienced some of the worst atrocities in recent decades. In addition to the relatively stable Zambia and Malawi, it shares borders with Mozambique, the Democratic Republic of Congo, Rwanda, Burundi, Uganda and Kenya – no fewer than six countries where massive tolls of suffering and death were exacted through genocide, massacres, protracted civil and transnational wars, and brutal dictatorships. The Rift Valley, which runs through mainland Tanzania, was witness to numerous periods of migration, which led to approximately 120 different language groups inhabiting the territory. Off the coast, a mixture of Arab, Persian and African populations inhabits the islands of Zanzibar. This particular diversity was a product of two and a half centuries of domination of the islands and surrounding coastal region by the Omani Sultanate (Yeager 1982: 7–8).

Tanganyika,[3] as Tanzania was formerly known, was colonized by Germany in 1885. It remained a German protectorate until 1920, when the League of Nations transferred administrative responsibilities to the UK. It became a United Nations trust territory in 1946, with the intention that this would quickly lead to independence. Although the expectation was that the British would facilitate such a change, in reality the administration of the territory reflected the colonial power's desire to maintain dominance through a 'multiracial' Legislative Council. This gave disproportionate representation to Europeans and Asians, with only token African membership (Klugman *et al.* 1999: 75; Yeager 1982). This apparent intractability of colonial rule, and the restrictions placed on African Tanganyikans both politically and economically, spurred a burgeoning independence movement in the early 1950s, advanced by Nyerere.

This opposition to colonial dominance was crystallized by the Tanganyika African National Union (TANU), formed by Nyerere. It incorporated the Tanganyika African Association (TAA), which was initially established in 1927 as a social club for civil servants and other professionals, as well as an independent welfare agency. Because it initially refrained from acting as a political organization, the colonial administration allowed it to exist and to expand to inland centres. Affiliating itself with mainland unions, as well as the Zanzibari African Association, the TAA's composition and character reflected the social diversity of both Tanganyika and Zanzibar, making it an invaluable resource for the mobilization of the population in the campaign for independence. Observing this, Nyerere, as the association's president from 1953, convinced senior members to disband the organization in the interests of using its well-established networks to herald a new, overtly political union. Thus TANU came into existence in 1954.

TANU's membership grew rapidly, and an increasingly diverse membership ensured that no particular identity group dominated the organization (Iliffe 1979: 523). The fact that Nyerere did not owe political allegiance to any group or region was also an advantage, enabling him to advocate national unity and transcend religious and social differences. This was the platform on which TANU premised its calls for independence (Iliffe 1979: 536–37). TANU actively supported strikes and other protests, campaigning against colonial policies that perpetuated the unequal provision of social services and the under-representation of Africans in the civil service (Klugman *et al.* 1999: 76; Yeager 1982: 19). The growing activism against colonial practices and related inequalities ensured that TANU became the focal point of the struggle for independence (Klugman *et al.* 1999: 75). This struggle was peaceful, characterized not by a desire for retribution over past injustices, but by a call for unity among all who regarded the territory as home. This was articulated by Nyerere as early as 1952:

> We appeal to all thinking Europeans and Indians to regard themselves as ordinary citizens of Tanganyika; to preach no Divine Right of Europeans, no Divine Right of Indians and no Divine Right of Africans either. We are all Tanganyikans and we are all East Africans. The race quarrel is a stupid quarrel, and it can be a very tragic quarrel. If we all make up our minds to live like 'ordinary sort of fellows' and not to think that we were specially designed by the Creator to be masters and others specially designed to be hewers of wood and drawers of water we will make East Africa a very happy country for everybody.
>
> (Nyerere 1967: 29)

Tanganyika became provisionally independent in 1961, with TANU completely dominating the Westminster-style elections, winning every seat with the exception of one independent, who was already technically a member and supporter of TANU. After a referendum in 1962, the country changed its constitution to become a republic, with Nyerere becoming the country's first president.

In Zanzibar, the road to independence was very different, marked by revolution and violence along social fault lines.[4] Formerly the capital of the Omani Sultanate, the death of Sultan Said in 1856 resulted in the archipelago forming a separate sultanate from Oman, and eventually becoming a British protectorate in 1890. The British ruled indirectly through the sultan, privileging the Arab population over those of African descent, and fostering an Arab elite in the process. Although Arab-African relations were more amicable on Pemba than on Unguja, the lead-up to independence was marked by political tensions along these ethnic lines. Despite the Arab domination of politics through their party, the Zanzibar Nationalist Party (ZNP), the African dominated Afro-Shirazi Party (ASP) received a majority of votes in the 1963 election. Owing to the distribution of parliamentary seats established by the British, the ZNP was able to form the first independent government in coalition with the Pemba-based Zanzibar and Pemba People's Party (ZPPP). In January 1964, a violent revolution, led by forces aligned with the ASP, overthrew the government, and a *coup d'état* placed ASP leader Abeid Karume in the president's office. While there have been conflicting reports about how many people were killed in the revolution, estimates range between 5,000 and 12,000, with most violence directed against the Arab population (Brown 2010: 622; Coulson 1982: 133; Ramadhani 2011: 9). In the same year, Tanganyika and Zanzibar merged to form the United Republic of Tanzania.

Nyerere vigorously pursued his vision of national unity immediately following independence. He initially embarked on an ambitious programme of industrialization and agricultural projects, but a shortfall in foreign investment prompted him to change direction (Kaiser 1996: 229). During his 1967

Arusha Declaration, he declared the establishment of 'African socialism' in an effort to establish self-reliance based on African values of egalitarianism and welfare. He set up 'villagization' programmes, encouraging (and also compelling) people to move to new settlements and engage in small-scale agricultural production. The policies of socialism and self-reliance were presented under the umbrella of *Ujamaa*, a KiSwahili word that means family and represented, according to Nyerere, the most basic and representative expression of African socialism. Arguing that Africa's absence of an industrial infrastructure called for a different approach to socialism, Nyerere claimed that the basic egalitarian principles of socialism were already inherent in African societies: 'We, in Africa, have no more need of being "converted" to socialism than we have of being "taught" democracy. Both are rooted in our own past – in the traditional society which produced us' (Nyerere 1968: 12). The Arusha Declaration instigated a series of five-year plans which aimed to balance investment in Tanzania's agricultural base with steady industrial growth (Svendsen 1970: 79).[5]

To augment this, TANU instigated a process of nationalization in 1969. It started with schools and expanded to include banks and a range of commercial enterprises and manufacturing companies (Cliffe 1969: 256). At the same time, the government introduced a number of policies to foster 'cultural integrity' (Kaiser 1996: 230), including the establishment of KiSwahili as the language of instruction in schools, a move which 'fostered cross-ethnic communication in a distinctly African context, and it also lessened linguistic dependence on the colonial language of English' (Kaiser 1996: 230).

These policies stemming from *Ujamaa* were widely regarded as successful in fostering social harmony and national unity. They brought about positive encounters between Christians and Muslims, and Tanzania was able to achieve 'a degree of cohesion that surpassed each and every neighbouring country' (Kaiser 1996: 231). While it is difficult to attribute this to any specific policy or action by the government, *Ujamaa* was catalytic in the way that it facilitated a common identity and corresponding positive interactions between various ethnic and religious groups. Uniquely, the 'villagization' programme provided opportunities for co-habitation and cooperation across these groups.

This social cohesion did not, however, translate into economic growth. Nyerere's grand vision of self-reliance was marred by serious inefficiencies, with most state-run enterprises overstaffed and operating at 10 to 30 per cent capacity. The country was increasingly dependent on foreign aid, to the extent that by the early 1980s, aid was paying for more than half of total imports, 60 per cent of the development budget and 16 per cent of gross national product (GNP) (Ayittey 2005: 202). The living standards of those in rural areas declined on average by 2.5 per cent between 1969 and 1983, and in urban areas real wages dropped by 65 per cent over the same period. Unsurprisingly, this affected household consumption, which between 1973 and 1990 fell by 43 per cent per capita (World Bank 1990: 42). By the mid-1980s, Tanzania's economy had suffered from nearly two decades of decline, was in severe crisis and largely dependent on foreign aid to feed its population, with per capita GDP falling to pre-1966 levels (Klugman *et al.* 1999: 87). Although there were a number of factors that influenced this decline,[6] Nyerere's *Ujamaa*-inspired policies were proving expensive and limiting. As Klugman *et al.* (1999: 89) point out, they 'caused a major resource drain from the costs of relocating a large segment of the population and difficulties efficiently managing central resource allocation'. Nyerere's final years in office were accompanied by a raft of changes to move Tanzania away from the state-controlled practices of *Ujamaa*. The government imposed its own structural adjustment and austerity measures, and slowly introduced a market approach while cautiously dismantling the old apparatus of state-owned firms (Kaiser 1996: 232).[7] The other significant political development occurred in 1977, with the merging of TANU with Zanzibar's ASP, to form Chama Cha Mapinduzi (CCM).[8]

As Nyerere retired from politics in 1986, his successor, President Ali Hassan Mwinyi took the crucial step of finalizing an agreement with the IMF which further formalized economic reform. It included the devaluation of exchange, the liberalization of trade, greater openness for foreign investment, and the privatization of a number of parastatal companies (Kelsall 2002: 610). In addition, Mwinyi established a commission to generate recommendations for political reform. The Nyalali Commission recommended a shift to a multi-party democratic system, despite 80 per cent of those surveyed indicating a preference for single-party rule. The recommendations resulted in the government changing the constitution in 1992 to legalize the formation of opposition parties (Ngasongwa 1992: 114). This was followed by the first multi-party elections in 1995. Subsequent elections were held in 2000, 2005 and 2010, with the CCM maintaining its hold on power. Mwinyi retired from politics in 1995, and was succeeded by Benjamin Mkapa, who in 2005 was succeeded by Jakaya Kikwete. Of the four presidents the republic has had, two have been Christian and two Muslim.

Multi-party politics has escalated tensions in three main ways. First, political and economic liberalization has led to the emergence of 'clientelism'. Vote buying and mutual back scratching between politicians and their constituents have become common features of local politics in the multi-party era (Kelsall 2002: 611–12). Second, claims of voting irregularities on the island of Zanzibar significantly increased the risk of violence there, although a recently formed government of national unity has eased these tensions. Third, the economic reforms that have shaped Tanzania's economy since the 1980s have done little to increase the overall wealth of the country, and have aggravated inequalities. In particular, there is a link between political-economic liberalization and growing tensions between Christians and Muslims on the mainland (Heilman 2002: 694).

Tanzania, like Zambia, has shown signs of growing social divisions over the last two decades. These divisions have coincided with the country's political and economic reforms, which suggest that both states showed an initial adeptness in managing social diversity, but not at developing economic prosperity. Nevertheless, Tanzania's social cohesion was strong enough to withstand the economic downturn of the 1980s. Unlike in Zambia, it did not precipitate a political crisis. The shift to a multi-party system was a proactive move by the government. Although it has not brought about a fully functioning multi-party democracy, the tensions triggered by the multi-party system and economic liberalization have not been transformed into ethnic or religious antagonism of the kind that has characterized politics in other neighbouring states, such as Kenya, Rwanda and Burundi.

Risk factors for mass atrocities in mainland Tanzania

Social division

Tanzania's diversity is characterized by a large number of relatively small linguistic and tribal groups – approximately 120 in total. The population is almost evenly divided among Christians, Muslims and followers of indigenous religions. Tensions between Muslims and Christians, and among regional groups on the mainland, are risk factors for future mass atrocities.

Ethnic and religious cleavages

Since the economic and political reforms of the 1980s and 1990s, social divisions have been aggravated in four ways. First, resentment against the country's Asian community has grown, and at times resulted in violence. Second, tensions between Muslims and Christians have increased, also at times leading to violence (Kaiser 1996: 233–34). Third, tensions between Zanzibar and the mainland have continued to simmer as unresolved differences between the Zanzibar-based political party Civic United Front (CUF) and the governing CCM, largely based on the issue of autonomy (Minorities at Risk 2011). Fourth, regional divisions (known as 'regional blocs') on the mainland are also becoming significant (Kelsall 2002: 613).

Following the structural adjustment measures of the 1980s, there were increased tensions between the African and Asian communities in Dar es Salaam. There was a growing perception that Asian merchants had profited from the privatization of parastatal industries at the expense of African Tanzanians. As the multi-party era took hold in the early 1990s, many opposition politicians publicly blamed Asians for taking advantage of this economic reform (Kaiser 1996: 232). This prompted small-scale attacks on Asian Tanzanians. On one occasion, street sellers removed from some parts of Dar es Salaam responded by looting shops of Asian merchants (Kaiser 1996: 233). Economic reform triggered some scapegoating and violence in Tanzania, although it was largely limited to Dar es Salaam.

Divisions between Christians and Muslims have grown more salient over the last 20 years. This stems in part from the ongoing political tensions between the predominantly Muslim Zanzibar and the mainland. Zanzibar's membership in the Organization of the Islamic Conference (OIC) in 1993 stirred controversy among many mainland MPs, who pointed out that the terms of the 1964 union did not allow either the mainland or Zanzibar to conduct their own foreign policy (Kaiser 1996: 233–34). These religious tensions brought the question of the union itself to the fore (Mesaki 2011: 256). In the same year, other Muslims in Dar es Salaam began pushing their agendas in a way that provoked the CCM. Many Muslim leaders opposed government controls on religious institutions, and sought to provoke division, with one notable example being the attack on two pork butcher shops in the city in 1993. In 1998, riots broke out in a mosque in Dar es Salaam, sparked by police entering to make arrests (Heilman 2002: 695). Violent demonstrations occurred again in 2001, after it was alleged that a Muslim preacher had insulted Christianity (Heilman 2002: 695). Such confrontations between some sections of the Muslim and Christian communities continued into the next decade. They attested to divisions not only between the two major religions, but also within the Muslim community – particularly between those who aligned with the state-recognized Supreme Council of Muslims and those who did not.

These isolated but growing divisions were largely the product of an 'Islamic revival' in the early 1990s, which posed a challenge to the CCM and its secular principles. It was premised on the belief among some Muslims that they had suffered discrimination by Christian-dominated former colonial states. This fostered suspicion of the Tanzanian state among many Muslims, and spawned a rise in membership of Muslim organizations with more pronounced international agendas. This trend is a distinct departure from the nationally aligned organizations sanctioned by the CCM (Heilman 2002: 695). Tension also exists at a grassroots level. While examples here are minor – including disputes over graveyard and burial practices, and evangelical Muslim organizations seeking to convert Christians – such instances demonstrate a potential for the 'political mobilization of identities along religious lines' (Heilman 2002: 697; Wijsen 2002: 238). However, despite the increased prominence of religious division since the liberalization of politics in Tanzania in the 1990s, inter-faith conflicts have not been as prevalent as intra-faith conflicts (Heilman 2002: 703).

Tension has also arisen over the formation of regional blocs in the CCM. The political and economic reform of the 1980s and 1990s catalysed new dynamics of regionalism and clientelism, made political elites more dependent on local support, and increased their capacity to mobilize such support by offering various financial incentives to voters (Kelsall 2002: 612). However, in Tanzania, this emerging clientelism has not led to mobilization along ethnic lines. As mentioned above, the country is too ethnically diverse for any single group to contest power on its own. Instead, what has emerged in Tanzania is a loose formation of regional blocs, which creates factional differences mostly within the CCM. These blocs – as the name suggests – are divided geographically, and 'have not yet congealed into coherent collective actors' (Kelsall 2002: 613). However, the process that involves political elites mobilizing support through rewards and incentives mirrors the pattern that has seen 'ethnic big men' mobilize both support and discontent in other parts of Africa (see Kelsall 2002: 612; Berman 1998).

In summary, in Tanzania, the tensions emerging from social divisions are largely the product of economic liberalization and political reform. There is also a growing tendency toward clientelism and regional factionalism. In addition, many Muslim organizations continue to question the need to align with the secular state, and identify more closely with pan-Islamist associations. Ongoing (albeit in recent times reduced) tensions in Zanzibar, and a culture of suspicion of the governing CCM, are still a cause for concern, as such tensions have at times triggered violence. As we have seen, ethnic and religious division is recognized almost universally by genocide scholars as a key risk factor for mass atrocities. In mainland Tanzania, religious and ethnic division has gradually become more pronounced since the mid-1980s.

Governance

Tanzania has a limited democracy and rule of law. These limitations have contributed to a higher risk of mass atrocities over the last two decades. Such risk is significant, particularly when viewed through the prism of the PITF's findings. These indicate that the nature of a country's political institutions is the most important risk factor with regards to future political instability (Goldstone and Ulfelder 2004: 14).

Limitations in democracy

Tanzania's limited democracy rewards incumbency and severely limits alternative political voices. Although it initiated a peaceful transition to a liberal democratic system, Polity IV still identifies it as a de facto one-party state, giving the regime a score of −1, an anocracy with tendencies towards autocracy (Polity IV 2008b). According to Freedom House, Tanzania is only 'partly free', because of the limitations of its democratic institutions, including the executive's excessive power and a range of electoral improprieties that have benefited the incumbent party, along with entrenched corruption and press restrictions (Freedom House 2010b). Clearly, there are limitations to Tanzania's democratic system, and despite major reforms in the early 1990s aimed at liberalizing the country's political institutions, the beneficiaries of these changes have been the incumbent CCM. This prompted one scholar to conjecture that these changes 'were generally intended to liberalize the political system without necessarily fully democratizing it' (Killian 2004: 192). In short, Tanzania's limited democracy has caused low-level violence in the recent past, and the CCM's continued determination to dominate the multi-party system could provoke future violence.

Like Zambia, Tanzania embarked on major, albeit incomplete, constitutional reforms in the early 1990s, as part of the transition from a one-party regime to a multi-party democracy (Gasarasi 2004: 78). Three key factors have contributed to the country's stalled democratic transition. First is the heavy concentration of power in the office of the president. Second is the CCM's continued manipulation of the political environment to maintain its power and undermine opposition parties. Third, social tensions were exacerbated by religious rivalry, by discrimination and political violence in Zanzibar, and by the emergence of regional blocs within the ruling CCM. These factors have increased the risk of political instability.

Despite Tanzania's shift to a multi-party democracy, power remains heavily concentrated in the office of the president. In 1992, the country's second president, Ali Hassan Mwinyi, allowed the formation of opposition parties, but the CCM remains firmly in control (Tambila 2004: 69). Freedom House describes the executive branch as one of the most powerful in Africa, pointing out that the president still has the power to overturn rulings in the Court of Appeal. The constitution also allows the president to appoint ten additional members of parliament, in addition to a large number of female parliamentarians (Freedom House 2010b).[9] Such a disproportionate amount of power in the hands of the executive is, according to the PITF, a major destabilizer, particularly in regimes that are undergoing democratic transition (Goldstone and Ulfelder 2004: 15).

The rise of multi-party political competition has also provoked deepening social tensions, through the advent of factional divisions within the CCM and the exacerbating of Christian–Muslim tensions. The PITF has identified political competition dominated by factional division as that can increase the risk of mass atrocities. In Tanzania, the constitution prohibits the formation of political parties along religious or ethnic lines (McHenry Jr 2004: 47). Nevertheless, at times such division emerges in less formal ways. For example, one trend that has recently surfaced, particularly within the dominant CCM, is the phenomenon of regional blocs. These blocs emerged as an expression of some MPs' dissatisfaction with the government, and at least one bloc is characterized by religious division: the coastal bloc has been referred to as the 'Islamic bloc'. In addition, 'northern', 'southern' and 'lake zone' MPs have formed loose and informal coalitions to increase their bargaining power in parliament (Polity IV 2008b). In 2001, the lake zone bloc began to pressure the government over the matter of royalties from mining concessions (Kelsall 2003: 65). Between 1995 and 2001, President Mkapa's Cabinet reshuffle saw power shift from coastal MPs to southern MPs, a move which then prompted some northern MPs to push for the finance minister, Professor Mbilinyi, to resign on the grounds of corruption. In an apparent act of revenge, the southern bloc forced Iddi Simba[10] to resign. This move was seen by his supporters as 'an anti-Muslim plot' (Kelsall 2003: 65). The tension between the southern and northern blocs, in particular, has sometimes resulted in MPs condemning their own government when reshuffles shift the balance of power away from their region (Kelsall 2002: 607; Polity IV 2008b). The growing presence of factionalism is significant here, as there are indications that religious identity is playing a growing part, potentially exacerbating tensions between Christians and Muslims.

While factionalism along the traditional social fault lines of ethnicity and religion is relatively new in parliament, the advent of political liberalization in Tanzania has coincided with an increase in religious tension more generally in the country. Although this fragmentation of social unity is also linked to the liberal economic reform that began in the 1980s (discussed in the next section), it also coincides with the country's democratic transition. Since the introduction of a multi-party system in 1992, political violence has surfaced on occasion, despite the continued rhetoric of national unity that characterized Nyerere's period of leadership (Kaiser 1996: 234). The first elections, held in 1995, were particularly tense and marked by violence, especially during the campaign phase. Much of this tension was dominated by ethnic rivalries, despite the fact that it was illegal to form political parties around social or religious identities. Some new parties implicitly expected support based on identity, with one example being presidential candidate Augustine Mrema. His party, the National Convention for Constitution and Reform – Mageuzi (NCCR-Mageuzi), became associated with the *Chagga* people of northern Tanzania, although a consequence was that it failed to gain support in opposition strongholds outside the traditional boundaries of this group (Kaiser 1996: 235). The frequent reports of police intimidation of opposition groups, and the denial of equitable media exposure, suggest that this diversity has been poorly managed.

Rule of law

Tanzania's rule of law is also limited. Since the advent of political liberalism in the early 1990s, both Freedom House and Polity IV have reported that while greater judicial independence from the government now exists, restrictions remain (Freedom House 2010b; Polity IV 2008b). Despite both Polity IV and Freedom House acknowledging improvements in this regard, the record of the country's courts over the last 20 years has been mixed. On some occasions, individual High Court judges have passed rulings challenging government policies, but many judges have readily done the government's bidding. In terms of law enforcement, numerous instances of police intimidation of opposition parties have come to light. Sometimes this has led to violence, especially, as noted, in Zanzibar.

The police in Tanzania often target opposition groups. In the country's first two multi-party elections – in 1995 and 2000 – there were numerous cases of intimidation by the police. Opposition leaders were arrested, and the police frequently blocked political rallies by opposition parties. When such rallies were permitted, there were often allegations of harsh treatment of partici-pants. According to Kelsall, these police actions, which clearly responded to the wishes of the government, effectively bolstered CCM domination (Kelsall 2003: 61). This further prevented opposition parties from gaining momentum to challenge this dominance.

In summary, Tanzania is a country with very limited democracy and rule of law. In addition, the country's shift to a multi-party democratic system occurred in the wake of the Nyalali Commission report, which despite recommending such a shift, acknowledged that 80 per cent of the population preferred to keep the one-party system (Ngasongwa 1992: 113). Thus this shift towards a more democratic form of representation itself ran counter to the will of the vast majority of Tanzanians. Although this can be interpreted as a government looking ahead in anticipation of future public pressure,[11] it also explains the tendency for democratic transition to occur on the terms of the ruling CCM, rather than as an expression of popular will. This limited democratic transition, coupled with judicial and law-enforcement bodies that lack independence, poses a significant risk of mass atrocities (see, for example, Harff 2003; Goldstone and Ulfelder 2004). As the era of political reform coincided with increased tensions between Christians and Muslims, these divisions have increased.

Economic weakness

Inequality of economic opportunity

Tanzania is one of the world's poorest states, with a per capita annual GDP of US$1,400 (CIA 2011c). Although this is comparable to Zambia, what places Tanzania apart from both Zambia and Botswana is its considerably lower level of inequality. In contrast to Zambia's Gini coefficient score of 50.8 and Botswana's very high 63.0, Tanzania scored 34.6, which is comparable to New Zealand, the UK and Switzerland (CIA 2011a). In addition, Tanzania's level of poverty, at 33.4 per cent, is markedly lower than Zambia's 59.3 per cent, and similar to Botswana's 30.6 per cent (World Bank 2011a, 2011b).[12] Superficially, Tanzania appears to have had greater success in managing the challenges of poverty and limiting the gap between rich and poor. However, in a predominantly rural country, poverty levels are often difficult to calculate in monetary terms. Tanzania is one of the world's highest recipients of foreign aid, with about 35 per cent of government spending provided for by donor money (Development Partners Group 2011). Half the population is under-nourished, and although the literacy rate is 69 per cent (CIA 2011c), only a small fraction of students go on to secondary school. Despite high economic growth over the last decade, poverty remains high. In this section I will out-line the impact of economic liberalization on the country, with emphasis on the risk of mass atrocities.

When Tanzania embarked on market-based reforms in the mid-1980s, the national unity and social cohesion fostered by *Ujamaa* began to fray.

Although inequality is low compared to neighbouring states, in the 1980s the gap widened considerably (Ferreira 1996: v), provoking grievances and at times violence (Kaiser 1996: 232–33). Widening inequality triggered tensions between Africans and Asians. In response to a prolonged economic decline in the 1970s and 1980s, Nyerere's successor, Mwinyi, adopted the Economic Recovery Programme in 1986, which heralded the end of *Ujamaa*. Government assets were sold, and the private sector expanded, exacerbating social inequalities in the process (Kaiser 1996: 232). Consequentially, wages declined and the cost of living skyrocketed as Nyerere's welfare state was dismantled. At the same time, it was the Asian community, predominantly based in and around Dar es Salaam, that was financially best positioned to take advantage of the privatization of government-owned enterprises. This fuelled a perception that a divide between rich and poor was developing along racial lines (Kaiser 1996: 232). Politicians who fed this perception gained in popularity. Eventually, such rhetoric led to violence, with a number of Asian shops being looted in Dar es Salaam in 1993. This 'anti-Asian sentiment' also threatened to upset the longstanding harmony between Christians and Muslims, as the tensions coincided with the controversy surrounding Zanzibar's membership in the OIC (Kaiser 1996: 233).[13]

The paradox of Tanzania's history is that the era that fostered social cohesion also yielded an expensive and unsustainable economic climate, producing nearly two decades of economic decline. By contrast, the current period of economic liberalization, which has culminated in over a decade of consistent economic growth (averaging 7 per cent annually), has aggravated ethnic and religious fault lines. Reforms have, therefore, increased (albeit marginally) the risk of mass atrocities. Another way of understanding this is by focusing on Nyerere's original intent in introducing *Ujamaa*. Socialism, he argued, was 'the application of the principle of human equality to the social, economic, and political organization of society' (Nyerere 1969: 303). Although the austerity measures of the 1980s and 1990s had purely economic goals, the dismantling of *Ujamaa* inevitably created unsettling ripples in the social and political organization of Tanzanian society.

Appraising risk in mainland Tanzania

Tanzania's limited democracy and rule of law displays characteristics often associated with a greater risk of mass atrocities. As stated in Chapter 3, the PITF's findings suggest that the greatest risk for political instability[14] is an authoritarian regime undergoing a limited democratic transition, characterized by excessive executive power and factional division. Tanzania has displayed both characteristics, but particularly the former. Although social division and economic inequality are not as significant as in Zambia and Botswana, Tanzania's authoritarian traits could conceivably allow a future leader to consolidate power on the basis of divisive policies and rhetoric. In short, Tanzania's limited democracy and government-biased judiciary and law enforcement could be instrumental in undermining the social cohesion on which the country was built. Yet for all of these potential risks, and despite the fact that Tanzania remains one of the world's poorest states, it is remarkably stable, particularly in its regional context. Exactly how such stability has come about, particularly in the face of these four risk factors, is the subject of the next section.

Resilience in mainland Tanzania

Despite the presence of four risk factors in mainland Tanzania, the territory has enjoyed decades of relative stability. Over the first two formative decades of independence, mainland Tanzania did not develop the enormous gap between rich and poor that was evident in the other two states. Unlike Zambia, the TANU government and the public sector did not experience factional division along ethnic lines (or any others); unlike Botswana, no ethnic minorities like the San or the Bakgalagadi were conspicuously marginalized in the newly independent state. However, the emergence of tensions along social lines over the last 20 years, Tanzania's very limited and stalled democratic transition and its poor economy demonstrate the existence of some risk factors. Most significant is the current condition of the country's regime. Despite the multi-party electoral system, it still displays the heritage of its one-party authoritarian past, giving the impression of a democracy in name but not in fact. This section identifies the factors that have mitigated this risk. They include the country's ethnic diversity, a history of cooperation between Christians and Muslims, the use of KiSwahili as the official language, Nyerere's inclusive ideology and equitable policies, and *Ujamaa*'s role in preventing any religious or ethnic group from gaining economic advantage in the two decades after independence.

Social cohesion

Ethnic diversity

Tanzania's ethnic diversity has been a positive factor in mitigating the risk of mass atrocities. In Tanzania, none of the 120 tribal groups dominates politically or economically, many tribal areas are sparsely populated, and the notion of chieftainship is not widespread (Klugman *et al.* 1999: 77). Furthermore, during the *Ujamaa* 'villagization' schemes, more than 85 per cent of the rural population was relocated to *Ujamaa* villages, to encourage rural development. The process encouraged coexistence among different ethnic and religious groups (Klugman *et al.* 1999: 84). In addition, it became standard practice for all secondary school students to travel away from their home region to attend a boarding school, and civil servants were also commonly located in regions away from their homes. In short, on the mainland at least, ethnicity has never been used to mobilize any section of the population politically.

The exception is in Zanzibar, where a tendency has been evident for Zanzibaris of Arab descent to support the CUF, and for those of African descent to support the CCM (Minorities at Risk 2011). The violence that erupted in Zanzibar in 2001 should not be understood merely as a clash between two ethnic groups. Rather, the initial demonstrations were a response to specific political and electoral grievances. Despite this, Zanzibar's violent ethnically driven revolution on the eve of independence continues to influence the dynamics, and more closely resembles Stanton's (1996) risk-laden bipolar society. This makes Zanzibar important to an investigation of how the palpable risk of mass atrocities has been mitigated.

Religious cohesion

Given that bipolar societies are said to be at greater risk of mass atrocities,[15] it is necessary to investigate why such violence has not erupted on a large scale due to religious difference. Tanzania's population has an even distribution of Christians and Muslims, and while tensions have increased between the two groups at times during the last 20 years, such violence has not escalated to alarming levels, and Christian-Muslim relations on the mainland are mostly cordial. Kelsall acknowledged the similarity to Nigeria, which has its own mixed heritage of Islam and Christianity. Such a mix is 'potentially explosive', yet Kelsall conjectures that religious differences in Tanzania have been 'managed relatively astutely since independence' (Kelsall 2003: 60). Likewise, Heilman points out that Tanzania should be a torn country, with its widespread poverty and significant populations of Christians and Muslims. Yet it is far from this (Heilman 2002: 691). One factor that favours the resilience of Tanzania's ethnic and religious diversity is the constitutional ban on creating parties or campaigning on the basis of ethnicity or religion (Kelsall 2003: 60). Such laws are a product of Tanzania's long-established culture of religious unity, which galvanized the struggle for independence and established a firm foundation for national unity. This foundation provides a context for understanding the relative harmony between Islam and Christianity in Tanzania, and why religious tensions that emerged during the political and economic reforms of the 1980s and 1990s did not escalate into widespread violence of the kind that continues to afflict Nigeria.

The provision of education, both before and after independence, was instrumental in maintaining a balance between Christians and Muslims, in no small part due to the use of KiSwahili as the language of instruction. Rasmussen highlights that the independence movement in Tanzania fostered unity among adherents of the two major religions by offering the prospect of equitable access to education and representation. This had begun under both colonial administrations, despite the presence of mission schools that largely catered to Christians (Rasmussen 1993: 44). The German colonial authorities initially set up state-run schools in the coastal area of Tanganyika, using KiSwahili as the language of instruction, a practice that the British continued after the First World War. The British administrators and Christian missionaries did not enjoy cooperative relations during this time, resulting in mission schools having less influence than state schools. Eventually the use of KiSwahili as the main language of instruction was also adopted by mission schools. Both KiSwahili and education spread from the coastal area to inland parts of Tanganyika, although the level of education offered to the indigenous colonial subjects remained limited (Rasmussen 1993: 45). While the presence of mission schools made education more widely available to Christians, the fact that Western education was extended to a broad cross-section of the population helped prevent major disparities in its provision, limited though it was. However, the need greatly to increase access to secular education (over the mission schools) prompted many Muslims to support TANU. Rasmussen notes that this desire to find balance in the provision of education between Christians and Muslims spurred the united struggle for independence (Rasmussen 1993: 44). As such, resistance to colonial rule offered an opportunity for both Christians and Muslims to unite around a common cause, while 'Swahili culture offered an alternative source of cultural values' (Rasmussen 1993: 45).

The foundations of religious unity can be traced back as far as the founding of the TAA, which aimed to eliminate all 'tribal, sectarian, political, cultural, educational, territorial, and other differences to promote a solid brotherhood of Africans' (Rasmussen 1993: 23). The aim to unite Christians and Muslims in this initial movement towards independence is reflected in its earliest leadership – its first president was a Christian and its first vice-president a Muslim. Upon incorporation into TANU in 1954, it aimed to win independence with the same ideal of unity, and achieved considerable popularity among both Muslims and Christians (Rasmussen 1993: 23–24). TANU's widespread support at independence was a product of this drive for unity, facilitated by the use of KiSwahili and the rapid expansion of state-run education.[16] After Nyerere (a Christian) retired in 1985, the office of the president was transferred to Mwinyi, a Muslim. Beyond representation in high office, TANU (and subsequently the CCM) were adept at ensuring that both Christian and Muslim communities actively contributed to the government's vision of *Ujamaa*. The Supreme Council of Tanzania Muslims, known as BAKWATA, was created as the principal Muslim body in the country. It had close ties to TANU, and had as its main goal assistance to Muslims in the social, religious and economic realms. It complemented the government's own nation-building agenda. Other organizations that promoted a more pan-Islamic identity were often viewed with suspicion by the government. Some were banned, including the East African Muslim Welfare Society (EAMWS), prohibited in 1968 for its resistance to government pressure (Rasmussen 1993: 58). Likewise, some churches were viewed with suspicion for failing to support *Ujamaa*, in particular the Jehovah's Witnesses, some Pentecostals, and the Seventh-Day Adventists (Forster 1997: 166). Although the state has been intolerant of religious organizations operating outside its established parameters, it has effectively fostered inter-faith dialogue, facilitating positive relations especially between Muslims and Christians (Forster 1997: 178). Furthermore, religious tension in Tanzania has usually been intra-faith in character, and this tension was largely the product of the political liberalization of the early 1990s. Those policies heralded a shift away from Nyerere's insistence on the complementarity of religion and the state in Tanzania's nation-building project.

This fostering of ethnic and religious harmony, and the widespread participation of the diverse population in the push for independence, created a strong foundation for national unity. Despite Tanzania's grinding poverty, it is rare for anyone to be scapegoated on the grounds of their perceived wealth.[17] There is no doubt that the country still faces enormous challenges, especially widespread poverty and malnutrition. Yet the lack of real or perceived horizontal inequality – a product of *Ujamaa* – has contributed to the country's ability to maintain relative political stability and social cohesion, even in the midst of such risk factors. This social cohesion was instrumental in building the country's resilience: economic decline and widespread poverty rarely triggered grievances against specific identity groups.

KiSwahili

Following decolonization, the adoption of KiSwahili as Tanzania's official language helped to foster national unity, as noted. KiSwahili is a fusion of Arabic and African Bantu languages. It developed gradually after the settlement of a number of Arab and Shirazi trading settlements on Zanzibar and the mainland coast, from approximately AD 900 onward. The language also spread inland with the expansion of trading outposts, becoming the region's lingua franca long before European colonization (Yeager 1982: 7). Tanzania's ethnic diversity meant great linguistic diversity as well, so Nyerere's TANU Party made KiSwahili the official language in order to safeguard the 'cultural integrity' of the new nation. In managing ethnic and religious diversity, the language 'facilitated the cross-ethnic communication in a distinctly African context, and it lessened linguistic dependence on the colonial language of English' (Kaiser 1996: 230). This laid a foundation for national unity in a territory characterized by heterogeneity. As Iliffe highlights, 'Swahili was TANU's sole official language, enabling leaders to speak directly to each other and to the people almost anywhere, permitting a transferable party bureaucracy, and preventing the emergence of an English-speaking elite of political patrons' (Iliffe 1979: 530).

Thus, since the advent of independence, the use of KiSwahili rather than English as the country's official language promoted national unity and social cohesion. By avoiding the creation of an elite class privileged to be educated in the colonial language, it also prevented an exacerbation of divisions between Muslims and Christians. Those who received an education in English did so at schools run by Christian missions, which meant that prior to independence, Western education in the colonial language was a privilege that Christians predominantly enjoyed. This was countered by the introduction of KiSwahili as the language of instruction and the nationalization of all mission schools. As Klugman *et al.* (1999: 77) point out, 'in many other colonies, the use of a colonial language contributed to the separation of a local elite from the rest of African society'. KiSwahili is also unique in that, unlike Setswana in Botswana, the national language is indigenous but not connected to a dominant ethnic group. As a hybrid language adopted for trade purposes over a long stretch of coastal territory from Somalia to Mozambique, it transcended the divisions associated with ethnic and tribal languages (Horton and Middleton 2000: 6–7). TANU's policy of promoting KiSwahili in this socially diverse territory was just one of many policies it adopted to manage difference and foster unity, in ways that still have currency today.

Political stability

Five decades of Tanzanian independence have posed myriad challenges to the country's stability. These include a wide range of potential social cleavages, widespread poverty, protracted periods of economic decline, and unsettling political and economic reform. Yet throughout the country's independent history, Tanzania has preserved political stability (Hughes 1963: 47; Klugman *et al.* 1999: 75; United Republic of Tanzania 2009: 176; Yeager 1982: 110). On the mainland, no major political or social crises have erupted, despite clear limits to the country's democratic transition. In this section, two key mitigating factors will be explored: TANU's and Nyerere's efforts to transcend social division through the forging of a unified national identity during the struggle for independence, and the consolidation of national unity following independence.

The move toward independence was anchored by Nyerere's inclusive ideology, which underpinned TANU's strategy of transcending ethnic and religious differences to forge a unified national identity. Nyerere was quick to promote the view of a future independent Tanganyika that was 'multi-racial', yet also to emphasize that its population was overwhelmingly African (Iliffe 1979: 517). This ran counter to Colonial Office policy at the time, which favoured European and Asian over African political representation (Iliffe 1979: 521). Nyerere's pro-African position gained widespread support, yet he was careful not to promote anti-European or -Asian sentiment in the process. Instead, he regarded all residents of the territory as equal citizens of an independent Tanganyika. As Nyerere himself stated, 'We are determined to see that those Asians and Europeans who have chosen to live permanently in Tanganyika shall enjoy the same political rights as everybody else' (Nyerere 1967: 43). Nyerere was effective in unifying the population around a largely African identity, but was also careful to include other minorities in the future of the territory, thus effectively steering TANU's independence campaign away from hatred or the stirring-up of grievances (Iliffe 1979: 536). Nyerere's relentless campaigning throughout the territory not only boosted his popularity, but gave rise to a campaign that was largely disciplined and peaceful. He insisted that the struggle for independence could not be won by conflict, pointing out that the independence movements of India and Ghana attained their goals non-violently. Nyerere's rhetoric won him popularity both in Tanganyika and at the UN, and ensured that relations with the colonial rulers remained cordial despite the clearly delineated differences (Iliffe 1979: 537). The transition of power from the former colonial rulers was implemented smoothly, without violence or upheaval. This created a strong foundation for post-independence stability.

After independence, the new government adopted a number of policies that aimed to promote greater equality (Klugman *et al.* 1999: 81). Such policies included the adoption of KiSwahili (as discussed earlier), the villagization schemes, and the establishment of numerous parastatals providing a wide range of services, including healthcare and education. The one-party government during the period of *Ujamaa* was ubiquitous from the capital to the local administration, and assumed the role of bureaucracy, party machine and civil society. Following the advent of *Ujamaa* in 1967, TANU consolidated its socialist approach to the historic neglect of the popular majority by dramatically expanding social services, particularly health and education. Using KiSwahili as the language of instruction, the government made the first seven years of schooling compulsory, and dramatically increased the provision of secondary schooling. It attempted to fast-track development by engineering more densely populated 'villages' and subsidizing the industrial sector. TANU, for all its failures during this period, did succeed in consolidating its role as the provider of the basic necessities.

TANU was also adept at both accommodating demands and limiting other alternatives by 'reducing or eliminating the autonomy of civil society organizations' (Klugman *et al.* 1999: 81). One example is the methods used for dealing with the union movement (Klugman *et al.* 1999: 81). Over time, TANU restricted the union movement and eventually succeeded in making it 'subordinate to government' (Klugman *et al.* 1999: 81). It outlawed organizations deemed incompatible with *Ujamaa*, particularly religious ones that prioritized internationalist agendas above the goal of national unity (Klugman *et al.* 1999: 81). Their balancing act of 'suppressing civil society' and 'accommodating demand' was effective for a time. In other words, during the first two decades of independence, the government did not neglect the concerns and activism of civil society; instead, it co-opted and monopolized them.

After *Ujamaa* was abandoned, some divisions did surface, occasionally resulting in violence. This mostly took the form of attacks against Asian Tanzanians (Kaiser 1996: 232–33), but it was never systematic, and never escalated into mass atrocities. One of the reasons why Tanzania's very limited democracy has not precipitated political instability on the mainland is the continued widespread support for the CCM. Hoffman and Robinson explored

Tanzanian citizens' complex approach to multi-party politics. Citing a 2008 Afrobarometer survey, they argue that although most Tanzanians (73 per cent) favour multi-party democracy, more than half (56 per cent) had little or no trust in opposition parties (Hoffman and Robinson 2010: 221). Although this lack of trust is in part a product of the constraints imposed on the opposition's ability to mobilize support, it is also due to the actions of the parties' members. For example, prominent mainland opposition leader Augustine Mrema, leader of the Tanzanian Labour Party (TLP),[18] spoiled his own electoral chances by erratic and sometimes illegal behaviour. NCCR-Mageuzi and the TLP accused him of housing CCM infiltrators. He also stole money and property from both opposition parties, using some of it to purchase a home. Consequently, his popularity dropped from 28 per cent in the 1995 presidential election to less than 1 per cent in 2005 (Hoffman and Robinson 2010: 233). The long tenure of the incumbent CCM since the first multi-party elections is a product of, among other things, broad electoral support, as well as the erstwhile failure of opposition parties to forge a credible challenge to power. Although a wide range of factors favour the incumbent government, the results of Afrobarometer's survey also suggest that the current status quo in politics reflects the will of the people. This raises doubt about the extent to which Tanzania's limited democracy poses a risk for the commission of mass atrocities.

In summary, as with Botswana and Zambia, Tanzania's stability owes much to its charismatic inaugural president, who similarly galvanized the population around a peaceful and inclusive independence struggle. Forging a new national identity, via an ideology that transcended division and effectively managed diversity, provided a strong foundation for the country in its formative years. With KiSwahili as the lingua franca, equitable provision of education and other services were instrumental in ensuring that when social divisions spilled over into violence in the post-*Ujamaa* era of structural adjustment and reform, such outbreaks were the exception rather than the norm. The legacy of national unity still permeates the political environment, and political parties based on ethnicity or religion are still prohibited. This has made it particularly difficult for social divisions to become formalized, and the relatively benign regional blocs reflect this. The risk of mass atrocities is mitigated by the inaugural leader's foundation of unity and inclusion.

Economic factors

As stated, three decades of economic liberalization have increased inequalities and deepened social divisions in Tanzania. Scapegoating by politicians in the early 1990s raised tensions between African Tanzanians and Indian traders, which on one occasion escalated violently. However, such scapegoating has been rare, and despite the benefits that some politicians have derived from it, such violence has been confined to a single incident in Dar es Salaam.

Moreover, an absence of horizontal inequalities has prevailed, despite popular perceptions. The inequality that emerged after economic liberalization was not, for the most part, manifested along ethnic, tribal or religious lines.

During the crucial decade of economic reforms beginning in the mid-1980s, rural inequality increased, but inequality in major urban centres did not. According to the World Bank, agricultural reform during this time benefited some farmers but disadvantaged others, leaving the very poor worse off in 1993 than they had been in 1983 (Ferreira 1996: 28–29). This inequality was 'due more to an increase of inequality within groups than between groups' (Ferreira 1996: vi). By the end of the 1990s, inequality had stabilized, remaining static throughout the first decade of the twenty-first century (United Republic of Tanzania 2009: xxii). Therefore, during the crucial period of economic decentralization and structural adjustment coinciding with the introduction of multi-party democratic reform, the increase in inequality for the most part did not provoke political or social division.

There are two major reasons for this. First, inequality increased in rural areas but not in urban centres, and had no pronounced horizontal character. This made it unlikely that political mobilization would occur around this issue. Those disadvantaged by such reforms were scattered throughout the country, rather than concentrated in large population areas where political mobilization was more likely. Moreover, the absence of an identity-based dimension to this inequality further decreased the possibility that it would trigger collective tensions and increase the risk of mass atrocities.

Second, the absence of scapegoating along ethnic and religious lines was a testament to Nyerere's and TANU's legacy of ensuring equitable opportunities, thereby creating a context where there were no visible economic differences among African ethnic groups, or members of different religions (Iliffe 1979: 571; Klugman *et al.* 1999: 80–81). Nyerere effectively prevented the emergence of a wealthy elite. Indian traders did have an advantage, but their position preceded the formation of the state of Tanzania, when the British colonial administration had favoured Indian involvement in commerce and trade, while prohibiting indigenous Africans from such economic activity (Klugman *et al.* 1999: 78).[19] The fact that no ethnic or religious group had been elevated since independence to take advantage of economic decentralization is a testament to Nyerere's nation-building project under the *Ujamaa* umbrella. *Ujamaa* promoted national unity through equitable provision of education and health, and its 'villagization' scheme compelled the coexistence of different ethnic and religious groups, particularly in rural areas where the rise in inequality was felt most acutely. Moreover, Nyerere was the architect of a national identity characterized by inclusion, not only of the diverse African groups, but also of Asian and British residents. This fostered an amicable change of power that was largely free of animosity and retribution (see, for example, Nyerere 1967). When Tanzania experienced its most profound shift in economic policy in the second half of the 1980s, this foundation of unity remained firm.

Risk factors for mass atrocities in Zanzibar

TANU's nearly two decades of socialist policies during *Ujamaa*, while failing to strengthen the country's economic credentials, did succeed in maintaining a relatively equitable foundation for social provision and economic opportunity. Tanzania's established record of low inequality also ensured that the level of inequality that emerged through structural adjustment and decentralization was limited, and considerably lower than other African states going through similar adjustments. Augmented by a broad range of inclusive policies of President Nyerere, including the fostering of cooperation between different ethnic and religious groups and the incorporation of KiSwahili as the national language, the first two decades of independence avoided elevating an elite group to take privilege in the spoils of rule and, consequentially, the emergence of economic inequality did not occur along identity lines. Collectively these processes mitigated the risk of mass atrocities.

Zanzibar, on the other hand, has experienced much greater political instability and risk of mass atrocities than any other region of Tanzania. According to Ramadhani, the archipelago displays 'most of the characteristics of a protracted and deep-seated ethnic conflict – the political divisions are superimposed on deeper racial/ethnic divisions embedded in territorially-defined horizontal inequalities' (Ramadhani 2011: 20). Zanzibar deserves a separate analysis for two reasons: first, it has a record of past atrocities, and second, in the last 20 years, it has experienced repeated election-related violence and widespread discrimination. This territory contains seven risk factors: social division, discrimination, human rights violations, past atrocities, limited democracy, limited rule of law and inequality of economic opportunity. This suggests a very high risk of the commission of mass atrocities in future. However, since 2001, tensions have significantly decreased, and by 2010 the political impasse that had crystallized division in the territory had been largely overcome. This section deploys the framework to examine risk in Zanzibar, and to account for why it did not escalate to the point of mass atrocity.

Social division

Prior atrocities

Zanzibar experienced a violent (albeit brief) revolution in January 1964, following independence in December 1963. The revolution followed the establishment of the Republic of Zanzibar and Pemba after an election strongly influenced by the former colonial rulers – the British gave the Arab population preferential treatment. Arab elites had ruled the islands under British supervision since 1890. The Arab-led ZNP, in coalition with the Pemba-based ZPPP, narrowly won the election, despite the African-supported ASP winning 54 per cent of the popular vote (Ramadhani 2011: 8). The African population, consisting of migrant workers and former slaves, had been repeatedly disenfranchised by the British, who had denied them representation on the Legislative Councils. Economically exploited, politically unrepresented and ethnically categorized through colour-coded identity cards (Brown 2010: 618), those in Zanzibar who identified as African (or of mixed African descent) mobilized around these grievances. As a consequence, ethnicity became the central variable by which political competition was defined (Lofchie 1965: 178–79). The ASP advocated for African majority rule, and regarded the election result as electoral manipulation by the British. The ZNP wanted to preserve the monarch in an Islamic state, and although they advanced a multi-racial platform, their leadership was exclusively Arab. Following ASP's electoral loss in 1964, a small group on the party's fringe instigated a revolution that overthrew the ZNP-ZPPP government and exiled the sultan. Following this, the revolutionaries inflicted violence on Arab and Indian citizens, killing between 5,000 and 12,000 (Brown 2010: 622; Coulson 1982: 133; Ramadhani 2011: 9). Thousands more were detained or expelled, property owned by Arabs and Indians was taken or destroyed, and larger properties were nationalized (Ramadhani 2011: 9). The ASP then established itself as the guardians of the revolution, a position which provided a basis for decades of retributive policies toward the Arab population.

Ethnic division

Social divisions on the two islands were entrenched not only by centuries of Arab economic and political dominance over the African population, but by the policies of the African-led ASP in the decades after the 1964 revolution. Despite this, ethnicity in Zanzibar is quite fluid. Many citizens who identify as African or Arab have a mixed heritage, and the ZNP attracted considerable African support on the island of Pemba. Thus, since the union with Tanganyika such division has also embodied a geographic dimension: the island of Pemba, with its diverse population of Arabs, Indians, Shirazis and Africans, has been marginalized politically and economically, apparently as punishment for its past support of the Arab-led ZNP (Ramadhani 2011: 12). Until 1992, all opposition parties in Pemba were banned, which resulted in the simmering of grievances that lacked any means of public expression. Consequently, when the ban on opposition parties was lifted, the CUF was established, with its support base largely in Pemba.

   The CUF consisted of key figures – predominantly of Arab background – who previously had been marginalized by the CCM (Minorities at Risk 2011). More broadly, political support for the CUF mirrored that of the former Arab-based parties of ZNP and ZPPP.[20] The constituencies that provided the support base for these parties in the early 1960s became enthusiastic supporters of the CUF (Kaiser 2003: 107).

   Like the ZNP-ZPPP coalition, the CUF drew much of its support from Pemba, while Zanzibar remained a stronghold for the CCM (Kaiser 2003:

107). While not ubiquitous, these social divisions were certainly prominent as tension between government and opposition increased throughout the 1990s. CUF supporters experienced ongoing harassment and intimidation by CCM supporters, whose actions had the 'implicit' support of the CCM government (Kaiser 2003: 108). CUF supporters also targeted CCM voters, attacking CCM offices and cars, and bombing government buildings (Hoffman 2010: 222–23). The new multi-party era of the early 1990s further entrenched social divisions as political competition and tensions between the two major political parties reignited older conflicts.

Discrimination and human rights violations

In 1964, a shift in the balance of power occurred, and the Arab and Indian populations of Zanzibar, along with the general population of Pemba, experienced widespread discrimination. Zanzibar's first president, Abeid Karume, introduced policies that oppressed non-African minorities. For example, it was compulsory for all Arabs and Indians to supply labour three nights a week and Sunday mornings. Although most of the region's revenue came from cloves (mostly grown in Pemba), the ASP diverted most of it to development projects on Unguja. There were no political representatives from Pemba, despite the fact that in 1964, many Pembans had voted for the ASP. Such discrimination widened divisions between the two islands to the extent that between 1964 and 1972, 10 per cent of the population fled Zanzibar (Brown 2010: 622–23).

From the outset of the multi-party era, CUF supporters experienced discrimination. Intimidation before the 1995 elections prompted many to flee Unguja to seek safety in Pemba, and hundreds lost their jobs on account of their support for the opposition party.[21] In addition, there was widespread harassment of CUF supporters, and CUF rallies were systematically banned (Amnesty International 2002: 4).

Discrimination and human rights violations against CUF supporters and Pemba residents at times spilled over into violence. The peak was the brutal crackdown on post-election demonstrations in January 2001, in which police (many of them brought over from the mainland) were ordered to use all necessary force to disband protestors on both islands. As a result, between 22 and 60 protesters were killed by police. Hundreds more were tortured, raped and sexually abused, and many reported police looting (Amnesty International 2002: 12–13; Brown 2010: 626; Human Rights Watch 2002: 3). Prior to the 2000 election, 18 members of the opposition were arrested and charged with treason, then held for three years without trial (Brown 2010: 625). Although such violations were not frequent, the CCM government demonstrated that it was prepared to intensify discrimination against opposition leaders and supporters – to incarcerate them and even to kill them. The escalation of violence and tension, and the entrenchment of social division, made the risk of mass atrocities acute.

Governance

These divisions were further aggravated when the incumbent government allegedly rigged successive elections in order to maintain the status quo enjoyed during the three decades of one-party rule. Consequently, the shift to multi-party democracy in Zanzibar was incomplete and marked by factional division. The rule of law was also limited in Zanzibar. These two characteristics of Zanzibar's governance further exacerbated the risk of mass atrocities, as it became clear that the Zanzibar government was prepared to use violence against opposition supporters.

Limited democracy

Zanzibar's limited democracy was most apparent in the CCM's determination to remain in power by manipulating the elections held in 1995, 2000 and 2005. Following the institutionalization of the multi-party system in 1992, the CUF was established in Zanzibar. It aimed to challenge both the elected members of the CCM,[22] and the position of president of Zanzibar. Although many of its key figures were former members of the Zanzibar branch of the CCM who had fallen afoul of the ruling party, the CUF also drew supporters from the mainland, in an attempt to broaden its support base beyond the Muslim-dominant population of the islands (Human Rights Watch 2002). Its losses in 1995, 2000 and 2005 were controversial, as all three elections were marked by allegations of irregularities. The campaigns preceding them produced numerous reports of intimidation by the army and police, with allegations ranging from arrests of CUF members to sacking of members from government posts. The incumbent government's complicity in elections deemed inadequate by international observers provoked major political instability on the islands, triggering an opposition boycott of parliament and numerous demonstrations, culminating in deadly violence in early 2001.

The 1995 elections in Zanzibar were marred by allegations of multiple irregularities (Commonwealth Secretariat 2000: 33; Lodge *et al.* 2002: 413–16; Masterson 2009: 546–49). These included irregularities in the voter registration process, hold-ups in the provision of voting materials, and interference by the police and army in vote counting (Human Rights Watch 2002: 6). In the run-up to the 1995 elections, it was clear there would be two main contenders: the CUF and the CCM. Both major parties disagreed on many aspects of the voting process, including the printing of ballots, the access the opposition should have to state-run media, the voter registration process and the composition of the Zanzibar Electoral Commission (ZEC) (Kaiser 2003). The CUF also complained about political intimidation during the election campaign. The most controversial issue was the way in which the ZEC handled the vote counting and the announcement of the results. Initial and unofficial results given to both parties indicated that the CUF chairman, Saif Sherif Hamad, had narrowly defeated the CCM leader, Salmin Amour. Contending that such a result would 'reverse' the revolution of 1964 and restore 'Arab' power, the CCM demanded that the ZEC not release the results straight away. After a four-day delay, the final results were declared by the ZEC. Amour had won the position of vice-president with 50.2 per cent of the vote, narrowly defeating Hamad (Anglin 2000: 43). The UN International Observer Group concluded that, given the slim margin of the CCM victory, the results were probably distorted (United Nations 1995). Of the 50 National Assembly seats reserved for Zanzibar, 26 went to the CCM, and the remaining 24 to the CUF. The legacy of the 1964 violent revolution was clear in the way the 1995 elections unfolded. Political competition occurred along the same social and territorial divisions of the pre-1964 period. When the CCM, which regarded itself as guardian of the revolution (Anglin 2000: 42), was confronted with the possibility of electoral defeat by a party perceived to represent the interests of the pre-revolutionary ZNP-ZPPP coalition, its strategy was to hold onto power at any cost.

The 1995 elections escalated tensions between the two main parties, creating a dangerous impasse. The CUF refused to recognize the results, and their elected MPs boycotted parliament. In 1997, 18 CUF leaders were arrested and charged with treason. With the ongoing intimidation of CUF supporters on both Pemba and Unguja, a political impasse was entrenched which lasted four years. In 1999, after talks mediated by the Commonwealth Secretariat, an agreement[23] was reached to review electoral laws and foster a more equitable environment for the 2000 elections. However, this agreement was ultimately ignored by Amour and the CCM (Commonwealth Secretariat 2010: 5).

The 2000 elections proved even more contentious. Election observers, both local and international, described them as 'more corrupt and more rigged than those in 1995' (Ramadhani 2011: 14). Many polling stations opened late, some as late as midday, causing tensions between voters and officials staffing the stations. The ZEC engaged in highly irregular practices, such as suspending counting at some polls and cancelling it at others. It nullified the vote in a total of 16 electoral areas (representing 42 per cent of the total electorate), and announced a re-run. When this occurred a week later, the CUF called for a boycott (Pottie 2002: 346–47). The official results firmly favoured the CCM, with their presidential candidate, Amani Abeid Karume, winning 67 per cent of the vote, and the CCM taking two-thirds of the seats in the National Assembly. These results were questioned by international observers. The report of the Commonwealth Secretariat stated that 'the conduct of the elections fell far short of minimum standards', and concluded that 'the cause was either deliberate manipulation or gross incompetence' (Commonwealth Secretariat 2000: 33). The CUF responded swiftly, with supporters organizing protest rallies on the islands of Pemba and Unguja. CUF leaders were then arrested and assaulted in custody. During the protests that followed, up to 70 people were killed by security forces. More than 2,200 residents fled from Pemba to Kenya, with a refugee camp being set up in Mombasa (FEWER 2005: 2).

Electoral violence in Zanzibar peaked in 2001. Subsequent elections have been more peaceful, although tensions simmered until 2010, when both parties agreed to a power-sharing arrangement. The election of 2005 was characterized once again by violence, with attacks by both opposition supporters against alleged CCM supporters and police against opposition supporters (Ramadhani 2011: 15). One fatality resulted. Irregularities in voting procedures resurfaced, prompting a re-run that the CCM vice-presidential candidate, Amani Abeid Karume, again won narrowly with 54 per cent of the vote. The CUF again refused to recognize the outcome (Commonwealth Secretariat 2010: 8; Polity IV 2008b). Despite this, the election did not provoke the kind of violence that occurred in 2000. Eventually, after talks between the CUF and the CCM in late 2009, a power-sharing arrangement – establishing a government of national unity – was reached. The move prompted bilateral support for a referendum on the introduction of such an arrangement. On 31 July 2010, 66.4 per cent of the population in Zanzibar voted in favour, and the Zanzibar Constitution was altered as a result (Commonwealth Secretariat 2010: 9). In the subsequent October elections, observers noted considerable improvement in the campaigning, registration and procedures on poll day, though some concerns remained (Commonwealth Secretariat 2010: 33).

The incumbent CCM's preference until 2010 was to deny the opposition CUF free and fair electoral competition through a combination of electoral irregularities and violent intimidation. As in the years preceding Zanzibar's independence, elections provided a forum for divisive political competition (see, for example, Kuper 1977: 162–67). This re-opened tensions that had been largely contained since the 1963 revolution. It also demonstrated how far the CCM was willing to go to ensure political dominance. Zanzibar's democratic limitations brought social cleavages to the surface. However, it was the limited rule of law that transformed these tensions into violence, with the police responding arbitrarily and with impunity to demonstrators, killing scores and injuring hundreds.

Limited rule of law

Over the last two decades, the rule of law in Zanzibar has been weak. Law enforcement has often been used by the ruling CCM to restrict the opposition's ability to campaign. In addition, it has frequently arrested opposition leaders, including CUF Chairman Hamad, and detained them for long periods without charge. This reached a nadir in early 2001, when the police turned on the islands' unarmed citizens. Police were brought over from the mainland to suppress opposition demonstrations on both Pemba and Unguja. According to Human Rights Watch, police were given explicit orders to use violence, with the regional police commissioner for Unjuga instructing them that killing was preferable to bringing back unused bullets. He was alleged to have commanded his forces: 'Kill, bring back bodies, then we will know that you have done your job' (Human Rights Watch 2002: 10–11). The police 'went on a rampage, indiscriminately arresting, beating and sexually abusing island residents' (Human Rights Watch 2002: 3). More than 35 people were killed and over 600 injured (Human Rights Watch 2002: 3). This was an extreme instance of the police doing the government's bidding – a tendency which existed throughout Tanzania, but with far greater brutality in Zanzibar. In short, a government reticent to engage in genuine democratic reform, coupled with a police force partial to the government's wishes, precipitated the violence that followed the 2000 elections. The police specifically targeted planned protests in four locations around Zanzibar. Thereafter, the crack-down eased, though in its immediate wake many were prevented from seeking medical attention, while others were arrested and charged with 'participating in an illegal demonstration' (Human Rights Watch 2002: 13–35).

This has had far-reaching effects on the two islands. Tension between police and voters was still evident in the most recent elections, held in 2010. The report of the Commonwealth Observer Group alleged that the army had also intimidated voters (Commonwealth Secretariat 2010: 9). While the police were less provocative in 2010, the general atmosphere of tension reflected the historical pattern of intimidation and partiality in favour of the ruling party.

Economic weakness

Economic inequality

Horizontal economic inequality was evident in the CCM's long-term neglect of Pemba Island. The re-surfacing of tensions during electoral competitions in the 1990s was underscored by decades of economic discrimination that deprived Pemba of wealth and disproportionately benefited Unguja – a trend that began with the 1964 revolution, even though Pemba's clove industry was Zanzibar's biggest source of revenue (see, for example, Ramadhani 2011: 12; Sheriff 2001: 315). Infrastructure on Pemba has been neglected, with the state of roads and tourist services, as well as air and sea transport, considerably inferior to Unguja (Ramadhani 2011: 12). The supply of electricity provides a particularly stark contrast between the islands. Unguja was connected to the national grid in the 1970s, whereas this did not occur in Pemba until 2007 (Mohamed 2007). Prior to that time, the island depended on diesel generators (Brown 2010: 627). The clove industry is tightly controlled by the CCM – the government sets the price for farmers' crops (often as low as 7 per cent of global prices), and uses much of the revenue for development on Unguja (Sheriff 2001: 315). These differences are reflected in poverty rates for both islands. Some 64 per cent of the population of Pemba lives below the poverty line, compared to 59 per cent in Unguja (Pearson 2009: 6). Since the 1964 revolution, the CCM/ASP has routinely punished both Zanzibaris of Arab descent, and Pembans in general. Arabs lost property and businesses in the 1960s, and Pemba was deprived of the fruits of its own wealth. These factors created new grievances in a period of autocratic one-party rule, at a time when no opportunity existed to voice them. Consequently, three decades of economic discrimination, coupled with political discrimination, deepened longstanding social cleavages, which then became the focal point for political struggle in the multi-party era. In short, economic inequality and discrimination further politicized identity on Pemba, renewing old tensions and increasing the risk of violence and mass atrocity.

Appraising risk in Zanzibar

A number of features place Zanzibar at high risk of future atrocity. These include a history of past atrocities, entrenched social divisions, discrimination and corresponding economic inequalities, an incumbent government unwilling to surrender power in an era of political reform and democratic transition, and a police force willing to resort to deadly violence on behalf of the government. The social cleavages that underscored the atrocities in 1964 were still apparent in the 1990s, with the new opposition party, the CUF, drawing much of its support from the same areas as the former ZNP-ZPPP coalition. However, violence peaked after the January 2001 crackdown, and although tension simmered (and the dispute remained unresolved) for nearly a decade after, violence never approached the levels seen in 1964. In 2010, the government and opposition came to a power-sharing agreement, and as a consequence the elections of that year were held with little violence reported. Tensions have subsided considerably, and the risk of atrocities has been reduced accordingly. The next section will explain both how the risk of mass atrocities was mitigated and managed over the last decade, and why the escalating tensions of the 1990s and the violence of 2001 did not produce atrocities on the scale of the 1964 revolution.

Resilience in Zanzibar

Since 2001, four major factors have effectively mitigated the risk of mass atrocities in Zanzibar. First, a political agreement, the *Maridhiano*, was reached based on a common vision of Zanzibar's autonomy. This was a significant development, given the long history of ethnic and racial divisions. Second, since 2001 the CCM under Karume's leadership has made genuine efforts to reach an accord with the CUF, opening the way to the negotiations that culminated in the *Maridhiano*. Third, the agreement of 2010 led to constitutional changes which strengthened democratic representation. Finally, in the decade following 2001, the CCM, under Karume, implemented policies that redressed many economic inequalities.

Social cohesion

Ethnic inclusion premised on Zanzibari unity

Rapprochement between the government and opposition was finally achieved after both sides agreed to abide by a shared idea of Zanzibari unity. Unlike previous negotiation processes, the *Maridhiano* yielded substantial changes – most significantly, a joint commitment to form a government of national unity. It was successful not only in resolving a longstanding political impasse, but in transcending decades of social division. One aspect of the *Maridhiano* that distinguished itself from other negotiations was the decision by Karume to bypass the mainland CCM by inviting Hamad to a private meeting at the State House in November 2009. The gesture was significant for two reasons. First, one of the obstacles in the previous failed processes was the CUF's suspicion of mainland CCM involvement, and a belief that negotiations would be steered toward the interests of the mainland. As Ramadhani points out, 'inter-party negotiations were seen to be driven by the Mainland and people in Zanzibar were not entirely happy about such a development' (Ramadhani 2011: 18). The CUF's political appeal was partly based on its strong position on Zanzibari autonomy, a factor that provoked the CCM to accuse it of seeking to secede and form an 'Arab-led' Islamic state. Second, the Zanzibar CCM has also insisted on Zanzibari autonomy. This has frequently led to tension between the archipelago and Dar es Salaam, but it is notable that both government and opposition support the autonomist stance and distrust the mainland CCM. Although it was CCM policy for all negotiations in Zanzibar to be approved by Dar es Salaam, the breakthrough came when this process was bypassed. For the local CCM, this was a way of asserting its autonomy credentials, while for the CUF it offered an assurance that terms were not being dictated by the mainland.[24]

Good governance

Change of leadership

The change of leadership from Amour to Karume in 2000 was instrumental in bringing about a gradual decline in tension and eventually a political resolution to the conflict. While Karume's inauguration preceded the deadly police crackdown of demonstrators in January 2001, the following decade was characterized by committed efforts to find common ground with the CUF, and moves to redress inequalities. This was in stark contrast to his predecessor, Amour, who had displayed intransigence and a determination to hold onto power at whatever cost, despite the return to multi-party politics.

Following the controversial 1995 election results, and the CUF boycott of parliament, Amour took a 'hard-line' position characterized by 'intolerance of any opposition, ... intimidation and outright thuggery' (Brown 2010: 626). He repeatedly refused offers of third-party mediation, even when the CUF expressed a willingness to agree to terms that clearly advantaged the CCM. Offers of mediation by the Organization of African Unity (OAU, later replaced by the AU), the UNDP, the EU and the Commonwealth Secretariat were categorically rejected (Anglin 2000: 46–50). Even the mainland CCM was reluctant to intervene, concerned that both the CCM and the CUF in Zanzibar 'were not above playing the separatist card' (Anglin 2000: 47). Nyerere went further, declaring that Amour refused to acknowledge that any problem existed. President Mkapa, dependent on Amour's bloc votes to secure his own position in 1995, declined to intervene. The Commonwealth Secretariat's special envoy, Dr Moses Anafu, finally persuaded Amour to endorse an agreement between the two parties in 1999, but the negotiations soon collapsed, mainly due to Amour's reluctance to implement changes and cease harassing opposition supporters (Anglin 2000: 47).

Karume, on the other hand, was open to third-party mediation, and far more willing to reach a mutual agreement. In his first year of office he created a commission to supervise negotiations that fostered joint talks for four years, ending in September 2005 (Brown 2010: 627). Although the talks were ultimately abandoned, they marked a substantial improvement on previous negotiations, for two reasons. First, Karume openly invited third-party involvement, which resulted in the Commonwealth Secretariat playing a more instrumental role. Second, the lead-up to the 2005 elections contrasted sharply with the period before the 2000 elections. There was less tension and far less violence. Although the results were again disputed, with international observers claiming widespread irregularities, it was also believed that the results were notably closer to reality than those of 2000. Despite the CUP's rejection of the results, the opposition party's rhetoric was far less inflammatory, and the CCM did not ordain a violent police crackdown along the lines of 2001. Although negotiations failed, they had made progress in addressing the grievances and tensions that had resurfaced in the early 1990s. In short, Amour's autocratic rule, and his belief that the CCM were guardians of the 1964 revolution,[25] escalated tensions and provoked violence. By contrast, Karume promised a greater willingness to negotiate and to engage in genuine democratic reform. This approach was even more notable considering the relations that Karume had with the mainland CCM. Karume was the first choice of the mainland CCM's Central Committee, which had the effect of overruling CCM Zanzibar's choice of Dr Gharib Bilal as Zanzibar's president in 2000 (Ramadhani 2011: 17). Karume sidelined his obligations to the mainland CCM when he acted independently to bring about a rapprochement with the CUF. As a key mitigator of risk, this helped to ease tensions between CCM and CUF supporters over the decade following the 2001 violence.

Democratic reform

Another factor that mitigated the risk of mass atrocities after 2001 was the major political reform that the *Maridhiano* heralded. This was the establishment of a Government of National Unity (GNU) to replace the existing 'winner-take-all' system. The agreement promised the kind of genuine power sharing that had been absent in previous agreements. A referendum held in

July 2010 resulted in 67 per cent of the electorate approving the new arrangement (Ramadhani 2011: 19). According to the GNU, the winning party took the office of the president, while the runner-up party became the 'first vice-president'.[26] The Cabinet would be determined by the proportion of seats won by each party (Ramadhani 2011: 19).

This new arrangement presaged the elections of 31 October 2010, which were reported to be the most peaceful since the re-introduction of multi-party political competition. Despite some confusion on Pemba, the widespread irregularities of previous elections were notably absent (Commonwealth Secretariat 2010: 30–31). The Commonwealth Observer Group also reported a much-improved political atmosphere in the lead-up to the elections, although it noted that a fully functioning multi-party system did not yet exist. The CCM continued to enjoy an overwhelming advantage, particularly in terms of access to campaign finances and media coverage (Commonwealth Secretariat 2010: 33). The improved conduct of all actors during the 2010 elections in Zanzibar indicated that the new power-sharing arrangement had muted longstanding political disputes and significantly decreased tensions on both Pemba and Unguja. The conduct of the election and the widespread acceptance of the results indicate that these democratic reforms have had a positive impact on the islands' political stability, mitigating the risk of future atrocities.

Economic inclusion

Since the early 2000s, Karume has sought to address the economic inequalities that had deepened on Pemba since 1964. These had been the result of ASP/CCM leaders punishing the island economically for its 'Arab-led' opposition movement. Karume increased spending on health and education, building new schools and medical centres. At the same time, he increased investment in the island's tourism industry, which had hitherto been concentrated on Unguja. After the collapse of negotiations in 2005, the renewed investment in Pemba continued, including a project finally to connect the island to the national electricity grid, begun in 2007 (Brown 2010: 627). The subsequent GNU arising out of the *Maridhiano* further consolidated this economic rebalancing through a change in the price paid for cloves, Pemba's main revenue source. With the island's trade restricted by the CCM-run Zanzibar State Trading Corporation (ZSTC), the price offered to producers remained significantly lower than global market prices (Nayar 2009). Now Zanzibar's vice-president, CUF leader Hamad, declared that farmers would receive 80 per cent of the world market price (Nyanje 2011). This move coincided with greater dialogue between the CUF and the CCM, as well as a substantial decrease in violence. Following the crafting of the GNU in 2010, economic reform in the clove industry raised further revenue for the island, in the process mitigating the risk of future mass atrocities.

Resilience in Zanzibar

Zanzibar's high level of risk highlights the province's greater political instability. The mitigation of such risk has been a long process of trial and error. Three series of negotiations were needed finally to bring about a mutually acceptable agreement. However, after two decades of tension and sporadic violence, three factors emerged that mitigated risk in Zanzibar. Karume's leadership heralded more genuine efforts to seek a workable agreement. Karume also initiated many projects to improve infrastructure and economic opportunity on neglected Pemba. Finally, the agreement between the CCM and the CUF was premised on Zanzibari unity and autonomy. This marked the first time that a sense of a shared yet distinct Zanzibari identity was embraced by both parties. The agreement led to democratic reform and the formation of a GNU. As a result, a more inclusive political regime now exists, and the tensions that characterized Zanzibari politics have, for now, subsided.

Conclusion

Tanzania displays many key risk factors for mass atrocities. On the mainland, it has experienced growing social divisions, limited democracy and rule of law, and growing economic inequality. In Zanzibar, risk has been more acute, with evidence of past atrocities, social division, discrimination, human rights violations, limited democracy and rule of law, and economic inequality. The limits to the democratic transition on both the mainland and Zanzibar are especially concerning. It is this factor, in particular, that led the CIDCM in 2012 to rank Tanzania ninth on its list of states at greatest risk of political instability (Hewitt 2012: 5). Compounding this risk is Tanzania's geographical location. For decades, the surrounding region has endured civil wars, genocides and other atrocities.

Despite these risk factors, Tanzania is regarded as a politically stable country (Klugman *et al.* 1999; Rasmussen 1993). The relative absence of discrimination and entrenched division was clearly the product of Tanganyika's particular process of decolonization and early nation building. TANU's incorporation of minorities into a unified nation during the struggle for independence set a precedent for a non-exclusive national identity. Nyerere's vision of inter-ethnic and religious harmony was also instrumental. Like Botswana and Zambia, mainland Tanzania benefited greatly from a charismatic inaugural leader with an inclusive ideology. Following independence, the use of KiSwahili as the national language, together with the policy of *Ujamaa*, ensured equitable access to education and other services. The socialist structures of *Ujamaa* meant that no significant gap between rich and poor emerged during the first two decades of independence. Even when market-based reforms and austerity measures produced greater inequality from the mid-1980s onward, the gap between rich and poor remained low compared to other states in the region. Overall, Tanzania's strong foundation of ethnic and religious harmony has been instrumental in managing diversity since the political and economic reforms of the 1980s and 1990s. While these changes contributed to greater tensions, on the mainland they rarely produced violence, and when they did, it was sporadic and exceptional.

Given its distinctive historical circumstances, it is unsurprising that the process of risk mitigation differed in Zanzibar. The establishment of a GNU in 2010 improved the archipelago's democratic system and made it more inclusive. Most influential here was Zanzibari President Karume. In marked contrast to his predecessor, he was committed to negotiations with the CUF. Investment in infrastructure on the neglected island of Pemba reduced economic inequalities. Tanzania also exerted a stabilizing influence over Zanzibar when tensions escalated into violence in early 2001. Although mainland police were partly culpable in the violence against demonstrators in January of that year, the union's resources and influence provided surety against violent regime change accompanied by atrocities like those of the 1964 revolution. Overall, however, differences between mainland Tanzania and Zanzibar demonstrate how important local dynamics are to understanding risk and resilience.

Like the cases of Botswana and Zambia, the case of Tanzania demonstrates that the framework's distinction between risk factors and mitigating factors is often unclear in practice. Nyerere's introduction of *Ujamaa* in 1967 fostered harmony and cooperation amongst the country's diverse tribal, ethnic and religious groups. The new regime favoured no particular identity group above others, creating a strong foundation for equality. However, *Ujamaa* was also responsible for costly and inefficient economic practices. Subsidized industries drained the resources of the government to the extent that it was no longer able to sustain its commitment to service provision. Consequently, poverty remained intractable and the country became increasingly dependent on international aid. This led to the introduction of structural adjustment programmes in the mid-1980s, prompting the privatization of much of the public sector. As a result, inequality grew, as did social divisions. Nevertheless, the preceding two decades of equitable service provision ensured that no particular identity group was positioned to capitalize on this privatization process, and thus that a gap between rich and poor did not coalesce along ethnic or religious lines. Although the Asian community was able to accumulate wealth from privatization, increasing tensions in Dar es Salaam, this did not result in widespread scapegoating. Clearly Nyerere's early socialist policies were ambiguous in their impact, but their unifying foundation cushioned the destabilizing potential of the risks they created.

Notes

1 Ethnic and religious division, limited democracy, limited rule of law, and a growing inequality of economic opportunity in the face of protracted and widespread poverty.

2   Social division, discrimination, human rights violations, past atrocities, limited democracy, limited rule of law and economic inequality.

3   Tanganyika refers to the mainland territory which did not include Zanzibar. When the two territories united in 1964, it was renamed the United Republic of Tanzania.

4   Zanzibar consists of a number of small islands and two large islands: Unguja, sometimes referred to as Zanzibar Island, and Pemba.

5   These reforms were instigated virtually unchallenged, despite the existence of opposition. The TANU government was structured in such a way that dissent by any MPs from executive-led legislation in the National Assembly would trigger expulsion from the party, which automatically resulted in dismissal from parliament, as the constitution sanctioned single-party rule. See, for example, Tambila 2004: 61.

6   The 1973 oil crisis and the war with Uganda in 1979 were both significantly draining for Tanzania.

7   This process was escalated considerably by Nyerere's successor, Ali Hassan Mwinyi.

8   Translated, it means Party of the Revolution.

9   The constitution states that 30 per cent of seats in the National Assembly must be held by women. This means that each party represented in the Assembly appoints women parliamentarians in proportion to the number of seats the party has won. Given the CCM's hitherto significant electoral advantage, they have appointed the vast majority of these women representatives.

10 The MP who had led the offensive against Mbilinyi.

11 The conversation about political reform occurred around the time that Eastern European socialist states were undergoing democratic change. A similar climate towards multi-party politics was also evident in Africa, with neighbouring Zambia changing its constitution in 1991 to permit the existence of opposition parties, prior to the resumption of multi-party elections in 1992.

12 It is important to note that the poverty line in Tanzania is determined by the cost of goods normally consumed by poor households. This is calculated to be 500 Tanzanian Shillings a day, or just over US$0.31. To put this into broader perspective, the proportion of Tanzania's population living on less than $1.25 a day is 88.52 per cent. See, for example, Policy Forum 2011; UNDP 2011.

13 This raised suspicion for two reasons. First, the OIC was a pan-Islamic organization, and therefore symbolized an Islamic shift away from the secular state. Second, it marked a radical departure from the traditional understanding that membership with international organizations was a foreign policy responsibility and could only be made by the union as a whole. This move was thus seen by many mainland MPs as compromising the integrity of the union.

14 Such instability includes revolution, civil war and military overthrow of a government – all associated with the commission of mass atrocities.

15 See Chapter 3.

16 All mission schools were nationalized by the late 1960s.

17 One exception, as mentioned previously, was Indian traders in 1993.

18 Prior to this he was leader and presidential candidate of the NCCR-Mageuzi, a party he joined after being a member of the CCM government, where he held three ministerial posts and was for a time deputy prime minister.

19 It is important to note that Indian traders and businesspeople constitute a very small minority in Tanzania, meaning their relative wealth has little statistical significance. Moreover, this economic advantage does not extend to politics. Thus, on one hand, the inclusiveness of the Tanzanian state ensured that Indian traders would not be the target of the kind of violence to which they were subjected in neighbouring Uganda, and on the other that economic advantage did not buy political advantage in the United Republic of Tanzania.

20 These parties won a disputed election in 1963, a result that triggered the violent revolution supported by African Zanzibaris. Up to 20,000 people were killed in the ensuing violence. Following the merging with Tanganyika in 1963, the African-dominated ASP formed a coalition with mainland TANU, eventually uniting to create the CCM.

21 This discrimination continued until the 2005 elections, although its frequency decreased after 2001.

22 In addition to having members elected to the National Assembly, Zanzibar has a separate House of Representatives with 50 seats. Like the National Assembly, members serve five-year terms.

23 Known as the *Muafaka*.

24 Much of this suspicion is a result of the 2001 violent crackdown on opposition demonstrations. Police were brought over from the mainland, and it was believed that this contingent did most of the killing. A religious dimension also featured, as most of the policemen were non-Muslim. See, for example, Human Rights Watch 2002: 10.

25 In addition to this, he believed that the CUF embodied the same Arab-led threat to power in Zanzibar, and thus a threat to reverse everything for which the 'guardian of the revolution' stood.

26 A second vice-president comes from the president's party.

Conclusion

In this book, I set out to understand why genocide and other mass atrocities have not been committed in three countries that have exhibited at least a moderate level of risk. In doing so, I sought to reveal the ways in which these countries utilize local and national sources of resilience to mitigate risk. I argued that a revised concept of structural prevention is needed, to understand the relationship between risk and resilience, because the commonly accepted approach – the identifying and addressing of root causes – tends to overlook domestic actors and processes that have a protective dimension. Limiting structural prevention to a focus on root causes puts such strategies at odds with the findings of key scholars in comparative genocide studies, who claim that the relationship between root causes and violent outcomes is tenuous at best. Despite the consensus that such structural risk factors do not lead inevitably to mass atrocities, until now very little attention has been paid to what goes on in countries where (a) such root causes exist, and (b) mass atrocities have not occurred. The analyses of Botswana, Zambia and Tanzania may help to shift scholarly attention onto negative cases. Moreover, asking why atrocities have not occurred supplies numerous insights into understanding how such violence has been prevented. This, in turn, yields greater knowledge about how similar processes of risk mitigation may proceed in the future.

I argued that the way that structural prevention has been conceptualized is too rigid and limited. There is a broad consensus in various reports and scholarly publications that long-term prevention involves identifying and ameliorating root causes. There is also a general agreement that prevention is carried out primarily by international actors. Another assumption is that the presence of risk factors suggests an inevitably violent outcome if the risks are not addressed. Consequently, there is little consideration of how local and national actors contribute to stability and resilience. Occasionally these gaps are mentioned in passing, or considered as an afterthought. Ban Ki-moon, for example, identifies it as an area that needs further research (Ban 2009a: 10–11), while Wolter (2007: 50), writing about the UN and conflict prevention, points out that little attention is given to what goes *right*. The Human Security Report also points out that while the causes of war receive much attention, very little is written about the causes of peace.

Scholarly research into the causes of genocide and mass atrocities appears to bolster such an approach in two ways. First, risk factors – or the pre-conditions of mass atrocities, as they are commonly referred to – are necessary but not sufficient causes. Most scholars contended that such factors do not directly cause mass atrocities, but instead provide a more fertile context for other, more alarming causal factors to take hold. Second, the research overwhelmingly identifies these risk factors as local and national in character – revolving around identity-based local dynamics, and the practices of local and national institutions. Accordingly, it is logical to derive solutions to such challenges from local contexts, not primarily from international actors, which have been prioritized in the prevention literature. I conclude, then, that the concept of structural prevention needs to be broadened to incorporate an understanding not only of risk factors, but of factors promoting resilience and stability. To test such an understanding, I devised an analytical framework that seeks to incorporate these complex dynamics, and sought to apply it to the cases of Botswana, Zambia and Tanzania. All these states are located in a region scourged by numerous civil wars and mass atrocities, and all exhibit some of the risk factors associated with mass atrocities.

The framework synthesizes two main strands of research: one on the risk factors of mass atrocities, and another on the factors that promote stability and resilience in states. While there is a wealth of knowledge to draw on regarding risk factors, research focusing on the causes of stability is much more scarce. Therefore, the framework itself has limitations. It cannot settle the question of which factors foster stability, nor can it isolate the precise relationship between risk and resilience. Indeed, the three cases reveal a range of processes that extend beyond the categories identified in the framework. The framework's value, perhaps, lies in its illumination of the relationship between risk and resilience in diverse communities and states.

Transition to independence: the inclusionary ideologies of inaugural leaders

The investigation yielded some key commonalities. First, in the decades pre-ceding independence, the liberation movements in each territory were led by individuals who worked to construct broad and inclusive national identities. In Botswana, Seretse Khama spearheaded the push for a modern centralized democratic state. He succeeded in gaining the consent of all the major chieftaincies to relinquish their political control and rights to mineral resources. In Zambia, Kenneth Kaunda stressed a new Zambian identity, transcending tribe and language. The UNIP-led struggle stressed the idea of 'One Zambia, One Nation', and was careful to secure the support of regional leaders across the territory. A similar unifying ideology was fostered by Julius Nyerere during the 1950s in colonial Tanganyika. More than a decade before independence, Nyerere was at pains to ensure that TANU reflected the territory's diversity, notably by ensuring that Muslims and Christians were fairly represented at both the grassroots and leadership levels. Even in Botswana, where limitations to this inclusiveness were evident, national identity was supported by eight major chieftaincies, without whose backing the state could not have been founded.

In all three states, the process of decolonization was characterized by amicable relations with the British colonial administrators. In Botswana, the transition to independence was characterized by a friendship between Seretse Khama and Resident Commissioner Peter Fawcus. They both advocated for a common voters' role, ensuring that Botswana would benefit from a more democratic foundation than neighbouring South Africa and Rhodesia, both of which disenfranchised the majority of their citizens. This amicable transition was instrumental in bolstering Khama's new government, as it encouraged many former colonial civil servants to continue their work under the new administration. This was especially crucial at the outset of the independence period, when Botswana's indigenous population lacked sufficient expertise in public administration. In Zambia, Kaunda and UNIP faced the challenge of a substantial expatriate population reluctant to relinquish its political privileges. Yet instead of mobilizing an independence movement with a call to overthrow the oppressive rulers, Kaunda emphasized the need for unity and peace. In Tanzania, Nyerere repeatedly stressed that an independent Tanganyika would welcome not only Africans, but also Europeans and Asians. While no group in Tanganyika would enjoy privilege over others, those who had been advantaged in colonial times – notably Asians and Europeans – would not be punished. The peaceful and amicable decolonization process allowed these new states to avoid wars of liberation, and likewise avoided the formation of national identities premised on division and retribution.

In all three states, a peaceful transition to independence was followed by the implementation of policies that prioritized the equitable provision of essential services. In Botswana, this was apparent in the rapid expansion of education and health services. Primary school was made compulsory, and within a decade this sparsely populated country had determined that every citizen, even in the remotest communities, was within 15 km of a health clinic. In addition, the country's merit-based system of recruitment for the public sector ensured that no position was reserved for members of the same tribe or ethnic group. As a consequence, members of minorities such as the Kalanga benefited enormously. Zambia's first decade of independence enjoyed strong economic growth, and a rapid expansion of public services to provide education and health for all provinces. At the same time, President Kaunda was engaged in a constant ethnic reshuffling of political and public-sector positions. This was done to avoid the tendency of members of particular ethno-linguistic groups stacking ministries and other public offices with members of their own group. Such a prospect would have undoubtedly fomented discontent and aggravated social division. In Tanzania, Nyerere's introduction of *Ujamaa* precipitated large-scale social planning that compelled members of different tribal and language groups, as well as Christians and Muslims, to live and work together.

The transition to independence and the consolidation of unifying national identities through inclusive policies were very much based on the visions held by Khama, Kaunda and Nyerere. This in itself highlights the importance of individual agency in the long-term prevention of mass atrocities. Much has been written about individual agency in relation to the perpetration of genocide and other mass atrocities, as architects of exclusionary ideologies, and as primary planners of genocidal actions. While the body of literature on rescuers and other resisters to genocide and mass atrocities is steadily growing, the role of individual leaders in preventing such violence, particularly in places where social fault lines could be exploited, is profoundly understudied. The three cases explored in this book highlight how significant were the ideas and actions of the three inaugural leaders in establishing broad and unifying national identities, and then in initiating a raft of inclusive social policies (albeit with varying degrees of success). In fact, these leaders were not only effective in fostering national identities that transcended tribal and religious differences; they were also able to appeal to an identity beyond the state, encapsulated in the idea of pan-Africanism.

Risk and resilience: a complex dynamic

These cases also demonstrate that some of the policies that sought to foster greater cohesion actually led to an increased risk of mass atrocities, through inequality, inefficiency, economic decline and limitations on democracy. In Botswana, gaining the support of the eight major chieftains was a critical achievement in establishing the new state, but many minority groups grew further marginalized, aggravating the immense economic inequalities that already existed between members of the larger chieftaincies and the smaller groups. The San, the Wayeyi and the Bakgalagadi were not represented in the newly established House of Chiefs. In addition, the process of land privatization initiated by the Tribal Grazing Land Policy further restricted the ability of the San and Bakgalagadi to access water and tend even small numbers of cattle or goats. Finally, the land policies of the Botswana government prompted the eviction of hundreds of San from their own ancestral territory in the Central Kalahari Game Reserve, a move that led to Botswana being characterized as at moderate risk on Genocide Watch's 2008 list.

In Zambia, the constant ethnic shuffling that occurred in the 1960s rendered government and the public sector highly inefficient, prompting Kaunda to ban political parties and further centralize power in the office of the president. For 18 years, he presided over an autocratic regime, a period of widespread nationalization of industries and institutions, and a subsequent period of economic decline. This deeply destabilized the country during the 1980s. Growing unemployment and rising food prices provoked popular unrest, which escalated into widespread rioting. In Tanzania, *Ujamaa* was abandoned in the mid-1980s, after being deemed a failure. The country's centralized economic policies impeded growth, and resulted in an increasing dependence on international aid. Poverty was widespread, and the Structural Adjustment Programmes of the late 1980s ended much of the welfare support that the government had been delivering. The country's high level of poverty and the inequality provoked by structural adjustment increased tensions between religious and ethnic groups in a way not seen previously. The trial and error of nation building in these three states clearly yielded conditions that fostered stability and cohesion, as well as others that increased the risk of mass atrocities. The experience of these states thus indicates that policies aimed at service provision, economic growth and good governance often have mixed results.

Yet the real test of each country's long-term resilience was how it managed the risk associated with mass atrocities as this risk evolved over time. In Botswana, the San Bushmen evicted from the CKGR challenged the government on two occasions – first in the High Court, and then in the Court of Appeal. Both times, the courts ruled in favour of the San, declaring the evictions illegal, and determining that they had the legal right to use boreholes to access water. The country's independent judiciary provided the means for this marginalized and discriminated group to have its grievances heard and redressed. While the modern state of Botswana aggravated their unequal position, it also provided the means for the San successfully to challenge discriminatory policies. Zambia's greatest challenge to stability occurred in the late 1980s when Kaunda's authoritarian regime came under pressure from widespread unrest. Protesters called for political reform, and rallied against the rapid increase in food prices. Although some riots resulted in a small number of fatalities, Kaunda opted against widespread repression of discontent. Instead, he agreed to major political reforms that saw the reintroduction of a multi-party democratic system, a move that prompted the defeat of the incumbent UNIP. What prompted Kaunda to choose compromise (and ultimately political suicide) over violent suppression of opposition voices was his guiding philosophy of 'humanism', which prioritized unity, non-violence and compassion. Kaunda's 'humanism' meant that growing unrest and instability in Zambia became an opportunity for reform and improvement.

The structural adjustment policies introduced in Tanzania in the late 1980s increased economic inequality, but the previous two decades of equitable welfare and service provision were effective in preventing any ethnic or religious group from gaining disproportionate advantage. As a consequence, the subsequent increase in inequality was not horizontal – because no group had benefited from the spoils of government after independence, no single collective was poised to monopolize the opportunities inherent in the privatization of public resources. Some Asian merchants did profit from this, provoking some public animosity as a result, but scapegoating was limited. In short, Tanzania's foundation of social cohesion and economic equality was instrumental in limiting the fallout from large-scale privatization. These examples of risk mitigation are contextually specific. Sometimes they are the product of inclusive government policy, sometimes a reaction to exclusionary government policy. They illustrate the complex nexus of problem and solution which casts further doubt on the notion that mass atrocities can be prevented simply by identifying and ameliorating risk factors. The process of risk mitigation in the three cases is ongoing and contingent upon specific circumstances and resources available.

The contextually specific nature of risk mitigation is further illustrated by the instability and unrest in Zanzibar. In this province, with its distinct historical experience, the risk of mass atrocities was far greater than in mainland Tanzania. Although both the mainland and Zanzibar were ruled by the same party – the CCM – Zanzibar's experience of democratization was different, marked by escalating tension and violence. Efforts to resolve this tension were fruitful only when the opposing party leaders negotiated in isolation from external influence. In the case of Zanzibar, risk mitigation was most effective when local elites agreed on mutually beneficial solutions. Both the nature of risk and its mitigation were contextually specific, even distinct from the rest of the country.

Comparing negative and positive cases

The analytical framework deployed in this volume assists in understanding not only why such atrocities do not happen, but why sources of resilience break down in countries where atrocities have been committed. This dimension of the causal path to war and mass atrocities until recently has been ignored. An exception to this is Kalyvas's seminal study of the nature of violence across changing and complex local civil war contexts. Kalyvas points out that it is not uncommon for some communities to be immune to violence, while others succumb to varying degrees. Why is violence limited in some areas but not in others? The OSAPG's list of eight risk factors for genocide incorporates 'circumstances that affect the capacity to prevent genocide', including such structures as an independent judiciary and effective national human rights institutions (OSAPG 2009). The effectiveness of such structures over time is important to understanding which grievances are heard and redressed – in addition to the nature of social dynamics and state-led discrimination.

Viewed through the theoretical lens of this book, the circumstances that produced two genocides in post-colonial Rwanda were decidedly absent in Botswana, Zambia and Tanzania. These countries acted to counter the risk of entrenched social division. Take Rwanda's multi-party democratic system, established upon independence. It quickly became an instrument for the further entrenchment of division and tension between Hutus and Tutsis. While ethnic division did actually emerge in Zambia's early parliament, Kaunda worked decisively against such tendencies. In Rwanda, democracy and ethnicity were quickly entwined under the Hutu-led government – partly in revenge for privileges afforded to the Tutsi elite during Belgian colonial rule. Violence soon emerged as a strategy for the 'silencing of the opposition' (Mayersen and McLoughlin 2011: 256; United Nations 1964).

Rwanda's economic growth throughout much of the 1980s certainly had a positive effect on the country's stability. However, this on its own was an inadequate source of resilience. Over-reliance on a single commodity for export revenue turned sour when the price of coffee collapsed. With this source of stability undermined, the country's ability to cope with further political upheaval diminished. A dramatic fall in GDP and the introduction of IMF-designed structural adjustment policies adversely affected living standards through rising inflation and unemployment, as well as the gutting of the health sector. In consequence, the fault line between Hutus and Tutsis reopened, and 'low-level anti-Tutsi rhetoric' increased (Mayersen and McLoughlin 2011: 260). Soon after, in October 1990, the Tutsi-led Rwandan Patriotic Front invaded from neighbouring Uganda, an upheaval that triggered a civil war in which extreme anti-Tutsi sentiments formed the ideological bedrock of the militia groups – most notably the *Interahamwe* – responsible for the preparation and orchestration of the genocide in 1994.

Key questions that this book has sought to explore include what coping mechanisms countries are able to develop in the face of risk, and what capacity exists to deal with shock or upheaval. In Rwanda, a dearth of options existed by 1990. This does not mean that such atrocities would not have unfolded had the price of coffee not dropped, but a combination of weaknesses, including Habyarimana's limited success in limiting ethnic tensions through suspending democratic competition and initiating policies aimed at restoring ethnic balance,[1] failed to decrease the very high risk of future atrocities generated by politicized social divisions, entrenched discrimination and recent past atrocities. This profoundly and negatively affected the risk-mitigation calculus.

Much in the tragic unfolding of events prior to the genocide in Rwanda could be compared with the three cases in this book. Zambia and Tanzania, for example, experienced profound economic decline – Zambia's economic fortunes were arguably even more dire than Rwanda's. Yet these declines did not exacerbate ethnic or religious divisions. The history of inclusive policies and definitive action aimed at negating ethnic/religious difference became a source of resilience decades later. Both Zambia and Tanzania experienced a withdrawal of services and a lifting of government food subsidies, as well as the privatization of many state-owned industries, yet these changes did not increase horizontal inequalities, nor did they trigger ethnic or religious antipathy. Such disruptions were not without their consequences – they provoked widespread dissent in Zambia, which led to rioting and a brutal government crackdown. However, such dissent was articulated and advanced by a coalition of civil society groups (the MMD), which eventually negotiated directly with the government, resulting in major democratic reform and the first regime change in the country's history.

What distinguished Zambia and Tanzania from Rwanda? Certainly there are differences with regard to colonial rule and demographics. Rwanda's

German, then Belgian rulers entrenched ethnic difference through identification papers, and created a Tutsi elite whom they educated and empowered. Moreover, Rwanda's ethnic division is largely 'bipolar', a fact that Stanton argues makes risk more acute. None of the three countries in this book had the same challenges.[2] Yet, instead of reinforcing divisions intensified by colonial rule, leaders of the independence struggle in Botswana, Zambia and Tanzania advanced new and inclusive ideas of nationhood.

Opportunities for prevention and further research

This investigation makes two major contributions to understanding how structural prevention is addressed in the scholarly literature. First, it argues that the concept of long-term prevention needs to move beyond risk factors. The assumptions embedded in the concept of long-term prevention are impractical, as no country is able to eradicate risk entirely. The three cases explored here demonstrate that in the presence of risk, complex processes of mitigation occur and effective prevention measures are developed. Furthermore, the framework of analysis used in this book does not assume the end result of prevention is a non-event. The processes of risk mitigation described in this book have a variety of benefits to communities and states. For example, policies that avoid favouring one identity group over others ensure more equitable benefits for all. The 2010 political settlement in Zanzibar illustrates this. It not only decreased the risk of mass atrocities, but also provided substantial economic benefits for the province. The government of national unity lifted controls on clove prices, which brought substantially better returns for the farmers on Pemba, further enhancing stability and public support. In Botswana, the merit-based approach to recruitment in the public sector distributed opportunities and economic benefits widely among the various ethnic groups. The motive of local and national actors in the three cases has never been primarily to prevent mass atrocities, but rather to improve living conditions through better social relations, greater economic opportunities and more representative government.

My analysis also questions the assumption that long-term prevention is a collection of policies and actions devised and implemented primarily by international actors. In the absence of mass atrocities, a complex array of activities is initiated by local and national actors to manage risk. The risk factors associated with mass atrocities are specific to their place and time, and domestic actors are best placed to understand such deeply contextual processes. Investigating what such actors do to build resilience and mitigate risk highlights their importance in preventing mass atrocities. It also emphasizes the need for international actors to play a more facilitative role in building resilience, rather than a prescriptive one in which problems and solutions are devised externally.

Further research is needed in four main areas. First, more study is needed to determine the precise relationship between risk and resilience. As highlighted in Chapter 3, the framework draws from a limited pool of research on the conditions that foster stability and build resilience. Research into the causes of mass atrocities is broad and comprehensive, yet the opposite can be said for research into the causes of peace and stability. This subject demands much greater emphasis, and with that will inevitably come fresh insights into the complex ways that risk is mitigated and mass atrocities are prevented. Understanding resilience is clearly a work in progress.

We need more detailed empirical studies of individual cases to advance further our understanding of the relationship between risk and resilience. The three cases provide illustrations of the complex processes that collectively mitigate risk, but these are far from exhaustive. More in-depth fieldwork would enable a better understanding of local-level dynamics and the role of civil society, as well as how local motivations and processes interact with national politics. Key insights into the causes and dynamics of civil war have arisen from Kalyvas's (2003, 2006) broad and detailed survey of the intersection between local and national dynamics. Similar interactions could be surveyed to locate the varied and complex sources of resilience.

A third area for further research is the ways in which the UN and regional organizations can support local resilience. Understanding risk and mitigation raises the possibility that such organizations can devise preventive policies to build resilience, rather than prescribing solutions aimed at eliminating risk factors. The framework could be used to identify processes in particular states that would be enhanced by international assistance. Processes and programmes that strengthen social cohesion, good governance and economic development are of particular value here. Strengthening Botswana's drought-assistance programme, aiding the development of tourist infrastructure on Pemba, and expanding the resources of Zambia's judiciary are examples of projects and institutions that foster stability and resilience. Although many projects are already focused on development assistance, strengthening the rule of law and crisis prevention, the challenge is to become more cognisant of local and national sources of resilience so that international assistance can further consolidate these dynamics. Beyond individual projects, the framework also clarifies how multiple processes interact, challenging international actors to examine how diverse programmes are linked, and to work collectively to manage risk. Identifying the capacity for such processes within organizations, and tracking the benefits of such programmes – including but not limited to the prevention of mass atrocities – provides an opportunity for the UN and regional organizations to invest in long-term prevention by applying a risk/resilience lens to a broad range of activities related to social and economic development. Such programmes are particularly relevant for the UNDP's projects related to governance, poverty reduction, crisis prevention and the Millennium Development Goals. The UN Research Institute for Social Development (UNRISD), the UN Children's Fund (UNICEF) and the UNDPA are also relevant here.

Finally, we need to investigate how the insights gained from building resilience and mitigating risk can be made accessible to those who most urgently need them: local and national civil society organizations, members and leaders of marginalized minority groups, public servants, political leaders and anyone else committed to building peace and stability in their states and communities. The three cases represent only the tip of the iceberg with regard to the multitude of risk-mitigation and resilience-building efforts around the world. If the lack of interest in the causes of peace in academic research is any indication, then there are numerous neglected stories of community and national resilience, and equally numerous opportunities for others to gain insight from their successes.

Notes

1 Habyarimana attempted to bring about a greater balance between the two main ethnic groups through policies that increased Tutsi inclusion – but only to a point. Continued quotas for education and employment in the public sector limited Tutsis' ability to advance. While they were allowed to participate to a limited extent in the one-party system, they were excluded from positions of power in both the government and the military (see, for example Mamdani 2001: 148, 141; Mayersen and McLoughlin 2011: 252–53).

2 Tanzania could also be regarded as bipolar in terms of religious division – there are equal numbers of Christians and Muslims. Also, Botswana's dominant ethnic group composes approximately 70 per cent of the population, roughly the same as the proportion of Hutus in Rwanda before 1994.

Bibliography

Ackermann, Alice. 2000. *Making Peace Prevail: Preventing Violent Conflict in Mace-donia.* Syracuse, NY: Syracuse University Press.

Ackermann, Alice. 2003. 'The Idea and Practice of Conflict Prevention'. *Journal of Peace Research* 40(3): 339–47.

Adolf, Antony. 2009. *Peace: A World History.* Cambridge: Polity.

African Union. 2011. 'The Peace and Security Department'. au.int/en/dp/ps/psd (accessed 3 December 2011).

Amnesty International. 2002. 'Tanzania: Human Rights Concerns Relating to Demonstrations in Zanzibar on 27 January 2001'. www.amnesty.org/en/library/asset/ AFR56/001/2002/en/5ce5b324-d89f-11dd-ad8c-f3d4445c118e/afr560012002en.pdf (accessed 5 April 2011).

Anglin, Douglas G. 2000. 'Zanzibar: Political Impasse and Commonwealth Media-tion'. *Journal of Contemporary African Studies* 18(1): 39–66.

Annan, Kofi. 2001. *Prevention of Armed Conflict.* A/55/985. New York: United Nations.

Annan, Kofi. 2003. *Interim Report of the Secretary-General on the Prevention of Armed Conflict.* A/58/365. New York: United Nations.

Annan, Kofi. 2006. *Progress Report on the Prevention of Armed Conflict.* A/60/891. New York: United Nations.

Ayittey, George B.N. 2005. *Africa Unchained: The Blueprint for Africa's Future.* New York: Palgrave Macmillan.

Ban Ki-moon. 2008. *Report of the Secretary-General on the Implementation of Security Council Resolution 1625 (2005) on Conflict Prevention, Particularly in Africa.* S/2008/18. New York: United Nations Secretariat.

Ban Ki-moon. 2009a. *Implementing the Responsibility to Protect: Report of the Secretary-General.* A/63/677. New York: United Nations Secretariat.

Ban Ki-moon. 2009b. *Implementing the Responsibility to Protect. The General Assem-bly Debate: An Assessment.* New York: Global Centre for the Responsibility to Protect. globalr2p.org/media/pdf/GCR2P_General_Assembly_Debate_Assessment. pdf (accessed 23 September 2010).

Bandow, Doug. 2013. 'Democracy is Under Challenge in Zambia'. *Forbes.* 11 Feb-ruary. www.forbes.com/sites/dougbandow/2013/02/11/democracy-is-under-challenge-in-zambia/ (accessed 24 April 2013).

Bartlett, David M.C. 2000. 'Civil Society and Democracy: A Zambian Case Study'. *Journal of Southern African Studies* 26(3): 429–46.

Bartoli, Andrea, Tetsushi Ogata and Gregory H. Stanton. 2009. 'Emerging Paradigms in Genocide Prevention'. In *Genocide Prevention*. Bern: Federal Department of Foreign Affairs, Confederation of Switzerland.

BBC News. 2006a. 'Botswana Bushmen Win Land Ruling'. news.bbc.co.uk/2/hi/africa/6174709.stm (accessed 14 March 2009).

BBC News. 2006b. 'Zambia Vote Count Sparks Violence'. news.bbc.co.uk/2/hi/5396884.stm (accessed 14 March 2009).

BBC News. 2011a. 'Botswana Bushmen Win Back Rights to Kalahari Water'. www.bbc.co.uk/news/world-africa-12300285 (accessed 5 November 2011).

BBC News. 2011b. 'Zambia Election: Sata Wins Presidential Race', BBC World. www.bbc.co.uk/news/world-africa-15029463.

Beaulier, Scott A. and J. Robert Subrick. 2006. 'The Political Foundations of Development: The Case of Botswana'. *Constitutional Political Economy* 17: 103–15.

Belbase, Krishna and Richard Morgan. 1994. 'Food Security and Nutrition Monitoring for Drought Relief Management: The Case of Botswana'. *Food Policy* 19(3): 285–300.

Bellamy, Alex J. 2008. 'Conflict Prevention and the Responsibility to Prevent'. *Global Governance* 14(2): 135–56.

Bellamy, Alex J. 2009. *Responsibility to Protect*. Cambridge: Polity.

Bellamy, Alex J. 2010. 'The Responsibility to Protect – Five Years On'. *Ethics and International Affairs* 24(2): 143–69.

Bellamy, Alex J. 2011. *Mass Atrocities and Armed Conflict: Links, Distinctions and Implications for the Responsibility to Prevent*. The Stanley Foundation: Policy Analysis Brief.

Bellamy, Alex J., Paul Williams and Stuart Griffin. 2004. *Understanding Peacekeeping*. Cambridge: Polity Press.

Berkes, Fikret, Johan Colding and Carl Folke. 2003. 'Introduction'. In *Navigating Social-Ecological Systems: Building Resilience for Complexity and Change*, ed. Fikret Berkes, Johan Colding and Carl Folke. Cambridge: Cambridge University Press.

Berkes, Fikret and Carl Folke. 1998. 'Linking Social and Ecological Systems for Resilience and Sustainability'. In *Linking Social and Ecological Systems. Management Practices and Social Mechanisms for Building Resilience*, ed. Fikret Berkes and Carl Folk. Cambridge: Cambridge University Press.

Berman, Bruce J. 1998. 'Ethnicity, Patronage and the African State: The Politics of Uncivil Nationalism'. *African Affairs* 97(388): 305–41.

Besançon, Marie L. 2005. 'Relative Resources: Inequality in Ethnic Wars, Revolution, and Genocides'. *Journal of Peace Research* 42(4): 393–415.

Bigelow, Katherine R. 1992. 'A Campaign to Deter Genocide: The Baha'i Experience'. In *Genocide Watch*, ed. Helen Fein. New Haven, CT: Yale University Press.

Bjorkdahl, Annika. 2006. 'Promoting Norms through Peacekeeping: UNPREDEP and Conflict Prevention'. *International Peacekeeping* 13(2): 214–28.

Bloxham, Donald. 2005. *The Great Game of Genocide: Imperialism, Nationalism, and the Destruction of the Ottoman Armenians*. Oxford: Oxford University Press.

Boothby, Derek and George d'Angelo. 2004. 'Building Capacity Within the United Nations: Cooperation on the Prevention of Violent Conflicts'. In *Conflict Prevention: From Rhetoric to Reality*, ed. David Carment and Albrecht Schabel. Lanham, MD: Lexington Books.

Boutros-Ghali, Boutros. 1992. *An Agenda for Peace*. A/47/277. New York: United Nations.

Boutros-Ghali, Boutros. 1995. *Supplement to An Agenda for Peace*. A/RES/51/242. New York: United Nations.

Bratton, Michael. 1992. 'Zambia Starts Over'. *Journal of Democracy* 3(2): 81–94.

Brown, Andrea. 2010. 'Political Tensions in Zanzibar: Echoes from the Revolution?'. *Canadian Journal of Development* 30(3–4): 615–33.

Buchanan, Allen. 2004. 'Reforming the International Law of Humanitarian Intervention'. In *Humanitarian Intervention: Ethical, Legal, and Political Dilemmas*, ed. L.Z. Holzgrefe and Robert O. Keohane. Cambridge: Cambridge University Press.

Burdette, Marcia M. 1988. *Zambia: Between Two Worlds*. Boulder, CO: Westview Press.

Burnell, Peter. 2002. 'Zambia's 2001 Elections: The Tyranny of Small Decisions, "Non-Decisions" and "Not Decisions"'. *Third World Quarterly* 23(6): 1103–20.

Burnell, Peter. 2003. 'Legislative-Executive Relations in Zambia: Parliamentary Reform on the Agenda'. *Journal of Contemporary African Studies* 21(1): 47–68.

Burnell, Peter. 2005. 'From Low-Conflict Polity to Democratic Civil Peace: Explaining Zambian Exceptionalism'. *African Studies* 64(2): 107–33.

Carment, David and Albrecht Schnabel. 2003. 'Conflict Prevention – Taking Stock'. In *Conflict Prevention: Path to Peace or Grand Illusion?* ed. David Carment and Albrecht Schnabel. Tokyo: United Nations University Press.

CDDR (Coalition for the Defence of Democratic Rights). 2013. 'Violations of the Harare Declaration by Government of President Michael Sata and the Patriotic Front Party'. www.scribd.com/doc/125093235/Zambia-Violations-of-the-Harare-Declaration-by-President-Michael-Sata-and-the-Patriotic-Front-Party (accessed 4 May 2013).

Central Statistics Office, Zambia. 2006. 'Poverty in Zambia 1991–2006'. Government of Zambia. www.zamstats.gov.zm/lcm.php (accessed 3 November 2010).

Chirot, Daniel and Clark McCauley. 2006. *Why Not Kill Them All? The Logic and Prevention of Mass Political Murder*. Princeton, NJ: Princeton University Press.

CIA. 2010. 'The World Factbook: Zambia'. Central Intelligence Agency. www.cia.gov/library/publications/the-world-factbook/geos/za.html (accessed 5 November 2010).

CIA. 2011a. 'Country Comparison: Distribution of Family Income – Gini Index'. www.cia.gov/library/publications/the-world-factbook/rankorder/2172rank.html?countryName=Tanzania&countryCode=tz&regionCode=afr&rank=88#tz (accessed 7 June 2011).

CIA. 2011b. 'The World Factbook: Botswana'. www.cia.gov/library/publications/the-world-factbook/geos/bc.html (accessed 7 June 2011).

CIA. 2011c. 'The World Factbook: Tanzania'. www.cia.gov/library/publications/the-world-factbook/geos/tz.html (accessed 7 June 2011).

Cliffe, Lionel. 1969. 'From Independence to Self-Reliance'. In *A History of Tanzania*, ed. I.N. Kimambo and A.J. Temu. Nairobi: Heinemann.

Cohen, Roger. 2008. 'How Kofi Annan Rescued Kenya'. *The New York Review of Books* 55(13).

Collier, Paul. 2007. *The Bottom Billion: Why the Poorest Countries are Failing and What Can Be Done About It*. Oxford: Oxford University Press.

Collier, Paul. 2009. *Wars, Guns, and Votes*. New York: Harper Perennial.

Collier, Paul, V.L. Elliott, Havard Hegre, Anke Hoeffler, Marta Reynal-Querol and Nicholas Sambanis. 2003. *Breaking the Conflict Trap: Civil War and Development Policy*. Washington, DC: World Bank and Oxford University Press.

Collier, Paul, Anke Hoeffler and Nicholas Sambanis. 2005. 'The Collier-Hoeffler Model of Civil War Onset and the Case Study Project Research Design'. In

Understanding Civil War, ed. Paul Collier and Nicholas Sambanis. Washington, DC: The International Bank for Reconstruction and Development/World Bank.

Commonwealth Secretariat. 2000. *The Elections in Zanzibar*. United Republic of Tanzania: Report of the Commonwealth Observer Group.

Commonwealth Secretariat. 2010. *Tanzania General Elections 31 October 2010*. Report of the Commonwealth Observer Group.

Connor, Walker. 1978. 'A Nation is a Nation, is a State, is an Ethnic Group, is a...' *Ethnic and Racial Studies* 1(4): 377–400.

Connor, Walker. 1998. 'Beyond Reason: The Nature of the Ethnonational Bond'. In *New Tribalisms: The Resurgence of Race and Ethnicity*, ed. M.W. Hughey. New York: New York University Press.

Coulson, A. 1982. *Tanzania: A Political Economy*. Oxford: Clarendon Press.

Cullis, Adrian and Cathy Watson. 2005. *Winners and Losers: Privatising the Commons in Botswana*. International Institute for Environment and Development (IIED), and RECONCILE.

Datta, K. and A. Murray. 1989. 'The Rights of Minorities and Subject Peoples in Botswana: A Historical Evaluation'. In *Democracy in Botswana*, ed. John Holm and Patrick Molutsi. Athens, OH: Ohio University Press.

Dedring, Juergen. 1998. 'The Security Council in Preventive Action'. In *Preventing Violent Conflicts: Past Record and Future Challenges*, ed. Peter Wallensteen. Stockholm: Department of Peace and Conflict Research, Uppsala University.

de Maio, Jennifer. 2006. 'Managing Civil Wars: An Evaluation of Conflict-Prevention Strategies in Africa'. *World Affairs* 168(3): 131–44.

Derlugian, Georgi M. 1998. 'The Tale of Two Resorts: Abkhazia and Ajaria Before and Since the Soviet Collapse'. In *The Myth of 'Ethnic Conflict': Politics, Economics, and 'Cultural' Violence*, ed. Beverly Crawford and Ronnie Lipschutz. Berkeley, CA: University of California.

Development Partners Group. 2011. 'Overview of Aid in Tanzania'. Development Partners Group Tanzania. www.tzdpg.org.tz/external/dpg-tanzania/overview-of-aid-in-tanzania.html (accessed 10 July 2011).

de Wilde, Jaap H. 2006. 'Orwellian Risks in European Conflict Prevention Discourse'. *Global Society* 20(1): 87–99.

DiJohn, Jonathan. 2010. *State Resilience Against the Odds: An Analytical Narrative on the Construction and Maintenance of Political Order in Zambia since 1960*. London: Crisis States Research Centre.

Dow, Justice U. 2006. *Judgement*. Lobatse, Botswana.

Dow, Unity and Max Essex. 2010. *Saturday is for Funerals*. Cambridge, MA: Harvard University Press.

Draman, Rasheed. 2003. 'Conflict Prevention in Africa: Establishing Conditions and Institutions Conducive to Durable Peace'. In *Conflict Prevention: Path to Peace or Grand Illusion?* ed. David Carment and Albrecht Schnabel. Tokyo: United Nations University.

Dress, Toby D. and Gay Rosenblum-Kumar. 2002. 'Deconstructing Prevention: A Systems Approach to Mitigating Violent Conflict'. In *From Reaction to Conflict Prevention: Opportunities for the UN System*, ed. Fen Osler Hampson and David M. Malone. Boulder, CO: Lynne Rienner.

Druckman, Daniel. 2005. *Doing Research: Methods of Inquiry for Conflict Analysis*. Thousand Oaks, CA: Sage Publications.

Duggan, Colleen 2004. 'UN Strategic and Operational Coordination: Mechanisms for Preventing and Managing Violent Conflict'. In *Conflict Prevention from Rhetoric to Reality*, ed. David Carment and Albrecht Schnabel. Lanham, MD: Lexington Books.

du Toit, Pierre. 1995. *State Building and Democracy in Southern Africa*. Washington, DC: United States Institute of Peace.

EISA. 2002. 'Zambia: 1996 General Elections'. Electoral Institute for the Sustainability of Democracy in Africa. www.eisa.org.za/WEP/zam1996election.htm (accessed 14 July 2010).

EISA. 2010. *Botswana Parliamentary and Local Government Elections*. Gaborone: Electoral Institute for the Sustainability of Democracy in Africa.

Ekeus, Rolf. 2003. 'Preventive Diplomacy'. Paper presented at the Muller Lecture, The Hague.

Ekeus, Rolf. 2006. 'Overcoming the Reluctance to Conflict Prevention'. New York: OSCE. www.osce.org/hcnm/20469 (accessed 13 September 2007).

Electoral Commission of Zambia. 2008. '2008 Final Presidential Results'. www.elections.org.zm/index.php?option=com_docman&task=cat_view&gid=22&Itemid=78 (accessed 23 November 2010).

Eliasson, Jan. 1996. 'Establishing Trust in the Healer: Preventive Diplomacy and the History of the United Nations'. In *Stopping Wars before they Start: Preventive Diplomacy*, ed. Kevin Cahill. New York: Basic Books.

Evans, Gareth. 1993. *Cooperating for Peace: The Global Agenda for the 1990s and Beyond*. Sydney: Allen & Unwin.

Evans, Gareth. 2007. 'Preventing Mass Atrocities: Making the Responsibility to Protect a Reality'. Paper presented at the Prevention of Mass Atrocities: From Mandate to Realisation, New York.

Fawcus, Peter and Alan Tilbury. 2000. *Botswana: The Road to Independence*. Gaborone: Pula Press and The Botswana Society.

Fearon, James D. and David D. Laitin. 2003. 'Ethnicity, Insurgency, and Civil War'. *American Political Science Review* 97(1): 75–90.

Fein, Helen. 1979. *Accounting for Genocide*. New York: The Free Press.

Fein, Helen. 1993. 'Accounting for Genocide after 1945: Theories and Some Findings'. *International Journal on Group Rights* 1: 79–106.

Feng, Yi. 1997. 'Democracy, Political Stability and Economic Growth'. *British Journal of Political Science* 27(3): 391–418.

Ferreira, M. Luisa. 1996. *Poverty and Inequality During Structural Adjustment in Rural Tanzania*. Washington, DC: The World Bank.

FEWER (Forum on Early Warning and Early Response). 2005. 'Electoral Violence and Reconciliation in Zanzibar'. Nairobi: Forum on Early Warning and Early Response – Africa. www.fewer-international.org/images/lib/July%2028%20press%20release%20Zanzibar_162.pdf (accessed 13 March 2011).

Fidzani, N.H. 1998. 'Land Reform and Primitive Accumulation: A Closer Look at the Botswana Tribal Grazing Land Policy'. In *Botswana: Politics and Society*, ed. W.A. Edge and M.H. Lekorwe. Pretoria: J.L. van Schaik.

Fine, Keitha Sapsin. 1996. 'Fragile Stability and Change: Understanding Conflict during the Transitions in East Central Europe'. In *Preventing Conflict in the Post-Communist World: Mobilizing International and Regional Organizations*, ed. Abram Chayes and Antonia Handler Chayes. Washington, DC: The Brookings Institution.

Forster, Peter G. 1997. 'Religion and the State in Tanzania and Malawi'. *Journal of Asian and African Studies* 32(3–4): 163–84.

Freedom House. 2010a. 'Country Report: Zambia'. www.freedomhouse.org/template.cfm?page=22&year=2010 (accessed 14 December 2010).

Freedom House. 2010b. 'Tanzania'. www.freedomhouse.org/template.cfm?page=363&year=2010 (accessed 21 January 2011).

Freedom House. 2011. 'Botswana'. www.freedomhouse.org/report/freedom-world/2011/botswana (accessed 23 December 2011).

Freedom House. 2013. 'Zambia'. www.freedomhouse.org/report/freedom-world/2013/zambia (accessed 12 July 2013).

Gagnon, V.P. 1994. 'Ethnic Nationalism and International Conflict: The Case of Serbia'. *International Security* 19(3): 130–66.

Gall, Sandy. 2001. *The Bushmen of Southern Africa*. London: Chatto and Windus.

Gasarasi, Charles. 2004. 'The General Environment in which the Members of Parliament Works'. In *People's Representatives: Theory*, eds R.S. Mukandala, S.S. Mushi and C. Rubagumya. Kampala: Fountain.

Geertz, Clifford. 1973. *The Interpretation of Cultures: Selected Essays*. New York: Basic Books.

Geloo, Zarina. 2012. 'Sata Stirs the Tribal Pot in Zambia'. Open Society Initiative for Southern Africa. www.osisa.org/general/blog/sata-stirs-tribal-pot-zambia (accessed 20 November 2012).

Genocide Prevention Advisory Network. 2009. 'Genocides, Politicides, and Other Mass Murder Since 1945 with Stages in 2008'. www.gpanet.org/content/genocides-politicides-and-other-mass-murder-1945-stages-2008 (accessed 1 April 2010).

Gertzel, Cherry. 1984. 'Western Province: Tradition, Economic Deprivation and Political Alienation'. In *The Dynamics of the One-Party State in Zambia*, ed. Cherry Gertzel, Carolyn Baylies and Morris Szeftel. Manchester: Manchester University Press.

Gloppen, Siri. 2003. 'The Accountability Function of the Courts in Tanzania and Zambia'. *Democratization* 10(4): 112–36.

Goldstone, Jack A., Robert H. Bates, Ted Robert Gurr, Michael Lustik, Monty G. Marshall, Jay Ulfelder and Mark Woodward. 2005. *A Global Forecasting Model of Political Instability*. Conference Paper. Washington, DC.

Goldstone, Jack A., Ted Robert Gurr, Barbara Harff, Marc A. Levy, Monty G. Marshall, Robert H. Bates, David L. Epstein, Colin H. Kahl, Pamela T. Surko, John C. Ulfelder and Alan N. Unger. 2000. *State Failure Task Report: Phase III Findings*. Arlington, VA: George Mason University, School of Public Policy.

Goldstone, Jack A. and Jay Ulfelder. 2004. 'How to Construct Stable Democracies'. *The Washington Quarterly* 28(1): 9–20.

Good, Kenneth. 1986. 'Systemic Agricultural Mismanagement: The 1985 "Bumper" Harvest in Zambia'. *The Journal of Modern African Studies* 24(1): 257–84.

Good, Kenneth. 1993. 'At the Ends of the Ladder: Radical Inequalities in Botswana'. *The Journal of Modern African Studies* 31(2): 203–30.

Good, Kenneth. 2005. 'Resource Dependency and its Consequences: The Costs of Botswana's Shining Gems'. *Journal of Contemporary African Studies* 23(1): 27–50.

Good, Kenneth. 2008. *Diamonds, Dispossession and Democracy in Botswana*. Woodbridge: James Curry, and Jacana Media.

Good, Kenneth. 2009. 'The Presidency of General Ian Khama: The Militarization of the Botswana "Miracle"'. *African Affairs* 1(10): 315–24.

Good, Kenneth and Ian Taylor. 2008. 'Botswana: A Minimalist Democracy'. *Democratization* 15(4): 750–65.

Grundy, Kenneth W. 1968. 'The Political Ideology of Kwame Nkrumah'. In *African Political Thought: Lumumba, Nkrumah, and Toure*, ed. W.A.E. Skurnik. Boulder, CO: University of Denver.

Gurr, Ted Robert. 1993. *Minorities at Risk: A Global View of Ethnopolitical Conflicts*. Washington, DC: United States Institute of Peace Press.

Hall, Richard. 1969. *The High Price of Principles: Kaunda and the White South*. Harmondsworth: Penguin.

Hamburg, David A. 2008. *Preventing Genocide: Practical Steps Toward Early Detection and Effective Action*. Boulder, CO: Paradigm Publishers.

Hamburg, David and Cyrus R. Vance. 1997. *Preventing Deadly Conflict – Final Report*. Washington, DC: Carnegie Commission on Preventing Deadly Conflict. www.wilsoncenter.org/subsites/ccpdc/pubs/rept97/finfr.htm (accessed 4 August 2007).

Hampson, Fen Osler and David M. Malone. 2002. *From Reaction to Conflict Prevention: Opportunities for the UN System*. Boulder, CO: Lynne Rienner.

Hampson, Fen Osler, Karin Wermester and David M. Malone. 2002. 'Introduction: Making Conflict Prevention a Priority'. In *From Reaction to Conflict Prevention: Opportunities for the UN System*, ed. Fen Osler Hampson and David M. Malone. Boulder, CO: Lynne Rienner Publishers, Inc.

Hanlon, Joseph. 2005. 'Is the International Community Helping to Recreate the Preconditions for War in Sierra Leone?' *The Round Table* 94(381): 459–72.

Hansen, Thomas Obel. 2009. *Political Violence in Kenya: A Study of Causes, Responses, and a Framework for Discussing Preventive Action*. Pretoria: Institute for Security Studies.

Harff, Barbara. 1987. 'The Etiology of Genocides'. In *Genocide and the Modern Age, Etiology and Case Studies of Mass Death*, ed. Isidor Walliman and Michael N. Dobkowski. New York: Greenwood Press.

Harff, Barbara. 1998. 'Early Warning of Humanitarian Crises: Sequential Models and the Role of Accelerators'. In *Preventive Measures: Building Risk Assessment and Crisis Early Warning Systems*, ed. John L. Davies and Ted Robert Gurr. Lanham, MD: Rowman and Littlefield Publishers.

Harff, Barbara. 2003. 'No Lessons Learned from the Holocaust? Assessing the Risks of Genocide and Political Mass Murder since 1955'. *The American Political Science Review* 97(1): 57–73.

Harff, Barbara. 2012. 'Assessing Global Risks of Genocide and Politicide: A Global Watch List for 2012'. In *Peace and Conflict 2012*, ed. J. Joseph Hewitt, Jonathan Wilkenfeld and Ted Robert Gurr. College Park, MD: University of Maryland.

Hegre, Havard, Tanja Ellingsen, Scott Gates and Nils Petter Gleditsch. 2001. 'Toward a Democratic Civil Peace? Democracy, Political Change, and Civil War, 1816–1992'. *The American Political Science Review* 95(1): 33–48.

Heilman, Bruce E. and Paul J. Kaiser. 2002. 'Religion, Identity and Politics in Tanzania'. *Third World Quarterly* 23(4): 691–709.

Heritage Foundation. 2013. '2013 Index of Economic Freedom'. www.heritage.org/index/country/botswana (accessed 10 December 2013).

Hewitt, J. Joseph. 2012. 'The Peace and Conflict Instability Ledger: Ranking States on Future Risks'. In *Peace and Conflict 2012*, ed. J. Joseph Hewitt, Jonathan

Wilkenfeld, Ted Robert Gurr, with Birger Heldt. College Park, MD: University of Maryland.

Hewitt, J. Joseph, JonathanWilkenfeld and Ted Robert Gurr. 2010. *Peace and Conflict 2010*. College Park, MD: University of Maryland.

Hilberg, Raul. 1985. *The Destruction of the European Jews. Vol. 1*. New York: Holmes & Meier Publishers.

Hillbom, Ellen. 2008. 'Diamonds or Development? A Structural Assessment of Botswana's Forty Years of Success'. *Journal of Modern African Studies* 46(2): 191–214.

Hintjens, Helen. 1999. 'Explaining the 1994 Genocide in Rwanda'. *The Journal of Modern African Studies* 37(2): 241–86.

HLP (United Nations High-Level Panel on Threats, Challenges and Change). 2004. 'A More Secure World: Our Shared Responsibility'. A/59/565. www.un.org/secure-world/report2.pdf (accessed 21 September 2007).

Hoffman, Barak and Lindsay Robinson. 2010. 'Tanzania's Missing Opposition'. In *Democratization in Africa: Progress and Retreat*, ed. Larry Diamond and Marc F. Plattner. Baltimore, MD: Johns Hopkins University Press.

Holm, John D. 1993. 'Political Culture and Democracy: A Study of Mass Participation in Botswana'. In *Botswana: The Political Economy of Democratic Development*, ed. Stephen John Stedman. Boulder, CO: Lynne Rienner Publishers.

Horowitz, Donald L. 1985. *Ethnic Groups in Conflict*. Berkeley, CA: University of California Press.

Horton, Mark and John Middleton. 2000. *The Swahili: The Social Landscape of a Mercantile Society*. Oxford: Blackwell.

Hughes, A.J. 1963. *East Africa: The Search for Unity – Kenya, Tanganyika, Uganda, and Zanzibar*. Harmondsworth: Penguin Books.

Human Rights Watch. 1998. 'Indonesia Alert: Economic Crisis Leads to Scapegoating of Ethnic Chinese'. www.hrw.org/news/1998/02/10/indonesia-alert-economic-crisis-leads-scapegoating-ethnic-chinese (accessed 3 March 2009).

Human Rights Watch. 2002. '"The Bullets were Raining": The January 2001 Attack on Peaceful Demonstrations in Zanzibar'. *Human Rights Watch* 14(3(A)).

Human Security Report Project. 2010. 'The miniAtlas of Human Security'. www.hsrgroup.org/docs/Publications/miniAtlas/miniAtlas_en_data_table.pdf (accessed 14 July 2011).

Human Security Report Project. 2011. *Human Security Report 2009/2010: The Causes of Peace and the Shrinking Costs of War*. New York: Oxford University Press.

Hunter, Helen Louise. 2009. *Zanzibar: The Hundred Days Revolution*. Santa Barbara, CA: Praeger.

ICISS (International Commission on Intervention and State Sovereignty). 2001. *The Responsibility to Protect*.

Iliffe, John. 1979. *A Modern History of Tanganyika*. Cambridge: Cambridge University Press.

Jacques, Gloria. 1995. 'Drought in Botswana: Intervention as Fact and Paradigm'. *Pula: Botswana Journal of African Studies* 9(1): 34–60.

Jahan, Rounaq. 1997. 'Genocide in Bangladesh'. In *Century of Genocide*, ed. William S. Parsons, Israel W. Charny and Samuel Totten. New York and London: Garland Publishing.

Jonassohn, Kurt with Karin Solveig Bjornson. 1998. *Genocide and Gross Human Rights Violations: In Comparative Perspective*. New Brunswick, NJ: Transaction Publishers.

Jones, Adam. 2006. *Genocide: A Comprehensive Introduction*. London: Routledge, 2nd edn, 2010.

Kaiser, Paul J. 1996. 'Structural Adjustment and the Fragile Nation: The Demise of Social Unity in Tanzania'. *The Journal of Modern African Studies* 34(2): 227–37.

Kaiser, Paul J. 2003. 'Zanzibar: A Multilevel Analysis of Conflict Prevention'. In *From Promise to Practice: Strengthening UN Capacities for the Prevention of Violent Conflict*, ed. Chandra Likha Sriram and Karin Wermester. Boulder, CO: Lynne Rienner.

Kaldor, Mary. 2006. *New and Old Wars: Organized Violence in a Global Era*. Cambridge: Polity.

Kalyvas, Stathis N. 2003. 'The Ontology of "Political Violence": Action and Identity in Civil Wars'. *Perspectives on Politics* 1(3): 475–94.

Kalyvas, Stathis N. 2006. *The Logic of Violence in Civil War*. Cambridge: Cambridge University Press.

Kapila, Mukesh and Karin Wermester. 2002. 'Development and Conflict: New Approaches in the United Kingdom'. In *From Reaction to Conflict Prevention: Opportunities for the UN System*, ed. Fen Osler Hampson and David M. Malone. Boulder, CO: Lynne Rienner.

Kasonde, Pixie. 2010. *Statement to the Media by the Chairperson of the Human Rights Commission, Mrs Pixie Kasonde on the Human Rights Situation and Matters of Public Interest or Concern in 2009*. Zambia: Human Rights Commission.

Kaufman, Stuart J. 2001. *Modern Hatreds: The Symbolic Politics of Ethnic War*. Ithaca, NY: Cornell University Press.

Kaunda, Kenneth. 1967. *A Humanist in Africa*. London: Longmans.

Keen, David. 1994. *The Benefits of Famine: A Political Economy of Famine and Relief in Southwestern Sudan 1983–1989*. Princeton, NJ: Princeton University Press.

Kelebonye, Greg. 2011. 'Kgafela Challenges the Validity of Botswana's Constitution'. Gaborone. www.mmegi.bw/index.php?sid=31&aid=419&dir=2011/December/Friday2 (accessed 2 March 2012).

Kelsall, Tim. 2002. 'Shop Windows and Smoke-Filled Rooms: Governance and the Re-Politicisation of Tanzania'. *Journal of Modern African Studies* 40(4): 597–619.

Kelsall, Tim. 2003. 'Governance, Democracy and Recent Political Struggles in Mainland Tanzania'. *Commonwealth and Comparative Politics* 41(2): 55–82.

Kiernan, Ben. 2007. *Blood and Soil: A World History of Genocide and Extermination from Sparta to Darfur*. Melbourne: Melbourne University Press.

Killian, Bernadeta. 2004. 'Comparing Performances: The 1990–1995 Single-Party Parliament and the 1995–2000 Multi-Party Parliament'. In *People's Representatives: Theory and Practice of Parliamentary Democracy in Tanzania*, ed. Samuel S. Mushi and Casmir Rubagumya Rwekaza S. Mukandala. Kampala: Fountain.

Kindra, Jaspreet. 2013. 'Understanding Resilience'. IRIN. www.irinnews.org/report/97584/understanding-resilience (accessed 4 April 2013).

Klugman, Jeni, Bilin Neyapti and Frances Stewart. 1999. *Conflict and Growth in Africa Vol. 2: Kenya, Tanzania and Uganda*. Paris: Organisation for Economic Co-operation and Development.

Krain, Matthew. 1997. 'State-Sponsored Mass Murder: The Onset and Severity of Genocides and Politicides'. *The Journal of Conflict Resolution* 41(3): 331–60.

Krain, Matthew. 2000. 'Democracy, Internal War, and State-Sponsored Mass Murder'. *Human Rights Review* 1(3): 1–24.

Kressel, Neil J. 2002. *Mass Hate: The Global Rise of Genocide and Terror*. Cambridge, MA: Westview Press.

Kuper, Leo. 1977. *The Pity of it All: The Polarisation of Racial and Ethnic Relations*. Minneapolis: University of Minnesota Press.

Kuper, Leo. 1981. *Genocide*. New Haven, CT: Yale University Press.

Kuper, Leo. 1985. *The Prevention of Genocide*. New Haven, CT: Yale University Press.

Langer, Arnim. 2008. 'When do Horizontal Inequalities Lead to Conflict? Lessons from a Comparative Study of Ghana and Cote d'Ivoire'. In *Horizontal Inequalities and Conflict: Understanding Group Violence in Multiethnic Societies*, ed. Frances Stewart. New York: Palgrave Macmillan.

Larmer, Miles. 2009. 'Zambia Since 1990: Paradoxes of Democratic Transition'. In *Turning Points in African Democracy*, ed. Abdul Raufu Mustapha and Lindsay Whitfield. Martlesham: James Currey.

Larmer, Miles and Alistair Fraser. 2007. 'Of Cabbages and King Cobra: Populist Politics and Zambia's 2006 Election'. *African Affairs* 106(425): 611–37.

Lederach, John Paul and R. Scott Appleby. 2010. 'Strategic Peacebuilding: An Overview'. In *Strategies of Peace: Transforming Conflict in a Violent World*, ed. Daniel Philpott and Gerard F. Powers. Oxford: Oxford University Press.

Leith, J. Clark. 2005. *Why Botswana Prospered*. Montreal and Kingston: McGill-Queen's University Press.

Lekorwe, M.H. 1998. 'Local Government and District Planning'. In *Botswana: Politics and Society*, ed. W.A. Edge and M.H. Lekorwe. Pretoria: J.L. van Schaik.

Lemarchand, Rene. 1968. 'Patrice Lumumba'. In *African Political Thought: Lumumba, Nkrumah, and Toure*, ed. W.A.E. Skurnik. Boulder, CO: University of Denver.

Lemarchand, Rene. 1997. 'The Burundi Genocide'. In *Century of Genocide: Eyewitness Accounts and Critical Views*, ed. William S. Parsons, Israel W. Charny and Samuel Totten. New York and London: Garland Publishing.

Levene, Mark. 1999. 'Introduction'. In *The Massacre in History*, ed. Mark Levene and Penny Roberts. New York: Berghahn Books.

Levene, Mark. 2004. 'A Dissenting Voice: Or How Current Assumptions of Deterring and Preventing Genocide May be Looking at the Problem through the Wrong End of the Telescope'. *Journal of Genocide Research* 6(2): 153–66.

Lillis, Joanna. 2009. 'Kazakhstan: Astana Refocuses Attention on National Unity and Economic Uncertainty'. www.eurasianet.org/departments/insightb/articles/eav011309.shtml (accessed 4 August 2010).

Lindemann, Stefan. 2010. *Inclusive Elite Bargains and Civil War Avoidance: The Case of Zambia*. London: Crisis States Research Centre.

Lipschultz, Ronnie D. 1998. 'Seeking a State of One's Own: An Analytical Framework for Assessing Ethnic and Sectarian Conflicts'. In *The Myth of 'Ethnic Conflict': Politics, Economics, and 'Cultural' Violence*, ed. Beverly and Ronnie Lipschutz Crawford. Berkeley, CA: University of California.

Lodge, Tom, Denis Kadima and David Pottie, ed. 2002. *Compendium of Elections in Southern Africa*. Electoral Institute of Southern Africa.

Lofchie, Michael F. 1965. *Zanzibar: Background to Revolution*. Princeton, NJ: Princeton University Press.

Londregan, John B. and Keith T. Poole. 1990. 'Poverty, the Coup Trap, and the Seizure of Executive Power'. *World Politics* 42(2): 151–83.

Luck, Edward C. 2002. 'Prevention: Theory and Practice'. In *From Reaction to Conflict Prevention: Opportunities for the UN System*, ed. Fen Osler Hampson and David M. Malone. Boulder, CO: Lynne Rienner Publishers.

Luck, Edward C. 2006. *UN Security Council: Practice and Promise.* New York: Routledge.

Lund, Michael S. 1996. *Preventing Violent Conflicts: A Strategy for Preventive Diplomacy.* Washington, DC: United States Institute of Peace Press.

Lund, Michael S. 2002. 'From Lessons to Action'. In *From Reaction to Conflict Prevention: Opportunities for the UN System*, ed. Fen Osler Hampson and David M. Malone. Boulder, CO: Lynne Rienner Publishers.

Lund, Michael S. 2004. 'Conflict Prevention is Happening: Learning from "Successes" as Well as "Failures"'. In *Conflict Prevention from Rhetoric to Reality*, ed. David Carment and Albrecht Schnabel. Lanham, MD: Lexington Books.

Mackenzie, John. 1969 [1883]. *Day Dawn in Dark Places.* London: Cassell & Company Ltd.

Macpherson, Fergus. 1974. *Kenneth Kaunda of Zambia: The Times and the Man.* Lusaka: Oxford University Press.

Magang, David. 2008. *The Magic of Perseverance: The Autobiography of David Magang.* Cape Town: The Centre for Advanced Studies of African Society.

Mamdani, Mahmood. 2001. *When Victims Become Killers: Colonialism, Nativism and the Genocide in Rwanda.* Princeton, NJ: Princeton University Press.

Mann, Michael. 2005. *The Dark Side of Democracy: Explaining Ethnic Cleansing.* Cambridge: Cambridge University Press.

Marr, Phebe. 2004. *The Modern History of Iraq.* Boulder, CO: Westview Press.

Marshall, Monty G. and Keith Jaggers. 2010. 'Polity IV Project. Systemic Peace'. www.systemicpeace.org/polity/polity4.htm (accessed 7 October 2011).

Masire, Quett Ketumile. 2006. *Very Brave or Very Foolish?: Memoirs of an African Democrat.* Gaborone: Macmillan.

Masterson, Grant. 2009. 'Tanzania and Zanzibar'. In *Compendium of Elections in Southern Africa 1989–2009: 20 Years of Multiparty Democracy*, ed. Denis Kadima and Susan Booysen. Johannesburg: EISA.

Mayersen, Deborah and Stephen McLoughlin. 2011. 'Risk and Resilience to Mass Atrocities in Africa: A Comparison of Rwanda and Botswana'. *Journal of Genocide Research* 12(3): 247–69.

McCulloch, Neil, Bob Baulch and Milasoa Cherel-Robson. 2000. *Poverty, Inequality and Growth in Zambia During the 1990s.* World Institute for Development Economic Research.

McHenry Jr, Dean E. 2004. 'Political Parties and Party Systems'. In *Democratic Transitions in East Africa*, ed. Paul J. Kaiser and F. Wafula Okumu. Aldershot, UK: Ashgate.

McLoughlin, Stephen and Deborah Mayersen. 2013. 'Reconsidering Root Causes: A New Framework for the Structural Prevention of Genocide and Mass Atrocities'. In *Genocide Risk and Resilience: An Interdisciplinary Approach*, ed. Bert Ingelaere, Stephan Parmentier, Jacques Haers and Barbara Segaert. Basingstoke: Palgrave Macmillan.

Meisler, Stanley. 1995. *United Nations: The First Fifty Years.* New York: Atlantic Monthly Press.

Melson, Robert. 1989. '"Genocide in the Twentieth Century". Revolutionary Genocide: On the Causes of the Armenian Genocide of 1915 and the Holocaust'. *Holocaust and Genocide Studies* 4(2): 161–74.

Melson, Robert. 1992. *Revolution and Genocide: On the Origins of the Armenian Genocide and the Holocaust.* Chicago: The University of Chicago Press.

Menkhaus, Ken. 2004. 'Conflict Prevention and Human Security: Issues and Challenges'. *Conflict, Security and Development* 4(3): 419–63.

Meredith, Martin. 2006. *The State of Africa: A History of Fifty Years of Independence.* London: Free Press.

Mesaki, Simeon. 2011. 'Religion and the State in Tanzania'. *Cross-Cultural Communication* 7(2): 249–59.

Miall, Hugh, Oliver Ramsbotham and Tom Woodhouse. 1999. *Contemporary Conflict Resolution: The Prevention, Management and Transformation of Deadly Conflicts.* Cambridge: Polity.

Midlarsky, Manus I. 2005. *The Killing Trap: Genocide in the Twentieth Century.* Cambridge: Cambridge University Press.

Miers, Suzanne and Michael Crowder. 1988. 'The Politics of Slavery in Bechuanaland: Power Struggles and the Plight of the Basarwa in the Bamangwato Reserve, 1926–1940'. In *The End of Slavery*, ed. Suzanne Miers and Richard Roberts. Madison, WI: University of Wisconsin Press.

Minorities at Risk. 2006a. 'Assessment for Bemba in Zambia'. www.cidcm.umd.edu/mar/assessment.asp?groupId=55101.

Minorities at Risk. 2006b. 'Assessment for Lozi in Zambia'. www.cidcm.umd.edu/mar/assessment.asp?groupId=55102.

Minorities at Risk. 2009a. 'Assessment for San Bushmen in Botswana'. www.cidcm.umd.edu/mar/assessment.asp?groupId=57101.

Minorities at Risk. 2009b. 'Minorities at Risk (MAR) Codebook Version 2/2009'. www.cidcm.umd.edu/mar/data/mar_codebook_Feb09.pdf.

Minorities at Risk. 2011. 'Assessment for Zanzibaris in Tanzania'. www.cidcm.umd.edu/mar/assessment.asp?groupId=51001.

Minority Rights Group International. 2007. 'World Directory of Minorities and Indigenous Peoples – Zambia: Overview, 2007'. www.unhcr.org/refworld/publisher,MRGI,ZMB,4954ce2823,0.html.

Minority Rights Group International. 2008. 'World Directory of Minorities and Indigenous Peoples: Wayeyi'. www.minorityrights.org/2593/botswana/wayeyi.html (accessed 16 May 2010).

Minority Rights Group International. 2010a. 'Peoples Under Threat 2010'. www.minorityrights.org/9885/peoples-under-threat/peoples-under-threat-2010.html (accessed 7 June 2011).

Minority Rights Group International. 2010b. 'Zambia Overview'. www.minorityrights.org/3922/zambia/zambia-overview.html (accessed 12 July 2011).

Mohamed, Mohamed Issa. 2007. 'Tanzania: Pemba Finally Gets Power from the National Grid'. allafrica.com/stories/200702130607.html (accessed 23 August 2011).

Molteno, Robert. 1974. 'Cleavage and Conflict in Zambian Politics: A Study in Sectionalism'. In *Politics in Zambia*, ed. William Tordoff. Manchester: Manchester University Press.

Moolakkattu, Stephen John. 2005. 'The Concept and Practice of Conflict Prevention: A Critical Reappraisal'. *International Studies* 42(1): 1–19.

Moyo, Dambisa. 2009. *Dead Aid: Why Aid is not Working and How there is Another Way for Africa.* London: Allen Lane.

Mucha, Witold. 2013. 'Prone to Conflict, but Resilient to Violence. Why Civil Wars Sometimes do not Happen: Insights from Peru and Bolivia'. *Journal of Peace, Conflict and Development* 20: 96–114.

Mueller, John. 2000. 'The Banality of "Ethnic War"'. *International Security* 25(1): 42–70.

Munshya wa Munshya, Elias. 2010. 'One Zambia, Many Nations: Politics of Tribe from Kaunda to Banda'. *Lusaka Times*. www.lusakatimes.com/2010/05/15/zambia-nations-politics-tribe-kaunda-banda/ (accessed 4 April 2011).

Murphy, J. and A. Cohn. 2008. 'Mental Health Innovations with the Australian Defence Force'. *Journal of Occupational Health and Safety in Australia and New Zealand* 24(6).

Nafziger, E. Wayne and Juha Auvinen. 2000. 'The Economic Causes of Humanitarian Emergencies'. In *War, Hunger and Displacement: The Origins of Humanitarian Emergencies Vol. 1*, ed. Frances Stewart, Raimo Vayrynen and E. Wayne Nafziger. Oxford: Oxford University Press.

Nayar, Anjali. 2009. 'Zanzibar Clove Farmers Still Await Free Market'. www.reuters.com/article/2009/01/26/us-zanzibar-cloves-idUSTRE50P08U20090126 (accessed 8 May 2011).

Ngasongwa, Juma. 1992. 'Tanzania Introduces a Multi-Party System'. *Review of African Political Economy* 54: 112–16.

Ngcongco, L.D. 1989. 'Tswana Political Tradition: How Democratic?' In *Democracy in Botswana: The Proceedings of a Symposium Held in Gaborone, 1–5 August 1988*, ed. John Holm and Patrick Molutsi. Athens, OH: Ohio University Press.

Nieuwoudt, Stephanie. 2008. 'Of Tourists, Bushmen – and a Borehole'. www.ipsnews.net/2008/05/development-botswana-of-tourists-bushmen-and-a-borehole/ (accessed 12 September 2010).

Nyanje, Peter. 2011. 'Tanzania: Clove Business to be Liberalized'. allafrica.com/stories/201107110324.html (accessed 25 February 2012).

Nyati-Ramahobo, Lydia. 2000. 'The Language Situation in Botswana'. *Current Issues in Language Learning* 1(2): 243–300.

Nyati-Ramahobo, Lydia. 2002. 'From a Phone Call to the High Court: Wayeyi Visibility and the Kamanakao Association's Campaign for Linguistic and Cultural Rights in Botswana'. *Journal of African Studies* 28(4): 685–709.

Nyerere, Julius K. 1967. *Freedom and Unity*. Dar es Salaam: Oxford University Press.

Nyerere, Julius K. 1968. *Ujamaa: Essays on Socialism*. Dar es Salaam: Oxford University Press.

Nyerere, Julius K. 1969. *Freedom and Socialism: A Selection from Writing and Speeches 1965–1967*. Dar es Salaam: Oxford University Press.

Nzongola-Ntalaja, Georges. 2004. 'Citizenship, Political Violence, and Democratization in Africa'. *Global Governance* 10: 403–9.

O'Malley, Pat. 2010. 'Resilient Subjects: Uncertainty, Warfare and Liberalism'. *Economy and Society* 39(4): 488–509.

O'Neill, Margaret and Necla Tschirgi. 2002. 'The Role of Research and Policy Analysis'. In *From Reaction to Conflict Prevention: Opportunities for the UN System*, ed. Fen Osler Hampson and David M. Malone. Boulder, CO: Lynne Rienner Publisher.

OSAPG (Office of the UN Special Adviser on the Prevention of Genocide). 2009. 'Analysis Framework'. United Nations. www.un.org/en/preventgenocide/adviser/pdf/osapg_analysis_framework.pdf (accessed 20 July 2011).

OSAPG (Office of the UN Special Adviser on the Prevention of Genocide). 2011a. 'Preventing Genocide'. United Nations. www.un.org/en/preventgenocide/adviser/genocide_prevention.shtml (accessed 20 July 2011).

OSAPG (Office of the UN Special Adviser on the Prevention of Genocide). 2011b. 'Preventing Genocide and Mass Atrocities'. United Nations. www.un.org/en/preventgenocide/adviser/un_role.shtml (accessed 20 July 2011).

Parsons, Neil. 1977. 'The Economic History of Khama's Country in Botswana 1844–1930'. In *The Roots of Rural Poverty in Central and Southern Africa*, ed. Robin Palmer and Neil Parsons. London: Heinemann.

Parsons, Neil, ed. 1985. *The Evolution of Modern Botswana: Historical Revisions. Evolution of Modern Botswana: Politics and Development in Southern Africa.* Lincoln, NE: Nebraska University Press.

Parsons, Neil, Willie Henderson and Thomas Tlou. 1995. *Seretse Khama: 1921–1980.* Braamfontein: Macmillan.

Pastor, Manuel and James K. Boyce. 2002. 'El Salvador: Economic Disparities, External Intervention, and Civil Conflict'. In *War, Hunger and Displacement: The Origins of Humanitarian Emergencies*, ed. Frances Stewart, Raim Vayrynen and E. Wayne Nafziger. Oxford: Oxford University Press.

Pearson, Anna. 2009. *Social Protection Policy: Responses to Older People's Needs in Zanzibar.* Dar es Salaam: HelpAge International.

Peck, Connie. 1998. *Sustainable Peace: The Role of the UN and Regional Organisations in Preventing Conflict.* Lanham, MD: Rowman & Littlefield Publishers, Inc.

Pettman, Jan. 1974. *Zambia: Security and Conflict.* Blandford: Davison Publishing Ltd.

Phiri, Bizeck Jube. 2006. *A Political History of Zambia: From the Colonial Period to the 3rd Republic.* Trenton, NJ: Africa World Press, Inc.

Phumaphi, Justice M.P. 2006. *Judgement.* Lobatswe, Botswana: High Court of Botswana.

Policy Forum. 2011. 'Growth in Tanzania: Is it Reducing Poverty?' www.policyforum-tz.org/files/GrowthTanzania.pdf (accessed 9 March 2012).

Policy Project for Bureau for Africa. 2001. *HIV/AIDS in Southern Africa: Background, Projections, Impacts, and Interventions.* Office of Sustainable Development, US Agency for International Development.

Political Terror Scale. 2011. 'About the Political Terror Scale'. www.politicalterror scale.org/about.php (accessed 23 January 2012).

Polity IV. 2008a. 'Polity IV Country Report 2008: Zambia'. Center for Systemic Peace. www.systemicpeace.org/polity/Zambia2008.pdf (accessed 25 September 2010).

Polity IV. 2008b. 'Polity IV Country Report: Tanzania'. www.systemicpeace.org/polity/Tanzania2008.pdf (accessed 13 January 2011).

Posner, Daniel N. 2003. 'The Colonial Origins of Ethnic Cleavages: The Case of Linguistic Divisions in Zambia'. *Comparative Politics* 35(2).

Posner, Daniel N. 2005. *Institutions and Ethnic Politics in Africa.* Cambridge: Cambridge University Press.

Posner, Daniel N. 2007. 'Regime Change and Ethnic Cleavages in Africa'. *Comparative Political Studies* 40(11): 5–24.

Posner, Daniel N. and David J. Simon. 2002. 'Economic Conditions and Incumbent Support in Africa's New Democracies: Evidence from Zambia'. *Comparative Political Studies* 35(3): 319–39.

Pottie, David. 2002. 'Party Strife and Political Impasse in Zanzibar's October 2000 Elections'. *Representation* 38(4): 340–50.

Power, Samantha. 2007. *A Problem from Hell: America and the Age of Genocide.* London: Flamingo.

Rakner, Lise. 2003. *Political and Economic Liberalisation in Zambia 1991–2001.* Stockholm: The Nordic Africa Institute.

Ramadhani, Lupa. 2011. 'Identity Politics and Complexities of Conflict Resolution in Zanzibar'. www.ucd.ie/ibis/publications/discussionpapers/identitypoliticsandcomplex itiesinzanzibar/#d.en.75024 (accessed 12 December 2011).

Rasmussen, Lissi. 1993. *Christian-Muslim Relations in Africa: The Cases of Northern Nigeria and Tanzania Compared.* London: British Academic Press.

Redvers, Louise. 2013. 'Zambia Cracks Down on Freedoms'. *Mail and Guardian.* 25 January. mg.co.za/article/2013-01-25-00-zambia-cracks-down-on-freedoms (accessed 14 March 2013).

Remy, Jean Philippe. 2011. 'Zambia: A Smooth Changeover at Last to King Cobra'. www.guardian.co.uk/world/2011/sep/27/zambia-election-win-for-sata?INTCMP=SRCH (accessed 11 February 2012).

RETENG. 2006. *Alternative Report Submitted to the UN Committee on the Elimination of All Forms of Racial Discrimination (CERD).* Gaborone: RETENG: The Multicultural Coalition of Botswana. www.ditshwanelo.org.bw/images/Reteng%202006%20Shadow%20Report.pdf (accessed 15 October 2009).

Richmond, Oliver P. 2005. *The Transformation of Peace.* Basingstoke: Palgrave Macmillan.

Roberts, Andrew. 1976. *A History of Zambia.* London: Heinemann.

Roeder, Philip G. 1998. 'Liberalization and Ethnic Entrepreneurs in the Soviet Successor States'. In *The Myth of 'Ethnic Conflict': Politics, Economics, and 'Cultural' Violence,* ed. Beverly and Ronnie Lipschutz Crawford. Berkeley, CA: Berkeley.

Rotberg, Robert I. 1965. *The Rise of Nationalism in Central Africa: The Making of Malawi and Zambia 1873–1964.* Cambridge, MA: Harvard University Press.

Rothchild, Donald. 2003. 'Third Party Incentives and the Phases of Conflict Prevention'. In *From Promise to Practice: Strengthening UN Capacities for the Prevention of Violent Conflict,* ed. Chandra Lekha Sriram and Karin Wermester. Boulder, CO: Lynne Rienner.

Royal Norwegian Ministry of Foreign Affairs. 2001. *Can Democratisation Prevent Conflicts? Lessons from Sub-Saharan Africa.* Solstrand, Norway: Royal Norwegian Ministry of Foreign Affairs.

Rummel, R.J. 1994. *Death By Government.* New Brunswick: Transaction Publishers.

Samatar, Abdi Ismail. 1999. *An African Miracle: State and Class Leadership and Colonial Legacy in Botswana Development.* Portsmouth: Heinemann.

Sambanis, Nicholas. 2001. 'Do Ethnic and Nonethnic Civil Wars Have the Same Causes?' *Journal of Conflict Resolution* 45(3): 259–82.

Saugestad, Sidsel. 2005. '"Improving Their Lives": State Policies and San Resistance in Botswana'. *Before Farming* 4(1): 1–11.

Schapera, Isaac. 1970. *Tribal Innovators: Tswana Chiefs and Social Change 1795–1940.* London: The Athlone Press.

Schnabel, Albrecht. 2004. 'Human Security and Conflict Prevention'. In *Conflict Prevention from Rhetoric to Reality, Volume 2: Opportunities and Innovations,* ed. David Carment and Albrecht Schnabel. Lanham, MD: Lexington Books.

Schnabel, Albrecht and David Carment. 2004. 'Mainstreaming Conflict Prevention: From Rhetoric to Reality'. In *Conflict Prevention: From Rhetoric to Reality, Volume 1: Organizations and Institutions,* ed. David Carment and Albrecht Schnabel. Lanham, MD: Lexington Books.

Seepapitso IV, Kgosi. 1989. 'The Kgotla and the Freedom Square: One-way or Two-way Communication?' In *Democracy in Botswana: The Proceedings of a Symposium Held in Gaborone, 1–5 August 1988,* ed. John Holm and Patrick Molutsi. Athens, OH: Ohio University Press.

Semelin, Jacques. 2007. *Purify and Destroy: The Political Uses of Massacre and Genocide.* London: C. Hurst & Co.

Shaw, Martin. 2007. *What is Genocide?* Cambridge: Polity Press.

Sheriff, Abdul. 2001. 'Race and Class in the Politics of Zanzibar'. *Africa Spectrum* 36 (3): 301–18.

Sichone, Owen and Neo Simutanyi. 1996. 'The Ethnic and Regional Questions, Ethnic Nationalism and the State in Zambia'. In *Democracy in Zambia: Challenges for the Third Republic*, ed. Owen Sichone and Bornwell C. Chikulo. Harare: Sapes Books.

Silberbauer, George B. 1981. *Hunter and Habitat in the Central Kalahari Desert.* Cambridge: Cambridge University Press.

Simon, David J. 2005. 'Democracy Unrealized: Zambia's Third Republic under Frederick Chiluba'. In *The Fate of Africa's Democratic Experiments*, ed. Leonardo A. Villalon and Peter VonDoepp. Bloomington and Indianapolis, IN: Indiana University Press.

Simpson, John. 2011. 'The Kalahari Bushmen are Home Again'. www.guardian.co.uk/commentisfree/2011/dec/13/kalahari-bushmen-home-again-botswana-diamonds (accessed 5 January 2012).

Smith, B.C. 2008. 'Models of Judicial Administration and the Independence of the Judiciary: A Comparison of Romanian Self-Management and the Czech Executive Model'. *Public Administration and Development* 28(2): 85–93.

Snyder, Jack. 2000. *From Voting to Violence: Democratization and Nationalist Conflict.* New York: W.W. Norton & Company.

Solway, Jacqueline S. 1994. 'From Shame to Pride: Politicized Ethnicity in the Kalahari, Botswana'. *Canadian Journal of African Studies* 28(2): 254–74.

Solway, Jacqueline. 2002. 'Navigating the "Neutral" State: "Minority" Rights in Botswana'. *Journal of African Studies* 28(4).

Solway, Jacqueline and Lydia Nyati-Ramahobo. 2004. 'Democracy in Process: Building a Coalition to Achieve Political, Cultural, and Linguistic Rights in Botswana'. *Canadian Journal of African Studies* 38(3): 603–21.

Somolekae, G.M. and M.H. Lekorwe. 1998. 'The Chieftancy System and Politics in Botswana, 1966–1995'. In *Botswana: Politics and Society*, ed. W.A. Edge and M.H. Lekorwe. Pretoria: J. L. van Schaik.

Southwick, S., M. Vyhiligan and D. Charney. 2005. 'The Psychobiology of Depression and Resilience to Stress: Implications for Prevention and Treatment'. *Annual Reviews of Clinical Psychology* 1: 255–91.

Sriram, Chandra Lekha and Karin Wermester. 2002. 'Preventive Action at the United Nations: From Promise to Practice?' In *From Reaction to Conflict Prevention: Opportunities for the UN System*, ed. Fen Osler Hampson and David M. Malone. Boulder, CO: Lynne Rienner.

Sriram, Chandra Lekha and Karin Wermester. 2003. 'From Risk to Response: Phases of Conflict Prevention'. In *From Promise to Practice: Strengthening UN Capacities of the Prevention of Violent Conflict*, ed. Chandra Lekha Sriram and Karin Wermester. Boulder, CO: Lynne Rienner Publishers.

Stack, John F. 1986. 'Ethnic Mobilization in World Politics: The Primordial Perspective'. In *The Primordial Challenge: Ethnicity in the Contemporary World*, ed. John F. Stack. New York: Greenwood Press.

Stanton, Gregory H. 1996. *The 8 Stages of Genocide.* Cambridge, MA. www.genocide watch.org/images/8StagesBriefingpaper.pdf (accessed 21 September 2008).

Stanton, Gregory H. 2004. 'Could the Rwandan Genocide have been Prevented?' *Journal of Genocide Research* 6(2): 211–28.

State House, Zambia. 2010. *I will not Tolerate Tribalism – President Banda*. State House, Zambia. www.statehouse.gov.zm/index.php/component/content/article/48-featured-items/2185-i-will-not-tolerate-tribalism-president-banda (accessed 12 December 2010).

Stevens, Richard P. 1967. *Lesotho, Botswana, & Swaziland*. London: Pall Mall Press.

Stewart, Emma. 2005. *The European Union and Conflict Prevention: Policy Evolution and Outcome*. New Brunswick: Transaction Publishers.

Stewart, Frances. 2000. 'The Root Causes of Humanitarian Emergencies'. In *War, Hunger and Displacement: The Origins of Humanitarian Emergencies*, ed. Frances Stewart, Raimo Vayrynen and E. Wayne Nafziger. Oxford: Oxford University Press.

Stewart, Frances. 2008. 'Horizontal Inequalities and Conflict: An Introduction and some Hypotheses'. In *Horizontal Inequalities and Conflict: Understanding Group Violence in Multiethnic Societies*, ed. Frances Stewart. New York: Palgrave Macmillan.

Straus, Scott. 2007. 'Second-Generation Comparative Research on Genocide'. *World Politics* 59: 476–501.

Straus, Scott. 2012. 'Retreating from the Brink: Theorizing Mass Violence and the Dynamics of Restraint'. *Perspectives on Politics* 10(2): 343–62.

Suny, Ronald. 2004. *Why We Hate You: the Passions of National Identity and Ethnic Violence*. Paper 2004-2001.

Survival International. 2009. 'The Bushmen'. www.survivalinternational.org/tribes/bushmen (accessed 4 March 2010).

Sutterlin, James S. 2003. *The United Nations and the Maintenance of International Security: A Challenge to Be Met*. Westport, CT: Praeger.

Svendsen, Knud Erik. 1970. 'The Present Stage of Economic Planning in Tanzania'. In *Nation-Building in Tanzania*, ed. A. Rweyamamu. Nairobi: East African Publishing House.

Swanstrom, Niklas L.P. and Mikael S. Weissmann. 2005. 'Conflict, Conflict Prevention, Conflict Management and Beyond: A Conceptual Exploration'. www.silkroad studies.org/new/docs/ConceptPapers/2005/concept_paper_ConfPrev.pdf (accessed 24 September 2007).

Talentino, Andrea Kathryn. 2003. 'Evaluating Success and Failure: Conflict Prevention in Cambodia and Bosnia'. In *Conflict Prevention: Path to Peace or Grand Illusion?* ed. David Carment and Albrecht Schnabel. Tokyo: United Nations University.

Tambila, Kapwepwe I. 2004. 'The Ups and Downs of the Tanzania Parliament'. In *People's Representatives: Theory and Practice of Parliamentary Democracy in Tanzania*, ed. R.S. Mukandala, S.S. Mushi and C. Rubagumya. Kampala: Fountain.

Taylor, Ian. 2006. 'The Limits of the "African Miracle": Academic Freedom in Botswana and the Deportation of Kenneth Good'. *Journal of Contemporary African Studies* 24(1): 101–22.

Tlou, Thomas and Alec Campbell. 1997. *History of Botswana*. Gaborone: Macmillan.

Toft, Monica Duffy. 2003. *The Geography of Ethnic Violence: Identity, Interests, and the Indivisibility of Territory*. Princeton, NJ: Princeton University Press.

Tordoff, William and Ralph Young. 2005. 'Electoral Politics in Africa: The Experience of Zambia and Zimbabwe'. *Government and Opposition* 40(3): 403–23.

UNHCR. 2011. 'ZAMBIA: Poverty Fuels Secession Bid by Western Province'. UNHCR. www.irinnews.org/Report.aspx?ReportID=91721 (accessed 21 January 2012).

United Nations. 1945. 'Charter of the United Nations'. www.un.org/aboutun/charter/ (accessed 23 September 2007).

United Nations. 1948a. 'Convention on the Prevention and Punishment of the Crime of Genocide'. www2.ohchr.org/english/law/genocide.htm (accessed 24 September 2007).

United Nations. 1948b. *The Universal Declaration of Human Rights.* New York: United Nations. www.un.org/en/documents/udhr/history.shtml (accessed 21 August 2007).

United Nations. 1964. *The Situation in Rwanda and Burundi: Summary of Reports Made to the Secretary-General by Mr. Max H. Dorsinville on his Two Missions to Rwanda and Burundi as the Secretary-General's Special Representative,* SG/SM/24, 3 March, para. 6.

United Nations. 1995. *Observations of the 1995 Tanzanian Elections: Report of the Team Leaders of the United Nations Electoral Secretariat in Tanzania.* Dar es Salaam: United Nations.

United Nations. 1998. *Rome Statute of the International Criminal Court,* A/CONF.183/9, 17 July, part 2.

UN News. 2011. 'Russia and China Veto Draft Security Council Resolution on Syria'. *UN News Centre,* 5 October.

United Nations General Assembly. 2005. *2005 Summit Outcome.* A/60/L.1, 20 September, paras 138–39.

United Nations Security Council. 2001a. *S/RES/1366 (2001).*

United Nations Security Council. 2001b. *UN S/RES/1366 (2001).*

United Nations Security Council. 2005. *UN S/RES/1625 (2005).*

United Nations Security Council. 2007. *S/RES/1769 (2007).*

UNDP (United Nations Development Programme). 2003. *Zambia Human Development Report 2003: Eradication of Extreme Poverty and Hunger in Zambia: An Agenda for Enhancing the Achievement of the Millennium Development Goals.* Lusaka: United Nations Development Programme.

UNDP (United Nations Development Programme). 2005. *Botswana Human Development Report 2005: Harnessing Science and Technology for Human Development.* Gaborone: United Nations Development Programme.

UNDP (United Nations Development Programme). 2011. 'International Human Development Indicators'. hdrstats.undp.org/en/indicators/38906.html (accessed 24 January 2012).

UNDPA (United Nations Department of Political Affairs). 2008. 'DPA's Budget and Trust Funds'. www.un.org.depts/dpa/budget.html (accessed 1 July 2008).

United Republic of Tanzania. 2009. *Poverty and Human Development Report.* Dar es Salaam: MKUKUTA Secretariat, Poverty Eradication Division, Ministry of Planning, Economy and Empowerment.

Valentino, Benjamin A. 2004. *Final Solutions: Mass Killing and Genocide in the Twentieth Century.* Ithaca, NY and London: Cornell University Press.

Valentino, Benjamin A. 2011. 'The True Costs of Humanitarian Intervention: The Hard Truth about a Noble Notion'. *Foreign Affairs* 90(6): 60–73.

Vayrynen, Raimo. 2000. 'Complex Humanitarian Emergencies: Concepts and Issues'. In *War, Hunger and Displacement: The Origins of Humanitarian Emergencies Vol. 1,* ed. Frances Stewart, Raimo Vayrynen, and E. Wayne Nafziger. Oxford: Oxford University Press.

Venter, Albert and Michele Olivier. 1993. 'Human Rights in Africa: Nyerere and Kaunda'. *International Journal on World Peace* 10(1): 21–33.

Verdeja, Ernesto. 2012. 'The Political Science of Genocide: Outlines of an Emerging Research Agenda'. *Perspectives on Politics* 10(2): 307–21.

Vogel, C.H. and J.H. Drummond. 1993. 'Dimensions of Drought: South African Case Studies'. *GeoJournal* 30(1): 93–98.

Wallensteen, Peter. 2002. 'Reassessing Recent Conflicts: Direct vs Structural Prevention'. In *From Reaction to Conflict Prevention: Opportunities for the UN System*, ed. Fen Osler Hampson and David M. Malone. Boulder, CO: Lynne Rienner Publishers.

Ware, Helen and Dele Ogunmola. 2010. 'Probing the Roles of Governance and Greed in Civil Strife in West Africa'. In *Economics of War and Peace: Economic, Legal and Political Perspectives*, ed. Ben Goldsmith and Jurgen Bauer. Bingley: Emerald Group Publishing Ltd.

Weitz, Eric D. 2003. *A Century of Genocide: Utopias of Race and Nation*. Princeton, NJ and Oxford: Princeton University Press.

Welsh, Jennifer M. 2010. 'Turning Words into Deeds? The Implementation of the "Responsibility to Protect"'. *Global Responsibility to Protect* 2(1–2): 149–54.

Werbner, Richard. 2004. *Reasonable Radicals and Citizenship in Botswana*. Bloomington, IN: Indiana University Press.

Wijsen, Frans. 2002. '"When Two Elephants Fight the Grass gets Hurt": Muslim-Christian Relationships in Upcountry Tanzania'. *Church and Theology in Context* 14: 235–48.

Wilmsen, Edwin N. and Rainer Vosen. 1990. 'Labour, Language and Power in the Construction of Ethnicity in Botswana'. *Critique of Anthropology* 10(1): 7–37.

Wolff, Stefan. 2006. *Ethnic Conflict: A Global Perspective*. Oxford: Oxford University Press.

Wolter, Detlev. 2007. *A United Nations for the 21st Century: From Reaction to Prevention*. Baden-Baden, Germany: Nomos.

Woodward, Susan L. 2007. 'Do the Root Causes of Civil War Matter? On Using Knowledge to Improve Peacebuilding Interventions'. *Journal of Intervention and Statebuilding* 1(2): 143–70.

World Bank. 1990. *World Development Report 1990: Poverty*. Oxford: Oxford University Press.

World Bank. 2011a. 'Botswana'. data.worldbank.org/country/botswana (accessed 10 July 2011).

World Bank. 2011b. 'Zambia'. data.worldbank.org/country/zambia (accessed 10 July 2011).

Yeager, Rodger. 1982. *Tanzania: An African Experience*. Boulder, CO: Westview Press.

Zartman, I. William. 2005. 'Need, Creed, and Greed in Intrastate Conflict'. In *Rethinking the Economics of War*, ed. Cynthia J. Arnson and I. William Zartman. Washington, DC: Woodrow Wilson International Center for Scholars.

Zenko, Micah and Rebecca R. Friedman. 2011. 'UN Early Warning for Preventing Conflict'. *International Peacekeeping* 18(1): 21–37.

Index